Lewis Mumford and American Modernism examines the career and writings of America's leading critic of architecture and urban planning. The author of numerous books and articles and a regular columnist for the *New Yorker,* Mumford focused on the roles that architecture, technology, and urbanism play in modern civilization. Although a key figure in the introduction of European ideas to the United States, he sought an American basis for modern architecture. Mumford was one of the first to write appreciatively of the achievements of the Chicago School, and he was a fervent supporter of Frank Lloyd Wright, whose buildings embodied the organic qualities that Mumford admired. Indeed, Mumford's writings have proved to be prescient, posing many challenging questions for architects and planners in a period of transition at the end of the twentieth century.

LEWIS MUMFORD AND
AMERICAN MODERNISM

LEWIS MUMFORD AND AMERICAN MODERNISM

EUTOPIAN THEORIES FOR ARCHITECTURE AND URBAN PLANNING

Robert Wojtowicz

Old Dominion University

CAMBRIDGE
UNIVERSITY PRESS

CAMBRIDGE UNIVERSITY PRESS
Cambridge, New York, Melbourne, Madrid, Cape Town, Singapore, São Paulo, Delhi

Cambridge University Press
The Edinburgh Building, Cambridge CB2 8RU, UK

Published in the United States of America by Cambridge University Press, New York

www.cambridge.org
Information on this title: www.cambridge.org/9780521639248

First published 1996
First paperback edition 1998
Re-issued in this digitally printed version 2009

A catalogue record for this publication is available from the British Library

ISBN 978-0-521-48215-8 hardback
ISBN 978-0-521-63924-8 paperback

To Sophia Wittenberg Mumford

CONTENTS

ILLUSTRATIONS

Illustrations follow page 112

Lewis Mumford, 1931

Lewis and Elvina Mumford, Atlantic City,
c. 1903

Charles Graessel

Patrick Geddes

Ebenezer Howard

Lewis and Geddes Mumford

Lewis Mumford, 1932

Geddes, Alison, and Sophia Mumford, Palo Alto,
1943

Catherine K. Bauer Wurster

Frank Lloyd Wright addressing the American Institute
of Architects' convention on receipt of the Gold
Medal, Dallas, 1949

Henry-Russell Hitchcock Jr.

Clarence S. Stein, New York City, c. 1960

Frederic J. Osborn

The Mumfords' House, Leedsville, near Amenia,
New York, c. 1955

Lewis and Sophia Mumford, Ledbury, England, July
1957

Lewis Mumford, Leedsville, New York

ACKNOWLEDGMENTS

I began this study of Lewis Mumford almost ten years ago. While a student worker in the Special Collections of Van Pelt Library at the University of Pennsylvania, I stumbled across the Mumford Papers in much the same way that Mumford himself first stumbled across the writings of Patrick Geddes. The sheer vastness of the papers (198 boxes!) was daunting but not insurmountable, and in the spring of 1990 I completed my dissertation, on which this present study is based.

Without the cooperation and assistance of Mrs. Sophia Mumford, I would never have been able to complete this study. She was always willing to answer questions, to clarify names or dates, and to enliven the written record of her husband's life with personal anecdotes. I always looked forward to our conversations over lunch, along with the company of her indispensable factotum, Richard Coons. Mrs. Mumford also graciously loaned me her personal "daybooks," a well-crafted series of journals that chronicle the years not covered by Mumford's autobiography, *Sketches from Life*. Alison Mumford Morss was also kind enough to share reminiscences about her father with me.

There are numerous friends and colleagues whom I would like to thank at the University of Pennsylvania, where I completed both my undergraduate and graduate educations. Chief among them is my dissertation adviser, David B. Brownlee, who kept his faith in my abilities through some very trying semesters. I was very fortunate in having David G. De Long serve as a second reader for my dissertation. I am deeply indebted to Nancy Shawcross, curator of manuscripts for Special Collections, for her support when I was researching this study, and especially now that I am geographically removed from the papers. Her assistants, Ellen Slack and Julie Reahard, provided valuable insights into the organization of the papers. Several of my graduate school colleagues who have since moved on to other institutions – Kathleen James, Michael Lewis, Peter Reed, and Marc Vincent – were kind enough to answer questions or to relay information discovered in the course of their own research. Robert Arbuckle and Robert Shepard provided helpful advice on the publishing industry.

My colleagues in the Art Department of Old Dominion University – Frederick Bayersdorfer, Patti Casper, Elizabeth L. Lipsmeyer, Linda McGreevy, Nancy Shelton, and Diana Tenckhoff – listened to innumerable talks about Mumford and read innumerable drafts of this manuscript. Wayne Burton of the Old Dominion University Library and Clay Vaughan of the Old Dominion University Art Library graciously extended their bibliographic expertise. Kristine Inchausti assisted with photography, and Nate Zeisler assisted with proofreading. Others who helped to bring this study to completion include K. C. Parsons, Mosette Broderick, and Vincent DiMattio. As always, I have been able to count on the support of my parents.

This study was funded in part by a summer faculty research award from the Old Dominion University Research Foundation and a grant from the College of Arts and Letters, Old Dominion University.

The letters of Harold Ross were reprinted by special permission of the New Yorker Magazine, Inc. (c) 1995. All Rights Reserved. The pagination cited in the notes for articles in the *New Yorker* may correspond to either the "New York City" edition or the "Out-of-Town" edition.

Robert Wojtowicz
Norfolk, Virginia
September 1995

LEWIS MUMFORD AND
AMERICAN MODERNISM

INTRODUCTION: THE STORY OF MUMFORD'S "EUTOPIA"

The foundations for eutopia can be laid, wherever we are, without further ado.

— The Story of Utopias

Utopian ideals played a central role in the writings of Lewis Mumford (1895–1990), although, somewhat paradoxically, he denied being a utopian thinker. His first book, *The Story of Utopias* (1922), marked his initial foray into the human condition, a theme that would preoccupy him for more than five decades. Mumford the pragmatist believed firmly in the betterment of society through sound design in architecture, practical reforms in housing, and comprehensive planning on the regional level. Yet Mumford the moralist also believed that physical change would not lead to a substantially better quality of life unless accompanied by personal renewal. In his writings, he repeatedly attempted to guide the reader not toward an impossible utopia, but rather toward "eutopia," the good place, brought down from the clouds and planted firmly on the ground.

For almost half a century, Mumford was the preeminent critic of architecture and urbanism in the United States and a leading advocate of modernism. He was the author of more than two dozen books and hundreds of articles and reviews that emphasized the social rather than the formal dimensions of the built environment. This book examines Mumford's eutopia as it developed out of his extraordinary written legacy. The first chapter traces Mumford's intellectual development from his youth to his initial publishing success with *The Story of Utopias*. The other three chapters are organized synchronously, each building upon the previous one. Chapter 2 discusses his contributions to American architectural history, chapter 3 his architectural criticism, and chapter 4 his writings on cities. Where appropriate, biographical information is provided. For a more conventional, chronological account of Mumford's life, there is Donald L. Miller's *Lewis Mumford: A Life* (1989).

A specialized study such as this necessarily does Mumford a great disservice. He thought of himself as a "generalist," an intellectual with no specialized academic training. Like his mentor, Sir Patrick Geddes, Mumford despised the barriers that had been erected between academic disciplines, and in his own work he attempted to synthesize disparate fields of inquiry into a meaningful whole. Such a comprehensive approach to knowledge may seem quaintly old-fashioned in this postmodern age, but Mumford's writings contain a great deal that is still relevant today. His dire warnings about technological warfare and environmental destruction have largely come to pass. His concerns about the human element in modern architecture and community planning have yet to be realized. Mumford did not live to see his eutopia realized, but this was never really his goal. It was in the striving toward eutopia, he argued, that society found its fulfillment.

* * *

As an intellectual, Mumford essentially invented himself, having come from a rather unexceptional family background in New York City. He had a keen awareness of his urban surroundings from an early age, and by the time he reached college, he was ready to embark on a writing career. On his own, he stumbled across the writings of Sir Patrick Geddes, the Scottish biologist, sociologist, town planner, and occasional utopian thinker. Geddes stressed the fundamental importance of studying one's environment from every possible angle through an interdisciplinary method that he called "regional survey." Another important early influence on Mumford was Sir Ebenezer Howard, the founder of the British Garden City movement. Howard advocated the building of new, self-contained garden cities that would combine the best aspects of rural and urban living. To a young man stuck in the dense gridiron of Manhattan's Upper West Side, such unorthodox approaches to planning must have seemed nothing short of revolutionary. Mumford never finished college, but in Geddes and Howard, he found the direction that he needed in life.

After World War I, Mumford rose to prominence quickly in New York's literary circles, especially after the publication of *The Story of Utopias*. The book was a direct outgrowth of a brief period of postwar optimism in America, when utopian ideas were being discussed avidly by New York's intellectuals. Near the book's conclusion, Mumford introduced the archaic term "eutopia" to describe a better, but necessarily imperfect, society that could be realized in the present. According to Mumford, this society would be replanned along regional lines with garden cities nestled into the countryside. He emphasized, however, that plans not accompanied by social and institutional change were rendered useless. Although Mumford offered no utopian blueprint of his own in the book, he urged his readers to work together for the greater good of their communities and the general betterment of life. Soon afterward, he became involved with the Regional Planning Association of America, a group of writers, architects, and planners dedicated to the development of eutopian communities in the United States.

Mumford spent the rest of his life outlining the path toward eutopia. His books and articles of the 1920s explored America's "usable past," so that his contemporaries might better understand their own intellectual and artistic forebears. *Sticks and Stones* (1924) and *The Brown Decades* (1931) established him as an unabashed critic of the Beaux-Arts tradition, which then dominated American architecture and planning. His criticism appeared frequently in the pages of the *Journal of the American Institute of Architects,* the *New Republic,* and, after 1931, the *New Yorker,* reaching a wide audience outside of the architectural profession.

In the 1930s Mumford embarked on an even more ambitious project, *The Renewal of Life* (1934, 1938, 1944, and 1951), an exhaustive study of Western civilization that focused on technology, urbanism, and the human personality. "Organic" renewal was the underlying theme of all four books. According to Mumford, if society was to achieve an organic balance, a blind faith in technology or planning was not enough. In his carefully crafted vision, technology would be harnessed for the common good, cities would be integrated carefully into their natural regions, and men and women everywhere would reach their fullest individual potential.

Mumford pursued this line of investigation even further in his last major books, *The City in History* (1961) and the two-volume *Myth of the Machine* (1967 and 1970), but with far more ominous conclusions drawn from the prevailing cold war climate. In these works, he explored the ancient origins of utopia, which he traced to the birth of the city itself. Moreover, he tied the utopian impulse to an authoritarian power structure that had culminated in the first human-powered "megamachine." Its destructive aspects were disguised in the present, Mumford argued, under the misleading banner of technological "progress," which promised a more perfect future. In particular, he was concerned that if nuclear weapons continued to multiply in the twentieth century, "Megalopolis" would quickly revert to "Necropolis." Still, Mumford would not relinquish his optimism that humankind would instead choose the more practical and humane path toward eutopia.

* * *

By his own example, Mumford sought to demonstrate the advantages of a eutopian lifestyle. He described his early life in great detail in his autobiography, *Sketches from Life* (1982), and in several published collections of his personal notes and letters. Mumford and his wife Sophia had a loving marriage that lasted for nearly seventy years. Although he admitted to a few infidelities, Mumford's relationship with his wife not only endured, it deepened over time. Sophia Mumford (1899–1997), a former assistant editor at the *Dial,* was her husband's indefatigable copyeditor, proofreader, and intellectual companion. The Mumfords had two children, Geddes (1925–1944) and Alison (1935–1993), whom they raised according to progressive educational methods. For eleven years, the Mumfords made their home in Sunnyside Gardens, Queens, a community designed by the Regional Planning Association of America that incorporated some significant garden city principles. They also spent part of every year upstate in Dutchess County where they owned a small house. Thus, the family enjoyed the advantages of both city and country life just as Ebenezer Howard had advocated; they moved to the country permanently in 1936. Many of Mumford's most pleasurable hours were spent digging in his garden, renewing his relationship with the earth.

Mumford saved almost every scrap of paper upon which he had written, thus providing an extraordinary challenge to any biographer. Out of the voluminous correspondence and autobiographical notes, the portrait that emerges is of a sensitive and thoughtful man, with a keen wit, a great deal of charm, and at times, a formidable ego. He was a natural diplomat, adept at working in groups, but more content to work alone. When required, Mumford would sacrifice everything on principle, even his closest friends. Such was the case when he advocated intervention on the Allies' behalf during World War II. A liberal democrat, he was profoundly disappointed by America's reluctance to enter the war. When his son Geddes was killed in combat, however, Mumford grieved openly. His memoir of Geddes, *Green Memories* (1947), relates not only the story of a troubled adolescent, but the self-doubts of a mature man unsure of his abilities as a father and husband. Although Mumford did not engage in partisan politics, in subsequent years he agitated vociferously against nuclear proliferation and the Vietnam War.

In many ways, Mumford's daily routine could be considered almost monkish in its ascetic self-discipline. An early riser, he would spend most mornings at his desk writing. In the more leisurely afternoons, he would work in his garden, take long walks, or catch up on his correspondence. His evenings were often devoted to reading in preparation for the next morning. He looked for ways to improve himself, as for example, when he taught himself to write more legibly while in his late fifties. If at times he seemed aloof, even to his children, this intense focus on his writing was absolutely essential for him to be productive. Except for those periods when he accepted academic appointments, including Dartmouth College (1929–1935), Stanford University (1942–1944), North Carolina State College (1948–1952), the University of Pennsylvania (1951–1956, 1959–1961), and the Massachusetts Institute of Technology (1957–1961), Mumford supported his family solely on his income as a writer and lecturer.

Mumford valued his independence, and he remained somewhat distant from the academy throughout his career. He accepted only a handful of the many honorary degrees offered to him in his lifetime. In general, Mumford did not seek publicity, and he only made occasional radio or television appearances. Ironically, for a renowned critic of architecture and urbanism, his favorite place was a small study in a white clapboard farmhouse, close to both family and nature. This was essentially Mumford's eutopia, and out of it developed one of the most remarkable written oeuvres of the twentieth century.

I

THE EDUCATION OF A CRITIC

My lack of a degree has become a valuable distinction in America. The Ph.D. is such an inevitable sign of mediocrity here that when the Carnegie Foundation for the Advancement of Art wanted someone to examine and report upon the various schools of art in America they tried to get hold of me – and this in the face of the fact that with their resources they had all the academic young men in the universities at their beck and call.

– *My Works and Days: A Personal Chronicle*

Few circumstances surrounding Lewis Mumford's youth suggest that he would develop into one of the most influential cultural critics of the twentieth century.[1] In searching for the roots of his intellectual development, however, three significant factors become apparent. First, although Mumford lacked a father during his formative years, his stepgrandfather assumed this role, becoming the first of a series of important mentors to the young boy. Second, Mumford exhibited an unusual precocity from a very early age, which manifested itself both in a voracious appetite for reading and in an unbounded curiosity about his surroundings. The third influence was New York City itself. The city underwent a period of unprecedented growth between 1898, when the five boroughs were consolidated, and the outbreak of World War I. Mumford participated fully in the cultural life of the city, finding it much more stimulating than his classroom experiences.

Mumford's childhood was atypical of a middle-class family in New York City at the turn of the century, but by no means was it deprived. He was born in Flushing, New York, in 1895, the illegitimate child of Elvina Mumford, a housekeeper, and Lewis Charles Mack, a businessman who was completely absent from the young boy's life.[2] He spent his youth on the Upper West Side of Manhattan, where he was jointly raised by his mother, his stepgrandfather, and his nanny in comfortable but reduced circumstances. The family finances gradually worsened during his child-hood, owing in part to his mother's imprudence, and they were forced to move to less expensive quarters on several occasions. For a time, Elvina Mumford had to take in what she called "paying guests" to supplement the family income.[3]

Perhaps because his family was constantly changing addresses, Mumford devel-oped an unusual sensitivity to his environment from an early age. In his autobiogra-phy, he railed against his mother's bourgeois, late Victorian taste in decorating. The rooms of his youth were dark, crowded, and musty, and he later claimed that such surroundings prompted him to embrace the more spartan design aesthetic of mod-ern architecture:

> One cannot properly understand the austere architecture of the period from 1930 to 1945 unless one remembers that the leaders in the modern movement and the critics like myself who abetted them were brought up in these chambers of esthetic horror and had no other thought, when at last they stood on their own legs, than to clear out the rubbish.[4]

Yet, despite Mumford's latent interest in his surroundings, he was not actively en-couraged by his mother to become an architect, as was the case with Frank Lloyd Wright, for example.[5] In fact, Elvina Mumford generally does not seem to have been a guiding force in her son's education, preferring instead to take him to card parties or to the stockbroker's office. On more than one occasion, she even pulled her son out of school to accompany her to the horse races.[6]

Fortunately for Mumford, he had a devoted nanny, Nellie Ahearn, whom he fondly referred to as "Nana" or as his "nurse." Ahearn more than compensated for his mother's inattentiveness. In addition to taking care of Mumford, Ahearn was the cook and housekeeper for his mother's extended household.[7] She even tried to instill in Mumford her Catholic values – Elvina Mumford did not pursue a religious education for her son – but to no avail.[8] Although in later years, Mumford em-braced a spiritual outlook, it was an amalgam of many world religions tempered by a humanist vision.

The most important adult influence in Mumford's early life was his mother's stepfather, Charles Graessel. A retired headwaiter from Delmonico's, the fashion-able New York restaurant, Graessel lived in the Mumford household until his death in 1906. In his former position, Graessel carefully observed New York Society, imitating its customs and appearances, but maintaining a critical distance that was not lost on the young Mumford. Moreover, it was Graessel who first introduced Mumford to the larger cultural and social life of New York by taking him on daily walks beyond the Upper West Side. Their favorite destination was Central Park, where, according to Mumford, they would "watch the procession of open victorias, pulled by pairs of fat, chestnut geldings with docked black tails."[9] On weekends, the two would travel all around Manhattan: to the bookbinder in Greenwich Village, the bootmaker on Canal Street, and the cigarmaker on the East Side. Graessel also introduced his stepgrandson to the collections of the Metropolitan Museum of Art and the American Museum of Natural History.[10] As Mumford reached young adulthood, these two museums, along with the New York Public Library, would become even more important to him, as he increasingly followed an autodidactic path.

Consciously or not, Mumford's social and aesthetic sensibilities were profoundly shaped by his stepgrandfather. His personal tastes remained modest and conservative throughout his life, owing no less to Graessel's example than to his mother's financial difficulties. In later years, Mumford was more a collector of books than of art or antiques. Moreover, it is no coincidence that connoisseurship would form only a small part of his writings.

* * *

In his autobiography, Mumford revealed that he was an avid reader, who at an early age favored the writings of Charles Dickens, Horatio Alger, and James Fenimore Cooper, among others.[11] He was a model elementary school student, but he derided his early education as intellectually unstimulating. His cramped school building seemed like a prison to him.[12] Despite his dissatisfaction, he advanced rapidly, skipping three grades; he was graduated first in his elementary school class in February 1909.[13]

Mumford attended the prestigious Stuyvesant High School in lower Manhattan, well known for its science-oriented curriculum, where he came into contact with students from all over New York City.[14] Unlike his elementary school, Stuyvesant greatly challenged Mumford, and several teachers became important mentors to him. In his autobiography, he maintained, moreover, that it was his science and technical courses at Stuyvesant that first started him on a lifelong interest in technology.[15] Mumford, however, was not the model pupil that he had been in elementary school. He maintained only a C average in high school, an indication of an increasing self-absorption in personal intellectual endeavors.[16] Mumford attributed his slackening interest in academics to his weakening health.[17] Although in his yearbook his classmates wrote, "Mumford is NOT going to be an engineer," his talent as a writer was clearly apparent to them; on a page of satirical class portraits, he was depicted as a scowling scribe.[18]

While in high school, Mumford maintained several extracurricular interests. He was an amateur wireless operator, and he began to submit short articles to *Modern Electrics,* a popular boys magazine of the period.[19] He was also an avid tennis player, and a member of the Stuyvesant team for two years. Central Park's 96th Street tennis courts were a familiar haunt to him as a setting for both athletics and romance.[20] On the paths by the courts, he caught his initial glimpse of Beryl Morse, his first serious girlfriend, with whom he would eventually collaborate on his early attempts at fiction writing.

Writing was the most time-consuming of Mumford's extracurricular activities. He wrote for several of Stuyvesant's student publications and was named literary editor of the *Caliper,* the school magazine, during his senior year.[21] Mumford also participated in student dramatic productions, both as an actor and as a writer. In 1911, he coauthored a play with three other students titled "Dr. Bilby's Aeroplane."[22] Mumford was himself a model airplane builder, and the play's subject reflected his developing interest in aviation technology.[23] He played the part of Benjamin Budd, "a thug," who harassed the eccentric Dr. Bilby.[24]

Mumford was graduated from Stuyvesant in June 1912.[25] He chose to attend the evening division of City College that following autumn because of his mediocre grades and uncertain financial situation. The tuition at the college was free to city residents, and he would be able to earn enough money during the day to meet his other expenses. He held several odd jobs during this period, including copy boy for the New York *Evening Telegram* and investigator for the Joint Arbitration Board of the Dress and Waist Industry.[26] These positions brought him into contact with some of the seamier aspects of life in Manhattan.

Mumford initially flourished at City College. In his autobiography, he fondly recalled the intellectual vigor of his professors and classmates at the evening session. Mumford improved academically in his first two years at City College, although he drifted without a major for several semesters, picking only courses that appealed to his intellectual appetite. He entertained notions of pursuing a Ph.D. in philosophy, but upon transferring to the day session in the fall of 1914, he found that he had to complete numerous required courses in which he had no interest.[27] At this stage of his life, the roots of his intellectual discontent ran deep.

In 1914, Mumford's college career was interrupted when a tubercular spot was diagnosed on his lung, and the matter of a degree and a future profession remained unresolved for several years.[28] Mumford would subsequently enroll in courses at Columbia University and New York University, in addition to a second interval at City College's evening division in 1917.[29] Although he assembled enough credits over the years to qualify for a baccalaureate degree, he never completed his undergraduate education.[30]

Mumford took great pride in the thoroughness of his self-directed education after he left college, an education conducted largely within the walls of the New York Public Library.[31] He read widely, absorbing the works of William James, Bernard Shaw, H. G. Wells, Samuel Butler, Leo Tolstoy, Henri Bergson, Peter Kropotkin, and Thorstein Veblen.[32] Veblen's *Theory of the Leisure Class* (1899) made an especially deep impression on Mumford, because of its scathing analysis of American class distinctions. Mumford was drawn to American literature as well, finding particular nourishment in the writings of Ralph Waldo Emerson and Walt Whitman.[33]

Significantly, it was at about this time that Mumford began to dabble in drawing.[34] Mumford had no formal training in art, except perhaps for some basic drawing manuals and a mechanical drawing class at Stuyvesant.[35] He made a number of competent portrait sketches of his family and friends and several of his City College professors. His favorite subject, however, was himself, and he seems to have carefully scrutinized his youthful features over and over again for some sign of his future destiny.[36] Brooding and handsome, Mumford depicted himself as the quintessential outsider. Soon he would expand his range of subjects to include architectural and city views. It is important to note, however, that even when these drawings were publicly exhibited in later years, Mumford did not consider himself an artist.[37]

As he grew older, Mumford considered his lack of a degree to be something of an advantage, and he thought of himself as belonging to a stellar company of intellectuals. In a random note from 1918, he wrote:

> It is impossible to examine the biographies of the leaders in Victorian science and art without coming to the conclusion that they owed some part of their vigor and originality to the fact that they escaped a formal education. Tyndall, Mill, Spencer, Dalton, Faraday, Dickens, and Shaw were none of them university bred. For that matter neither were Plato and Aristotle![38]

This passage also revealed Mumford's increasing awareness of his intellectual potential. That he dared to think of himself in the company of such luminaries was indicative not only of a youthful hubris but also of a determination to succeed. Moreover, as an outsider to the academic establishment, he would emerge as one of its most vociferous critics.

The continuous thread that connected Mumford's formal and informal studies was an unusual Emersonian self-reliance. Whether he was delving into literature, tinkering with radios, writing fiction, or studying philosophy, he immersed himself completely into his subject for its sheer intellectual pleasure. Yet, his inability to concentrate on his studies in high school and in college was indicative of a rebellious streak against established institutions. Mumford evidently did not regret abandoning his pursuit of a college education; he believed that his energies could be put to better use, especially at a time when an undergraduate degree was not yet a prerequisite for professional success.

Just before leaving academic life, Mumford encountered the writings of Sir Patrick Geddes, an unorthodox Scottish professor who would deeply influence the young American.[39] Geddes disavowed the separation of knowledge into academic disciplines and instead argued for an interdisciplinary approach to the study of civilization. A polymath who never earned a university degree, Geddes was the perfect role model for Mumford at a time when the young man could not settle on a single career path.

* * *

Mumford discovered Geddes's writings in the fall of 1914 while studying biology at City College.[40] Geddes's book *Evolution* (1911), coauthored with J. Arthur Thomson, had a profound effect on the young student. Geddes, a botanist by training, espoused an evolutionary approach to the study of both the natural and built environments. This approach was rooted in the Spencerian belief that society itself was an organism and that social progress was analogous to biological change. *Evolution* was thus a succinct application of natural selection to all aspects of cultural development. Geddes viewed evolution as a life process, and thus it was a fitting, all-encompassing label for his comprehensive theory of knowledge. In the introduction to *Evolution,* he attempted to clarify his broad definition of the term: "Changing order, orderly change, and this everywhere – in nature inorganic and organic, in individual and in social life – for this vast conception, now everywhere diffusing, often expressed, rarely as yet applied, we need some general term – and this is Evolution."[41] Following a general discussion of evolutionary theories that ranged from the Chevalier de Lamarck to Charles Darwin and Herbert Spencer, Geddes concluded that man and his environment were both mutually interactive agents and that the best means by which to study this complex relationship was the "regional survey." In the introduction to *Evolution,* Geddes discussed the regional survey and its interdisciplinary basis:

> Nature studies and social studies must again be generalized, and this not only separately but in unison. How so? By and from Regional Survey. Relief and climate, geological and botanical surveys, anthropological, archaeological and historic surveys all underlie our social studies. Our concrete science thus generalizes into a comprehensive regional survey, natural and social, rural and urban; as our abstract sciences advance and unite into a philosophy of evolution.[42]

In Geddes's unorthodox, interdisciplinary philosophy, Mumford found reinforcement for his own skepticism regarding academic overspecialization. Mumford was also reassured that it was permissible to have a variety of intellectual interests, and that these in turn could be synthesized into a meaningful career path. He wrote in his autobiography of the liberating effect Geddes's thought had upon him at this "unfocused" stage of his development:

> What Geddes's voice did was to lead me away from the well-paved avenue to professional success: his was the Song of the Open Road. By his own example he revealed a different approach: one full of pitfalls I could not anticipate, even had I

known his life story better than I then did, but also full of generous rewards, equally unpredictable.[43]

Geddes was a formidable role model for Mumford. Born in Scotland in 1854, he left his native Perth when he was twenty years old to study biology under Thomas H. Huxley at the Royal School of Mines in London. There Geddes also came into contact with Charles Darwin. At about the same time, Geddes became fascinated by the nascent field of sociology, absorbing the writings of John Ruskin and Herbert Spencer and the Positivist philosophy of Auguste Comte. Geddes was particularly influenced by Comte's hierarchical classification of the various "preliminary sciences," such as mathematics, biology, and chemistry as they culminated in the advanced study of sociology. A research trip to France in the winter of 1878–1879 brought Geddes into contact with the followers of Frederic Le Play, the originator of the social survey, which Geddes would subsequently adapt into the regional survey. In Le Play's sociological categories of family, work, and place, Geddes found striking analogies in the biological categories of organism, function, and environment. In his own work, Geddes later substituted the more anthropological term "folk" for Le Play's "family."

Geddes's interest in sociology had already begun to supersede that in biology when, in 1879, he experienced a temporary bout with blindness while conducting field research in Mexico. His eyesight was permanently weakened as a result, and he was effectively prevented from carrying out sustained microscopic research in the laboratory. Rather than hampering his career, however, this experience led Geddes to branch out in many directions. During his recuperation, Geddes devised the first of his "thinking machines," a system of shorthand on folded paper by which he could chart and synthesize relationships between ideas, objects, places, and fields of knowledge. What were comprehensive systems of classification to Geddes, however, were for the most part incomprehensible diagrams to the uninitiated. This inability to convey the complexity of his thoughts dogged the Scotsman throughout his life.

Upon returning to Scotland from Mexico, Geddes channeled his extraordinarily diverse intellectual energies into such fields as statistical analysis, economics, art criticism, town planning, and sociology. In 1888, he secured an unusual professorial appointment at University College, Dundee, which required him to teach only during the summer term, thus allowing him to pursue his numerous interests at other times during the year. Geddes initiated several social and educational programs in Edinburgh, including a series of privately financed building renovations in the city's notorious slums. He also traveled widely, taking his unusual philosophy and social agenda to Cyprus, Palestine, France, India, and America. Through his thinking machines and writings, but primarily through his personal contacts, Geddes sought to eliminate the barriers between various academic disciplines. Like

Comte, he firmly believed that each specialty had something valuable to contribute to a comprehensive system of knowledge under the heading of sociology. Studied together, these various fields of inquiry would yield fruitful information about the future direction of modern society.

In Geddes's view, the practical starting point for the study of society was the analysis of its physical structure, primarily as it was manifested in the development of cities. The regional survey, which combined the study of a region's topography, economy, history, and folkways, was his prescribed means of gathering this necessary information. Geddes first worked out his approach in theory through a series of comprehensive surveys of Edinburgh, and in practice through the various housing projects that he carried out in the city's Old Town. Alarmed by the blight that marred the center of Edinburgh, Geddes launched a counteroffensive, combining aspects of urban preservation and social reform. He founded several halls of residence for students at the University of Edinburgh, and he spearheaded the renovation of tenements on the model established by the English housing reformer Octavia Hill. Wherever Geddes could secure an open space in the congested Old Town, he advocated the planting of gardens to improve the health and the outlook of its residents. Geddes was also the driving force behind the building of Ramsay Gardens (1893–1894). This was an imposing range of apartment flats next to Edinburgh Castle designed by S. Henbest Capper in the Arts and Crafts mode. Geddes and his family lived in the topmost flat with its commanding view of the city's Old and New Towns.

One of Geddes's most visionary undertakings was the establishment in the 1890s of his combined cities exhibition and index museum in the Outlook Tower. Described at the turn of the century as "The World's First Sociological Laboratory," the Outlook Tower was situated in a crenelated structure next to Ramsay Gardens on Castlehill.[44] A camera obscura had previously been installed atop the structure, and Geddes seized upon this device as the centerpiece of the museum. Geddes renovated and reoriented the tower so that the visitor first ascended a staircase to the rooftop, where he absorbed a breathtaking view of the entire city. The visitor next entered the camera's enclosure, where he was given a detailed visual analysis of the surroundings as projected through the camera's lens. From there, he descended through the Outlook Tower, where at each level an exhibition detailed the human environment in increasing scope. From the level of the city and its region, the visitor passed into the country, the continent, and finally the world.

The explanation of the regional survey method was the key to understanding the various exhibits in the Outlook Tower. One of the most vivid visual elements of the regional survey was the "valley section," an idea inspired by the writings of the French geographer Elisée Reclus.[45] This was a schematic geographical cross section of a region into which were slotted the various occupations of society, ranging from the miner at the summit to the fisherman at the coastline. This model was particularly well suited to the hilly topography of Scotland. The Outlook Tower was also home to the Edinburgh Summer Meetings, an innovative series of courses covering a vast array of topics related to the regional survey.

Mumford's first exposure to Geddes's ideas in *Evolution* effectively changed the course of the young man's thinking, especially since Geddes considered education and the attainment of knowledge a lifelong process rather than a series of stifling classroom exercises. Mumford was also a quick convert to the regional survey. "From this time on, in my new explorations of the city, the shadowy figure of this new teacher accompanied me," Mumford wrote in his autobiography.[46] He next read Geddes's *City Development* (1904), a planning report prepared for the Scottish city of Dunfermline. Geddes's work in urban planning struck a deeply personal chord within Mumford. "[*City Development*] brought fully into consciousness my own growing interest in the city, for which my strolls with my grandfather had long ago prepared me," Mumford wrote.[47] Geddes's *Cities in Evolution* (1915), his most comprehensive treatise on city and regional planning, was next on Mumford's list. This book exposed Mumford to advanced European ideas, including those of Camillo Sitte, Raymond Unwin, and Ebenezer Howard. More important, Geddes's main thesis that society is an organism, whose development is analogous to biological evolution, permanently shaped Mumford's philosophical outlook. As Geddes explained in the first chapter of the book:

> For it is surely of the essence of the evolution concept – hard though it be to realise it, more difficult still to apply it – that it should not only inquire how this of to-day may have come out of that of yesterday, but be foreseeing and preparing for what the morrow is even now in its turn bringing towards birth....
>
> In short, then, to decipher the origins of cities in the past, and to unravel their life-processes in the present, are not only legitimate and attractive inquiries, but indispensable ones for every student of civics.[48]

Geddes looked optimistically toward the future. He argued that civilization was on the threshold of a "neotechnic" era in which clean industries, powered by electricity and supported by the region's resources, would replace the coal-driven, "paleotechnic" era of the previous century. Mumford would quickly appropriate these and other Geddesian terms into his own writings.

Mumford's contact with Geddes, initially through books and, beginning in 1918, through correspondence, cannot be underestimated as the single most important influence in Mumford's early intellectual development and the formation of his life's philosophy. Geddes's theory of evolution would guide Mumford's thought in a variety of fields. In his autobiography, Mumford recalled that Geddes himself was not fully aware of the effect he had on the young American beyond the field of urban planning. "How blind Geddes was not to realize that from the beginning it was in biology that he had made his most lasting contribution to my education – and even more profoundly to my life," Mumford wrote, noting that he had never even seen the Scotsman's cities exhibition in the Outlook Tower.[49] Geddes's evolutionary approach provided the underpinning for Mumford's books on utopias, American culture, technology, and cities. Not least through Geddes's peripatetic example, Mumford acquired a certain confidence about his own diverse interests that he had been lacking previously.

* * *

Geddes's writings soon led Mumford to the other leading figure in British planning circles, Sir Ebenezer Howard, the originator of the garden city.[50] Geddes had made a passing reference to Howard's ideas in *Cities in Evolution;* by 1916 Mumford was already familiar with Howard's seminal planning treatise, *To-morrow: A Peaceful Path to Real Reform,* first published in 1898 and revised in 1902 as *Garden Cities of To-morrow.*[51] A stenographer by profession, Howard approached the study of cities as an amateur sociologist. He was so deeply distressed by the social problems affecting his native London that he formulated an alternative, the garden city, based in part on his knowledge of nineteenth-century utopian tracts and experimental communities.

Howard envisioned the building of new, self-contained garden cities outside existing metropolitan centers. They were to be privately financed by the sale of mortgage debentures. A board of trustees would manage the ground leases, collecting modest rents from the tenants, paying interest to the debenture holders and other necessary expenses, and reinvesting the remaining funds into the community. Each garden city would have a population of about 30,0000 inhabitants on a site of 6,000 acres, large enough to foster cultural activity, but small enough to prevent social problems. The garden city itself would be developed on 1,000 acres, and the remaining land set aside for an agricultural greenbelt. This would ensure a steady supply of food to the garden city and at the same time would prevent metropolitan sprawl. The completed network of garden cities would be linked together via an efficient rail system.

What must have piqued Mumford's interest most about the garden city was Howard's sociological analysis of the benefits to be derived from combining the best features of rural and urban life, as symbolized by the well-known diagram of the three magnets. In the introduction to *Garden Cities of To-morrow,* Howard wrote:

> Neither the Town magnet nor the Country magnet represents the full plan and purpose of nature. Human society and the beauty of nature are meant to be enjoyed together. The two magnets must be made one.... Town and country *must be married,* and out of this joyous union will spring a new hope, a new life, a new civilization.[52]

Despite formidable economic obstacles, Howard founded two garden cities to the north of London during his lifetime: Letchworth (1903–1904) and Welwyn (1919–1920).

As Mumford soon realized, there were fundamental differences in the approaches of Geddes and Howard. Whereas the latter advocated the construction of new garden cities, the former recommended the rehabilitation of existing cities. True to his biological training, Geddes treated older cities as dying patients, calling for "conservative surgery" in treating their life-threatening slum conditions, and "diagnosis before treatment" in addressing their broader replanning. Yet Mumford found much that was complementary in their ideas, chiefly that architecture and planning without a carefully considered social underpinning remained just a collection of empty forms. One can discern an emerging synthesis in Mumford's mind in the following random note from 1916:

> City development, if one takes up the subject rigorously and follows its ramifications, is no simple re-adjustment of terminal facilities or block-layout, no mere provision of parks and playgrounds: it becomes more and more evident that there can be no thoro [sic] development of cities except on a regional scale, in a manner that shall comprehend not merely the dweller-within but also the dweller-without.[53]

At about the same time that he discovered Geddes and Howard, Mumford began reading architectural journals, keeping abreast of new developments in Europe and America. At this point, he had no clear allegiance to any particular style or movement, just a desire to know more about the subject. Yet, in a brief essay written in 1916 on architectural "eyebrows," his nickname for cornices, Mumford expressed an early disdain for needless ornament:

> Very often, when they are pinioned onto the bricks three qua[r]ter[s of the] way up the building they are positively eyesores; and when at their best the only just comment that can be made is that they do not disfigure the building. The point has been answered effectively by various architects who have created buildings both in America and in Germany and Austria in which these archaic survivals have been elim[i]nated.[54]

Inspired by his reading, Mumford was soon transformed into a roving architectural critic, conducting a series of regional surveys in and around New York City.

* * *

Mumford began writing to the Outlook Tower in 1915 in the excitement that followed his discovery of Geddes's teachings.[55] At the time, however, Geddes was involved in town planning projects in India, and he did not acknowledge Mumford's letters until 1918. Nevertheless, Mumford was spurred enough by Geddes's published writings to begin exploring the New York metropolitan region on his own, armed with a pencil and a notepad. These excursions also provided Mumford with much-needed exercise following his brush with tuberculosis.

While conducting these explorations, Mumford put his observations to paper in a series of notes that slowly evolved into more developed critical essays. "These surveys laid a firm basis for all my further studies in architecture and urbanism," he recalled in his autobiography.[56] Mumford supplemented these written notes with drawings that ranged from quick, on-the-spot graphite sketches to more developed compositions in watercolor, and his subjects included skyscrapers, tenements, streets, and parks.

New York City had expanded vastly in area in the years leading up to World War I. Fueled by successive waves of European immigrants, residential neighborhoods were extended deep into the outlying boroughs. Downtown Manhattan experienced a surge of skyscraper construction, culminating with Cass Gilbert's Gothic-revival Woolworth Building (1913), then the world's tallest. Closer to the ground, several important Beaux-Arts landmarks in the neoclassical style were also completed during this period, including McKim, Mead, and White's Pennsylvania Station (1906–1910) and Carrère and Hastings's New York Public Library (1911).

True to Geddes's call for regional surveys, Mumford explored the city from all possible angles: architecture, planning, geography, geology, sociology, and economics. Although he had no formal training in the history of art, he began to develop a sense of connoisseurship in the dating and attribution of architectural forms and styles. The late nineteenth century had left its distinctive stamp on most areas of New York City, and it was in this period of American architecture that Mumford became most expert. At this point in his critical development, he favored the architectural styles of the first half of the century to the eclecticism that followed. In a description of South Brooklyn written in 1916, for example, Mumford focused on a pair of Protestant churches to illustrate what he perceived as the decline in architectural taste over the course of the nineteenth century:

> As a contrast between the aspirations and artistic ideals of two periods an old M[ethodist] E[piscopal] church rebuilt in 1889 and an old Presbyterian Church rebuilt in 1846 are suggestive. The second is a sound, well-proportioned, simply designed structure of red sandstone (hewn, so the caretaker told me, out of the quarries at Belleville, N.J.); the other is a hideous jumble of turrets, arches, and gratuitous elaborations, a building that carries Victorian gothic and romanesque down to its last degrading level.[57]

Mumford took a particular interest in housing and its improvement largely because of Geddes's work in the rebuilding of Edinburgh's slums. While generally dismayed by contemporary conditions in New York City, Mumford sought out housing that departed from the usual speculative pattern. At Sylvan Terrace in upper

Manhattan, for example, Mumford discovered an unusual site plan, in which the houses were oriented around a garden away from the street. Nevertheless, he noted, they exhibited "the naive ugliness of that period of early jerry-building."[58] In describing a series of model tenements in Brooklyn Heights in 1916, Mumford noted that while the exterior was "curiously well-done in a sober, restrained way," the generous courtyard was "all-too-well fenced, and the amount of space given up for children's plays was too little."[59] His contemporaneous analysis of Upper East Side apartment buildings yielded virtually the same conclusion:

> Our rich people have ample incomes and yet allow themselves to be herded in lofty tenements whose sole outlook is upon the walls or courtyard of – another lofty tenement. We have not merely to redistribute cash, we must refix values. Nothing short of new ideas of heaven and hell – those orientation marks – will be satisfactory.[60]

These new values, Mumford continued, must result from "a change in habits of thinking, habits of acting, in the whole way and conduct of life."[61]

Mumford's exploration of the outer boroughs of New York coincided with a period of intense real estate speculation in what were still semirural districts. In his notes, he pondered the evils of jerry-building, as he watched the new subdivisions overrun the landscape, much as they had overrun the Upper West Side of his youth. A visit to the Queens neighborhoods of North Beach, Elmhurst, and Astoria left him wondering how a new planning strategy might be devised to reverse this dismal trend:

> The question we must ask is: how can we burke this development, get control of it, set it on healthier, better-considered foundations. We cannot too hastily arrive at our decision, if we have any to make. For while we are pondering the matter the jerry-building is being extended, the influx of population will quickly follow; and for another couple of decades, perhaps another century, Queens will be the scene of a lost cause and an abandoned idealism.[62]

Mumford, however, did single out nearby Forest Hills Gardens, Queens, for its exceptionally high standards of planning and design. Forest Hills Gardens was developed by the Russell Sage Foundation between 1909 and 1912 and designed by architect Grosvenor Atterbury; its curvilinear plan was devised by the Olmsted brothers. Following the example of many of Geddes's planning reports, Mumford began his analysis of Forest Hills Gardens from the "strikingly beautiful" train station, the initial point of reference for most visitors to the community.[63] While he described the houses as "individually superb," he did not find the village to be "collectively imposing."[64] Above all, he sensed that the opportunity to plan a genuine garden city had been lost. "The impression remains that Forest Hills must be made a flourishing *Garden* City before it can even pretend to be a city," Mumford concluded.[65]

Mumford soon extended his excursions beyond the New York City limits, roaming across Westchester County, the Palisades, and the New Jersey waterfront in an effort to acquaint himself with the entire topography of the metropolitan region. Eventually, he traveled as far afield as Boston; Portland, Maine; Philadelphia; Pittsburgh; and Washington, D.C. Pittsburgh made a particularly strong impression on him. In the summer of 1917, Mumford was employed as a laboratory assistant at the Pittsburgh office of the U.S. Bureau of Standards. During the day, he worked in a cement laboratory where he sketched chunks of architectural ornament before they were smashed.[66] At night, he continued his self-directed course of study in the Carnegie Library, reading works by Aristotle, Plato, John Ruskin, William Morris, John Dewey, and Jane Addams.[67]

Although Mumford spent most of his free time reading, the city's industrial character and unusual topography lured him into taking long walks in his new environment, notepad in hand. Late that summer he wrote: "Potentially the hilliness of Pittsburgh is full of benefits; it has prevented mass proliferations in housing, and helpt [sic] maintain the integrity of neighborhoods; at the same time it has resulted in unsightliness and hygienic negligence which wouldn't be tolerated in more plainly laid out cities."[68] Yet, time would even temper the impressions of a budding young critic like Mumford. In December 1917, he reminisced about his experiences the previous summer: "I shall not forget the little boxes of houses on the Laurenceville side, their smoke stained haze-softened walls and their gleaming slate roofs and the intermingling green or gold of poplar trees and locusts. The city showed the ruddy cheek of a lively urchin under its grimy daubs and discolored hair."[69]

Mumford spent several days exploring Washington, D.C., in the fall of 1919, and this city impressed him more than any other so far during his explorations. "In the broad layout of things Washington is surely the finest city on the North American continent and doubtless one of the spectacularly good cities of the world," he wrote.[70] While Mumford approved of the overall design of the city, his impression of its architecture was decidedly mixed. He disliked the "post-bellum hideousness" of Alfred Mullet's State, War, and Navy Building (1871–1888) and the "second hand beauty" of Smithmeyer and Pelz's Library of Congress (1886–1897), but at the same time, he admired Henry Bacon's Lincoln Memorial (1914–1922) and Paul Cret's Pan-American Building (1910).[71] Mumford did not restrict his observations to public architecture. His analysis of Washington's residential areas was written with an almost geological precision, drawing upon his previous observations of other cities:

> The capital seems to be the point of convergence of two regional modes: first, the two-story house, on a sixteen foot front, as occurs typically in Philadelphia and Baltimore, and second, the two or three story and dormer red brick house with an awkwardly designed and decorated mansard roof, such as one notes universally in the older part of Pittsburgh. On top of this widespread domestic foun-

dation are such later strata as the eight and ten story apartment houses in the heart of the northwest district, and the detached and semi-detached frame, brick, or stucco houses that fill up the outlying sections which I explored.[72]

During this period of intensive urban exploration, Mumford attempted to re-write his copious notes and longer essays into a form suitable for publication. In 1916, he began writing a long essay titled "A Regional Policy for Manhattan," which would have applied the Geddesian categories of place, work, and folk to the Garden City movement.[73] The following year, Mumford considered writing a comparative study of Boston, New York, Philadelphia, and Pittsburgh, an under-taking that he described in his autobiography in Dickensian terms as "a kind of sociological Tale of Four Cities"; he even submitted a synopsis to Appleton's, a publishing house that specialized in books about American cities.[74] Although Appleton's rejected his proposal, he continued to revamp his notes and ideas for even-tual publication.

In 1920, Mumford outlined another book based on his studies of New York City. Tentatively titled "Counter-Tendencies: An Outline of Regional Policy," it would have included chapters headed "The Regional Approach," "The Manhattan Region," "The Imperial City," "The Incipient Citizen," "Industry and Decentral-ization," and "The Regional Prospect."[75] Like Mumford's proposed "Tale of Four Cities," "Counter-Tendencies" never coalesced into a book, but its chapter titles hint at ideas that would be incorporated into his future published writings.

* * *

During this period of intense urban and regional exploration, Mumford was actively pursuing a career both as a playwright and as a screenwriter for the young, New York–based, motion picture industry. As mentioned earlier, he had been involved in dramatic productions while a student at Stuyvesant High School, and after he was graduated, he was encouraged to keep writing scripts by his girlfriend at the time, Beryl Morse. Morse became an active collaborator on some of these pieces during Mumford's first year in college, and one of their screenplays was produced in 1913 by the Edison Company. A print no longer survives, but Mumford described it in his autobiography as "a sentimental film" inspired by Edgar Allen Poe's poem "The Bells."[76] Despite some encouraging responses from publishers and a per-forming arts group in Baltimore, none of Mumford's remaining plays or screenplays was ever produced.[77] This was a source of great disappointment for Mumford throughout his life.

One reason that Mumford's dramatic works did not meet with much success was that they were often too autobiographical in content, and in style they strove too hard to emulate George Bernard Shaw, Mumford's favorite writer at the time. Unfortunately, Mumford's romantic plots lacked the sophistication of his Shavian models. Another overriding defect in his plays and screenplays was that he spent more energy on developing his settings than his characters. It was almost inevitable that he would provide a detailed backdrop for his fictional narratives, especially considering the amount of time that he spent wandering about the city and countryside. Although this tendency to dwell upon settings hindered his creative writing, it had the unintentional effect of strengthening his architectural criticism.

For the most part, Mumford's architectural analyses are contained in lengthy stage directions written with a Shavian flair. A number of these passages revealed Mumford's dislike of Victorian interiors. Around 1914–1915, while under the additional influence of H. G. Wells, Mumford wrote a screenplay for a science fiction fantasy called "The Survival of the Fittest," in which he described a futuristic room, freed from Victorian clutter:

> Night. Interior of the communal sitting room. Everything in perfect taste: chairs comfortable, buff walls simply decorated with border, floors bare. Every object has a utilitarian value – simplicity run riot. There are no windows; the room is lighted with what looks to be a Moore vapor lamp – the light is yellow, soft, and very pleasant. In the background a set of parallel tubes throwing out a warm, red glow, occupy what used to be the fireplace....
>
> Conspicuously absent are rugs, curtains, pictures, ornamental bric-a-brac and gew-gaws. The room is so unendurably neat that ... one might imagine the place to be paradise.[78]

An entirely different setting was envisioned for "The Invalids," a play written around 1916. The interior might well have been Mumford's own house:

> The living room on the second floor of a certain brownstone dwelling on the upper West Side: a sombre reminder of the architectural crimes that were rampant in the middle eighties. The furniture is essentially modern, of the better Grand Rapids type, altho [sic] here and there remain vestiges of the days that chafed the tender soul of Oscar Wilde.[79]

The protagonist of "The Invalids," Regius Storm, is a semiautobiographical character who is unable to seize life's opportunities at their fullest because of his sedentary lifestyle. Curiously, Mumford denied any personal connection to Regius Storm in a twenty-two page postscript that he wrote as a commentary on the play in 1917. Nevertheless, in the conclusion to the postscript, Mumford ultimately betrayed himself as the direct model for his protagonist:

> Assuming now that Regius knows how to do good work, with a good spirit: assuming that from his personal standpoint his life has become, in the words of Geddes (with whom Regius is by now I hope anxious for a more intimate acquain-

tance) eutechnic and euphysic.... Let him spend the rest of his days as a citizen helping to build the good place, verdant, beautiful, life-throbbing, out of the region in which he has chosen to live.[80]

Architecture itself was the central metaphor of another play written between 1917 and 1919, and it was one of Mumford's first developed pieces of architectural criticism. Originally titled "The Rundown House," it was later revised as "The Brownstone Front." The breakdown of the Victorian family is told through the deterioration of a brownstone dwelling as it is converted from residential to other uses. Mumford relied upon his mother's and his uncle's memories in reconstructing how a brownstone would have originally appeared.[81] Mumford's analysis of the use of brownstone in nineteenth-century architecture may have also been colored by Thorstein Veblen's *The Theory of the Leisure Class*. Veblen wrote:

> The endless variety of fronts presented by the better class of tenements and apartment houses in our cities is an endless variety of architectural distress and of suggestions of expensive discomfort. Considered as objects of beauty, the dead walls of the sides and back of these structures, left untouched by the hands of the artist, are commonly the best feature of the building.[82]

As filtered through the opinions of Veblen, Mumford viewed the pretentiously ornamented architectural facade as just another manifestation of upper- and middle-class conspicuous waste.

In act one, Mumford established brownstone as a drab, menacing material that was slowly taking over Manhattan in the late 1850s and supplanting the pleasant, red-brick architecture of earlier periods. Mumford took a Ruskinian stand against this kind of facadism:

> The secret of its use is given away in the very name applied to the buildings that this style created: they were not brownstone dwelling[s], but pre-eminently Brownstone *Fronts*. To live b[e]hind one of those gloomy chocolate walls, and to reside on a street that gave one the prospect of walls equally turbid and gloomy was the aspiration of every respectable family.[83]

Mumford's keen perceptions of class distinctions and bourgeois tastes, as imparted to him earlier by his grandfather, now made their way into his stage directions. Mumford deliberately noted that the house in question was built by the striving Langhorne family, who had not yet arrived in society: "Not everyone can keep the pace set by the families on Union and Stuyvesant Squares . . . and the Langhorne establishment is only near enough to the Square to get occasional whiffs of its festivities, and to bask in its reflected glories."[84]

The first act transpired in Mr. Langhorne's smoking room, located on the front side of the second floor of the house. Mumford described a high-ceilinged dark chamber with heavy moldings, a hanging gasolier, and heavy walnut furniture. Act two was set almost twenty-five years later. Although the Langhorne house was still intact, the neighborhood was threatened by commercial development at its edges. Moreover, the family's declining fortunes required that they take in boarders, a situation quite familiar to Mumford. The scene shifted to the now shabby downstairs parlor, which had been altered for use as a bedroom.

The third and final act transpired in the first decade of the twentieth century, when the Victorian brownstone had been supplanted by gleaming, white Beaux-Arts classical facades. In creating the context, Mumford offered perhaps his first mature observation on contemporary American architecture:

> Two conditions have contributed to this downfall [of brownstone]. New York architects, led by the cultured triumvirate, McKim, Mead and White, have turned aside from the misleading archaisms of [Henry Hobson] Richardson and the blank uglinesses of contemporary anonymity, and are reviving the Renascence, only to discover . . . that a more lustrous fabric than sand was necessary to their effects. . . . The second event that led to the arrest of the brownstone crime was the cheapening of steel girders, and the application of the american [sic] principle of skeletal construction to the economical building of skyscrapers.[85]

The Langhorne's house had been almost completely turned over to commercial purposes by this time, with a loft addition extending from the rear of the property. The house now contained a furrier, a woodworking shop, "the Alpha Transparency Company," an electrical contractor, an artistic novelties dealer, a photography studio owned by a descendant of the original residents, and "the Butterfly Waist and Dress Company."[86] The crowding of businesses within the house was not atypical during the period that Mumford was exploring the city and working as an investigator for the Joint Arbitration Board of the Dress and Waist Industry. The decline and partitioning of the house, moreover, paralleled the fragmentation of the Langhorne family, although a new marital union was forged by the play's conclusion. "The Brownstone Front" was never published or produced, but the color and form of its subject stayed with Mumford, resurfacing in his later books.

Mumford's plays and screenplays were useful literary exercises for the young writer, despite his inability to secure their production. His sentimental plots and underdeveloped characters did not prevent him from sketching out such ambitious social themes as the role of the model citizen and the breakdown of the American family. In these almost forgotten scripts, Mumford proved himself to be an insightful young critic of contemporary society.

* * *

Mumford's indecision regarding his future profession persisted well into his early twenties. Although he found his regional explorations and his fiction writing to be equally enjoyable, he was unsuccessful at publishing the latter, while the former did not suggest a clear professional direction. His frustration regarding his future seemed to have reached a turning point during a visit to the Maine resort of Ogunquit in the summer of 1916:

> The satire I was struggling to develop came to nought in Ogunquit, for every little witticism of sally was silenced by the ocean whose constant reminder was: cease this trifling and dabble no more with plots and puny fancies: deal with the elements: return to my bosom: otherwise your breed will perish and time and the tide which wait not for man will bury them forever. In that mood I left Ogunquit and traveled to Portland, with the dramatist's art further than ever from my mind, but with regionalism ever developing more clearly in my conceptions.[87]

Although Mumford continued to work on his plays after 1916, he did so with perhaps less conviction and fewer expectations of publication.

In the spring of 1917, Mumford had a personal epiphany that convinced him that his unfocused interests would eventually coalesce into a useful and varied life, not unlike the one led by Geddes. While he was crossing the Brooklyn Bridge to Manhattan, the combination of the weather, the Manhattan skyline, the East River, and the bridge itself seemed to act in concert upon his senses. In his autobiography, Mumford recalled this exhilarating moment in vivid terms:

> The world, at that moment, opened before me, challenging me, beckoning me, demanding something of me that it would take more than a lifetime to give, but raising all my energies by its own vivid promise to a higher pitch. In that sudden revelation of power and beauty all the confusions of adolescence dropped from me, and I trod the narrow, resilient boards of the footway with a new confidence that came, not from my isolated self alone but from the collected energies I had confronted and risen to.[88]

At that moment, a bond was forged between Mumford and New York City that lasted until the end of his life. The city, and Manhattan in particular, would become the dominant subject of his architectural and urban criticism. Mumford understood New York City more completely than any other urban area, and it became the touchstone for his broader views on architecture and urban planning.

* * *

Before Mumford's career as a writer and critic could even begin, it was interrupted by World War I. He had initially avoided enlisting in the armed services because of his health, but in April 1918 he passed a physical examination for the navy.[89] Before long, Mumford began training as a radio operator, putting his adolescent hobby to good use. Although he disliked the regimentation of navy life even more than college, he used his free time wisely, reading and exploring his environment. Mumford began his training in Newport, Rhode Island, where he spent "a few blissfully indrawn hours in the Redwood Library."[90] He was soon transferred to Cambridge, Massachusetts, where he began training at the radio school the navy conducted on the Harvard University campus. Classes were held in the law library of Henry Hobson Richardson's Austin Hall, bringing Mumford into direct contact with Richardson's work for the first time.[91]

Mumford had taken rooms in a boardinghouse in Cambridge, and there he made the fortuitous acquaintance of William B. Bigelow, a former principal in the short-lived architectural partnership of McKim, Mead, and Bigelow.[92] Little is known about Bigelow as an architect, except that he was an unusually talented draftsman. In 1879, Stanford White replaced Bigelow in the partnership, and the firm soon emerged as a national leader in the neoclassical revival. Although retired, Bigelow was Mumford's first real contact with a professional architect. Through conversations with the older man, Mumford was at last able to discuss his ideas in some detail, since until this point, architecture and urban planning issues seem to have been a solitary interest for him. He recalled, moreover, that it was Bigelow who first directed him to such periodicals as the *Century* and *Scribner's* magazine. "Bigelow opened a fresh path for me, in a way that no American book or university course on architecture then in existence could have done," Mumford wrote appreciatively in his autobiography.[93] From Bigelow's files, Mumford was also able to assemble a bibliography on New York City.[94]

One can only speculate about the interaction between the two men, since Mumford left no written notes about their conversations.[95] Bigelow may have opened Mumford's eyes to the beauty and richness of late-nineteenth-century architecture. During the period when Bigelow was a partner with Charles Follen McKim and William Rutherford Mead, the firm was designing residences in the informal shingle style. It is not difficult to imagine the older man reminiscing about his practice to the young sailor who had just seen so many shingled houses in Newport.

While living in Cambridge, Mumford continued the regional explorations that he had begun in the Boston area in 1915. Housing continued to be a dominant focus of his excursions, and he particularly admired Boston's lack of tenements and apartment blocks. His surviving notes delved into the social and economic forces that had shaped the Boston area:

> The impression I got was of a great melange of highly individualized communities, in which age and tradition gave to the present little more than a breath of the living past, and in which all the bleak delapidations of a fierce, humanity-scorning industrialism were set off, as between the spacious South Boston promenade and the mean tangle of streets adjacent, between the [Massachusetts] Institute of Technology and the refuse ridden backwaters of Cambridge, against vital socio-technic impulses which had already proved themselves capable, in the great park

system and in isolated public improvements of renovating the traditional order of free communities and replacing the mushroom enterprise of "unhampered industrial opportunity."[96]

During this ten-month interlude in the navy, Mumford also found time to enter a design competition for model housing sponsored by the *Journal of the American Institute of Architects* in 1918. Despite his lack of professional drafting skills, Mumford recalled that in the "first prospectus the sociological and economic sides were so plainly stressed that I formed forwith [*sic*] the notion of entering the competition."[97] Even after the printed rules governing the project plainly emphasized its design aspects, Mumford persisted. His working environment was hardly ideal. As he would later relate to Patrick Geddes, Mumford developed his project "while under restriction in barracks during an influenza epidemic."[98]

A fragmentary copy of Mumford's essay survives, and in it he proposed not just a design for a model house, but for an entire community to be built across the East River from Manhattan, a community based largely upon his reading of Ebenezer Howard, Geddes, and Thorstein Veblen. Mumford derided the standard American pattern of real estate speculation based upon the gridiron plan. If housing and the quality of life for American workers were to be improved, he reasoned, a new interdisciplinary approach to community design was needed. In his conclusion, Mumford stressed that economic, sociological, and architectural issues were inextricably bound together:

> It is for the living and evolving community that the artist must plan and the builder must build, and it is as much his privilege to shape that community into what it may be as to find out as a preliminary to this what it is. Freed from the money purpose, with its demands for irrelevant archaisms at one moment and sterile modernisms at the other, he has now set before him the task of working out a social purpose, whose ideals shall be embodied in fresh varieties of architecture and in [n]ew adaptations of form.[99]

Mumford called his proposed community "Garment Gardens." It was based on his previous experience as an investigator in the New York garment industry, whose workers were at the time largely clustered in slums on Manhattan's Lower East Side.[100]

Mumford's preliminary sketches for the competition survive, and they depict a typical two-family, two-story house that may have been conceived as a part of a larger terrace block.[101] His design is unusually modern in appearance, and it may have been based upon images of European housing that he had gleaned from American architectural journals.[102] It is characterized by unornamented geometrical wall planes, horizontal window openings, and low roofs that are almost flat in profile. He devised a flexible floor plan with rooms that could be expanded or used for multiple purposes.[103] Calculations that he made in the borders of his sketches indicate his preoccupation with ideal population densities for the community. Mumford did not win the competition, and in his autobiography he called this one and only attempt at architectural design "bold but inevitably amateurish."[104] Still, he was emboldened enough to begin sending written pieces to the *Journal*.

In general, this period away from New York City seemed to have increased Mumford's resolve to pursue a career as a writer. Just how much his writing meant to him is revealed in a note from January 1919, in which he recalled a visit home while on furlough: "Back in my old room, surrounded by my manuscripts (by means of which I drank huge draughts of Myself with great refreshment) the whole [naval] discipline dissipated itself into the mere memory of a nightmare of regimentation."[105]

* * *

Mumford's entrance into the field of journalism was a gradual process, and he did not experience an overnight literary success. Although he called the period of his enlistment in the navy "the hardest part of my literary apprenticeship," upon his discharge in February 1919, he already had published more than a half dozen articles, book reviews, and short stories.[106] In fact, 1919 was a watershed in his fledgling writing career. He more than tripled his literary output, and he established himself as a rising journalist at more than one periodical and in more than one field.

Many of Mumford's earliest published writings were heavy-handed expositions of Geddes's theories, which had not been widely circulated in the United States. For example, one of Mumford's most important early pieces, "The Marriage of Museums," attempted to impose Geddes's evolutionary framework upon the organization of exhibitions in museums of both natural history and fine arts. One can also discern the influence of Thorstein Veblen in some of the article's more satirical passages. Although it was published in the September 1918 issue of the *Scientific Monthly*, Mumford had made notes for the article at least two years earlier.[107]

The impetus for writing "The Marriage of Museums" was undoubtedly Geddes, who in *City Development* had advocated the planting of museums in landscaped parks.[108] These included buildings devoted to natural history, the fine arts, and assorted regional crafts, and they were part of a larger scheme to encourage the direct participation of the general public in the museum environment. Mumford utilized Geddes's ideas in a proposal that would introduce the standard evolutionary presen tation of the natural history museum into the fine arts museum. Using the familiar examples of the Metropolitan Museum of Art and the American Museum of Natural History, Mumford called for a "marriage" between the collections of the two museums. This new spirit of cooperation would be symbolized by reviving an unrealized proposal to connect the two museums via a path across Central Park.[109] Mumford wrote:

> The physical connection will serve to emphasize a cultural borrowing which has at once introduced the presentments of graphic art into the nature museum, and the organic conception of life into the art museum: with the result in certain galleries that the absent-minded visitor will be at loss to recall which museum he is making an inspection of.[110]

In the analysis that followed, Mumford satirized both institutions' methods of acquisition and display using terms and phrases that recalled Veblen's analysis of the predatory instincts of the upper classes. Mumford characterized museums in general as either "the robber's cave, the receptacle for princely loot, or the hunter's cache, the repository for animal skins and bleached bones."[111] In Mumford's view, their acquisition policies stressed quantity over quality, mainly serving to inflate the ego of "every rich ignoramus who has cared to perpetuate his name to posterity through a respectable interest in cultural activities."[112] While he realized that museums were dependent upon such collectors, he proposed that they abandon their "warehouse" mentality and provide the viewer with a better understanding of the object's original context.[113] In natural history museums, he endorsed the use of the painted mural as the appropriate means for providing such a context, and he urged that period rooms and models be used more frequently in fine arts museums for essentially the same purpose. Rather than dwelling on the isolated formal beauty of an object, the viewer would be enlightened as to its place in the larger historical and cultural continuum.

The second major article by Mumford to expound upon Geddes's views was "The Heritage of the Cities Movement in America: An Historical Survey," published in 1919 in the *Journal of the American Institute of Architects*. The article marked Mumford's critical debut in the architectural press. In the piece, he assailed what he viewed as the shortcomings of the "City Beautiful" movement in the years following the 1893 World's Columbian Exposition in Chicago. The City Beautiful, led by architects such as Daniel H. Burnham, Charles Follen McKim, and others who had trained at the Ecole des Beaux-Arts in Paris, urged a return to academic classicism in architecture and in planning, the building of axial boulevards, monumental civic centers, and other municipal improvements. Although Mumford did not attack the work of individual architects or the programs of specific cities in his article, his target was clearly Burnham.

Mumford's main thesis was that the City Beautiful was all form and no content, an argument that he had previously made in his play "The Brownstone Front." He viewed the many monumental projects as mere facadism, masking a whole variety of urban problems without correcting them. Neither the aesthetic nor the economic forces that lay behind the City Beautiful movement were spared his wrath:

> The new idea was that beauty could be superimposed upon the work of the jerry-builder and the speculator by getting an electrician to light up the main thor-

oughfares, an architect to rear up a classic city hall, a sculptor to sprinkle a few monuments, and the local municipal engineer to carve up a public place. And the result was, of course, not beauty to satisfy the artist, but conspicuous expenditure to satisfy the businessman. The aim was simply to "put on a front."[114]

According to Mumford, the major shortsightedness of the City Beautiful movement was its ignorance of the historical forces that shaped and threatened to destroy urban centers. Following the model of Geddes's valley section, Mumford argued that although cities developed from the confluence of various geographical and economic forces that cut across their regions, their peaceful and balanced development was largely subverted by the hunter-warrior class at the top of the hill. This resulted in the emergence of national capitals in the postmedieval period, whose political and territorial expansion only reinforced this destructive pattern, since they sapped the vitality from regional centers.

In light of these historical factors, Mumford criticized the City Beautiful movement for ignoring the role of the local community:

> Civic life cannot be carried on effectively until … the *meeting-places* of a new community are founded.
>
> The weakness of our plans for city extension in America, with their debasing imitations of Paris and Berlin, lies in our failure to perceive the significance of this fact.[115]

Mumford concluded his article with a seemingly radical call for "reconstituted cities," which would be the result of "reconstruction" and "political engineering."[116] Thus, power would be transferred from national capitals to regional centers, and a more viable urban pattern would emerge.

Mumford's criticism must have seemed unduly harsh to the *Journal*'s professional readership. That the *Journal* would even print such a controversial article was a testament to the vision of its editor, Charles Harris Whitaker.[117] The magazine was founded as the professional organ of the American Institute of Architects in 1913 with Whitaker as its first editor. He molded the *Journal* into a magazine that addressed a wide range of contemporary, historical, and, most importantly to Mumford, sociological issues. In a letter to Whitaker from March 1920, Mumford wrote: "There [is] . . . more live sociology in the J.A.I.A. than goes into the American Journal of Sociology. I fancy that you occasionally encounter undercurrents of opposition [to this] within the profession."[118] To this assertion Whitaker responded rather modestly: "There are a number of quite eminent American sociologists who read the Journal."[119] Still, Mumford's forceful writing style must have initially made even Whitaker wary. Architectural periodicals were constantly open to the threat of lawsuits, and as the official organ of the American Institute of Architects, the *Journal* had to be particularly careful in this regard.[120]

Although Mumford was not a regular contributor to the *Journal* at this point, the correspondence that developed between Whitaker and Mumford provided the aspiring writer with some much-needed direction. Their exchange of letters had begun with Mumford's unsuccessful submission to the housing competition in 1918. Whitaker was clearly impressed by Mumford's interest in architecture, and perhaps even more by Mumford's persistence in writing to the magazine. For his part, Mumford introduced Whitaker to the writings of Geddes and his circle of sociologists in Great Britain.[121]

In March 1919, Whitaker offered Mumford the opportunity to review books for the *Journal*.[122] When Mumford made his first trip to England in the spring of 1920, Whitaker arranged to have Mumford write pieces for the magazine on developments in British architecture and planning.[123] Mumford did not have the time to take advantage of these opportunities, since at this point in his career his writing was equally in demand from literary periodicals. Significantly, his architectural criticism did not initially flourish in professional journals; rather, it was part of a larger body of criticism that viewed the literary, dramatic, and visual arts as interrelated aspects of modern culture.

* * *

Between 1919 and 1922, Mumford produced a flood of articles and book reviews for various periodicals on a vast array of subjects ranging from architectural criticism to political commentary. The three publications with which Mumford was most closely associated during this period were the *Dial*, the *Sociological Review*, and the *Freeman*. With the exception of the *Sociological Review*, an academic journal, these were small periodicals oriented toward an intellectual readership, combining political commentary with artistic and literary reviews. They were not specifically oriented toward architecture or planning, although they occasionally printed pieces that dealt with these issues. Mumford's association with these periodicals brought him into contact with a number of influential individuals who would shape the direction of his career. At the same time, he was able to develop his characteristic writing style in an informed, popular manner.

The *Dial* was a fortnightly literary and political review with a rich publishing history that reached back to the last decades of the nineteenth century. Mumford joined the staff upon his discharge from the navy in 1919.[124] He was initially assigned to reviewing books, but he was soon promoted to the position of associate editor. Mumford's colleagues on the *Dial*'s staff included John Dewey, Thorstein Veblen, the prominent feminist Helen Marot, and his future wife, Sophia Wittenberg. At the time, the *Dial*'s staff was in the thick of the intellectual debates surrounding postwar reconstruction. "Our 'activism' was what specially distinguished us from 'The New Republic' and 'The Nation,'" Mumford wrote in his autobiography. "'Reconstruction' was our watchword."[125] According to Mumford, reconstruction encompassed not only the rebuilding of war-torn Europe, but the eventual government ownership of industry, progressive education along the lines formulated by Dewey, and a widespread moral reshaping of cultural institutions.[126]

Of all the members of the editorial staff, Mumford most admired Veblen. As has been already noted, the influence of Veblen can be detected in Mumford's earliest writings. In particular, Veblen's *Theory of the Leisure Class* seems to have held an extraordinary personal relevance for Mumford because of his bourgeois back-ground; Veblen essentially provided Mumford with the intellectual lens by which he could distance himself from his upbringing. Moreover, Veblen's economic phi-losophy was based on the principle of social evolution in human institutions. Such a philosophy meshed well with Geddes's views, and, in fact, the two men had crossed paths in Chicago in 1900.[127] Furthermore, at about the time that Mumford joined the *Dial's* staff, he enrolled in a course on modern economic development under Veblen at the New School for Social Research.[128] Mumford adhered closely to Veblen's ideas, remaining skeptical of the material benefits to be gained under a purely capitalist system.

During Mumford's seven-month tenure at the *Dial*, he wrote numerous book reviews, unsigned editorials, and articles on a variety of topics, although only a few were concerned directly with architecture and planning issues. He wrote two cap-sule reviews of new books on town planning for the September 20 issue. Mumford dismissed Frederick Noble Evans's *Town Improvement* for its "simplification of facts and formulae already notorious," but he was more receptive to the garden city ideas promoted in *New Towns after the War,* a tract published by Charles B. Purdom, Ebenezer Howard, Frederic J. Osborn, and W. G. Taylor under the collective pseudonym, "The New Townsmen."[129]

Another brief review that Mumford wrote of Claude Bragdon's *Architecture and Democracy* (1918) is particularly revealing, for it seems to have had a great influence in shaping Mumford's architectural criticism. A student of Louis Sullivan, Bragdon belonged to the more progressive wing of the architectural profession, standing apart from the Beaux-Arts classicism of the early twentieth century. Bragdon quoted extensively from Sullivan in *Architecture and Democracy,* and this seems to have been Mumford's first introduction to Sullivan's writings. In the book, Bragdon also di-vided modern American architecture into two categories: "arranged" and "or-ganic."[130] Bragdon's definition of organic architecture, as it was adapted from Sulli-van, stressed that a building's form should follow its function. Conversely, arranged architecture was rooted in the styles of the past. In his review of *Architecture and Democracy,* Mumford endorsed the organic approach:

> [Bragdon's] criticism of pre-war architecture, with its pretentious "period" fa-cades and its imbecility in design, the contrast between arranged architecture and organic, should doubtless be familiar to members of the profession who are acquainted with the literature of non-academic criticism from Ruskin to Mr. L. March Phillips. But the call to forget the solutions of other ages and to confront

the problems of one's own has not been adequately heeded, and it is well that architects should hear this exhortation from such eminent work-fellows as Mr. Bragdon and his master, Louis Sullivan.[131]

Although "organic" was a term that Geddes used frequently in his writings to describe all sorts of life processes and relationships, Bragdon's use of the term was more specifically tied to an American architectural tradition headed by Sullivan.[132] Mumford would become one of the chief proponents of this antiacademic tradition in his later writings.

Mumford's position and the positions of several of his editorial colleagues at the *Dial* were abruptly terminated in November 1919 when it was acquired by Scofield Thayer and James Sibley Watson and recast as a monthly literary and arts review.[133] Disconsolate, Mumford floundered for several weeks until he was offered the position of acting editor of the *Sociological Review,* the journal of the London-based Sociological Society.[134] The offer was extended by Geddes's colleague Victor Branford, who wished to revive the journal after its wartime hiatus. Branford was then busy reestablishing the society in its new headquarters in Pimlico, christened Le Play House, after the French sociologist. Although Mumford's tenure at the *Sociological Review* was even briefer, lasting only five months, it brought him close to one of Geddes's chief collaborators, and to the spirit, if not the person, of the Scotsman himself.

In fact, several years would pass before Geddes and Mumford actually met. At the same time that Branford offered Mumford the editorial position, Geddes had formulated other plans for the young man. Geddes hoped that Mumford would eventually turn out to be a suitable assistant. Toward that end, Geddes asked Mumford to travel abroad with him, first to Palestine, where he was planning the University of Jerusalem, and afterward to India, where he had teaching commitments. Mumford instead chose Branford's offer in London, which promised more secure financial remuneration, but with the hope that he might join Geddes later.[135]

Although Mumford had corresponded with Branford for less than a year prior to this, the letters that Mumford exchanged with Branford on the sociological applications of architecture were both encouraging and enlightening. In September 1919, Branford wrote to Mumford: "Your Heritage of American Cities [article] breaks new ground in applying the Geddes–LePlay formula [i.e., place–work–folk] in a sphere where most people in America, I fancy, would altogether fail to see its applicability."[136]

Mumford, in turn, kept Branford apprised of the state of American sociology and the activities of Veblen at the *Dial* and Whitaker at the *Journal of the American Institute of Architects.* "The Journal is a meeting place for the architects, as the Dial is in some sense for the socialized engineers," Mumford wrote to Branford in October 1919, but adding that "the respective groups are not yet in effective communication."[137] Several months later, Mumford wrote to Branford with more encouraging news: "The sociological outlook is achieving a position for itself with remarkable swiftness among the architects, town planners and engineers, and the only place where I can as yet discover no very sturdy signs of it is in the universities."[138] Through his contacts with Veblen, Whitaker, Branford, Geddes, and others, Mumford attempted to bridge these gaps in communication across disciplines and across oceans with somewhat limited success. Nevertheless, Branford was clearly impressed by the young man's potential. Branford excerpted some of Mumford's *Dial* pieces in the autumn 1919 issue of the *Sociological Review*.[139] With the pressures of revamping both the society and the journal, Branford welcomed the opportunity to take on an assistant.

Upon his acceptance of Branford's offer in April 1920, Mumford embarked upon his first trip abroad. In his autobiography, Mumford called this short interlude in London "a sort of postgraduate education that rounded off all I had learned, formally and informally, in my native city."[140] Yet, although he welcomed the opportunity to be on his own in a new city, his thoughts remained in New York, where he had become romantically attached to Sophia Wittenberg of the *Dial* staff before his departure.

As acting editor of the *Sociological Review*, Mumford was responsible for assembling material for future issues. He contributed book reviews to the journal, and he also assisted Branford with a graphic survey of Westminster.[141] Perhaps more important than Mumford's editorial output were the contacts and the invitations that his friendship with Branford and his position at the *Sociological Review* made possible. Mumford met the town planners Raymond Unwin and S. D. Adshead, prominent leaders of the generation following Patrick Geddes and Ebenezer Howard.[142] The trip also provided him with other professional opportunities. Mumford attended the Inter-Allied Conference of Town Planners as an observer for the *Journal of the American Institute of Architects* and the Labour Party Conference as an observer for the *Freeman*, although he failed to write the promised articles for these publications.[143]

Still, Mumford's editorial responsibilities were limited at the *Sociological Review*, and with financial concerns unresolved with the Sociological Society, he soon made plans to return to the United States. He had already become too stubbornly independent a thinker to be anyone's assistant, as his first difficult meeting with Geddes would confirm a few years later. It was a more mature, self-confident young man who returned to New York in October 1920 to meet his future wife, Sophia. After a stormy courtship that lasted almost a year, the two were married and set up an apartment in Greenwich Village.[144] There they moved freely in avant-garde intellectual circles, maintaining these friendly ties even after they relocated to an apartment in Brooklyn Heights in 1922. Sophia Mumford kept her job as an editorial assistant at the *Dial* until the birth of their son in 1925.[145] Despite this connection, Mumford sought regular writing posts at other periodicals.

Mumford eventually landed an ongoing free-lance position at the *Freeman*. With its broader editorial policy, the *Freeman* allowed Mumford to mature more fully as a critic with a clearly defined viewpoint. With equal facility, he reviewed books, plays, and art exhibitions in a consistently fair, but often irreverent and satirical style. Mumford's association with the *Freeman* lasted from 1920 until its demise in 1924, and while there he made numerous important literary connections. With Walter Fuller, the managing editor, Mumford shared an admiration for Geddes; it was also at the *Freeman* that he first met Van Wyck Brooks, who would encourage Mumford to plunge into the study of American culture during the mid-1920s.[146]

Mumford began writing for the *Freeman* just prior to his departure for England in the spring of 1920. Many of his early pieces were unsigned contributions to the "Miscellany" column under the byline "Journeyman," a title that Mumford regarded as emblematic of his whole literary apprenticeship.[147] He began by writing art criticism, a field for which he had no particular preparation beyond his reading and his visits to museums. What he did possess was a healthy skepticism about the field. In his first "Miscellany," for example, he irreverently mocked the art historical tradition:

> No one except a boarding-school "flapper" need view a Raphael under the impression that it is a supreme masterpiece of all time. We know better than that now. We feel that if Michelangelo had lived in the twentieth century he might have designed dynamos or skyscrapers: but we are sure that if Raphael were now on earth he would continue, as a successful illustrator, to palm off his madonnas and popes as magazine covers and portraits of successful business-men.[148]

In another piece, signed with Mumford's own initials, he wryly attempted to discern order within the chaos of modern schools of painting. He wrote:

> Every view of a modernist painting is an interview, and you cannot behave comfortably in its presence unless you are prepared to accommodate yourself to the peculiarities of the artist's personality. If he is a cubist, you must enter an angular world; if he is an ovularist you must enter an egg-shaped world; if he is a phallicist you must journey into a region where Mons Veneris has become Mont Blanc. Instead of seeking to convey an aesthetic emotion the modernist is satisfied to contain it, and this gratification of his private self has been the ruin of his ability to achieve adequate expression.[149]

While abroad Mumford submitted other pieces to the *Freeman* whose topics ranged from the design of public parks to the birth of Dada.[150] The reopening of the Tate Gallery provided him with the opportunity to reflect on J. M. W. Turner's extraordinary use of light: "No one apparently has ever taken so much pleasure as Turner in putting the effects of light on canvas; he was the solitary pupil of his own school and the tradition he created was not carried on until Whistler discovered in fogs and twilights the ecstasy that Turner found in radiance."[151]

Mumford wrote architectural criticism less frequently for the *Freeman*, developing his ideas on this subject only occasionally in book reviews and other small pieces. Although short in length, a review that he wrote of Charles Moore's *Daniel H. Burnham: Architect, Planner of Cities* in February 1922 was particularly significant for its cogent analysis of the deficiencies of neoclassical architecture and the City Beautiful movement as seen in the microcosm of Burnham's life. According to Mumford, Burnham and his colleagues practiced a kind of architectural pillage in recreating the great monuments of Europe: "[The American architect's] crude impulse was to transplant some of this plunder and set it up along Michigan Avenue and Riverside Drive: a Doric architrave here, a Parisian Champs Elysées there – why should the American city starve for beauty when the architect had only to 'help himself'?"[152] The bulk of Mumford's review concerned Burnham's famous 1909 plan for Chicago, which Mumford faulted for its vast, inhuman scale, its avoidance of slum rehabilitation, and its monotonous uniformity. He concluded with what was by now a familiar Geddesian diagnosis:

> Our chief ground for quarrel with this Augustan architect is that these monumental city plans are a projection of their environment and not a creative effort to remould that environment: Burnham did not perceive, apparently, that in order to reconstruct the city it might be necessary to revaluate its activities and to redirect the currents of its life into other channels.[153]

That Mumford had more critical leeway in a nonarchitectural journal like the *Freeman* was borne out by Charles Harris Whitaker's response to the review. "That's a bully review of Burnham's life!" Whitaker wrote to Mumford soon after it appeared. "Wish to God I could have published it in the *Journal* – where it belongs – but my hands are tied in such cases."[154]

* * *

During part of the summer and fall of 1922, Mumford and his wife Sophia traveled to Europe, in part to celebrate the acceptance of the manuscript for his first book, *The Story of Utopias*.[155] This initial literary success ended Mumford's tumultuous introduction into the publishing world, and the favorable reviews that it received firmly established him in the American literary community. Researched and written in less than three months in the spring of 1922, the book appeared in November upon the Mumfords' return from Europe.[156] In content and structure, *The Story of Utopias* laid the foundation for many of Mumford's later writings in architecture and planning.

The Story of Utopias was a broad historical survey whose territory ranged from Plato's *Republic* to H. G. Wells's *A Modern Utopia*. Mumford had been interested in utopias since studying philosophy at City College, where he wrote a term paper on the subject.[157] Not surprisingly, the project was largely inspired by Patrick Geddes, who called Mumford's attention to the fact that "Utopia" was a pun by Sir Thomas More on "Eutopia," the good place, and "Outopia," no-place.[158] Moreover, in Geddes's postwar tracts, co-written with Victor Branford, Mumford found numerous references to eutopia, which would be built from the ruins of the great conflict in Europe. To both Geddes and Branford, the eutopian ideal was the end result of social evolution, and the regional survey was the best means by which the progress of society could be measured. In their book *The Coming Polity* (1919), Geddes and Branford wrote:

> For Eutopia is an environment ensuring the survival not merely of the fittest but of the best.... [T]he Eutopian ideal is concerned with the well-being of communities in their regions, cities and nations; with the friendly coming together of national groups, and so on increasingly, up to the growing establishment of the Human Commonwealth.[159]

Around 1920, Mumford was searching for a book topic, and it only remained for his colleague at the *Freeman,* Van Wyck Brooks, to suggest that he collect his ideas on utopias for publication.[160] The book elaborated upon themes already expressed in Mumford's writings, chiefly the postwar reconstruction of society along progressive lines, but it allowed him to develop these themes at greater length. Furthermore, as historian Casey Nelson Blake has shown, Mumford also had a political motivation for writing the book.[161] In the period following the demise of the old *Dial,* Mumford was attempting to refocus what he saw as the emptiness and disillusionment of postwar radical thought, toward what his late colleague Randolph Bourne had affectionately called the "Beloved Community."

In organizing *The Story of Utopias,* Mumford divided utopian writings into two broad categories: utopias of escape and utopias of reconstruction. According to Mumford, the former sought refuge from the world and the latter sought more positively to change it. He called the inner world of human ideas that generated the utopian impulse the "idolum," through which "the facts of the everyday world are brought together and assorted and sifted, and a new sort of reality is projected back again upon the external world."[162] His historical survey of utopias included among others discussions of Plato's *Republic,* Sir Thomas More's *Utopia,* Johann Valentin Andreae's *Christianopolis,* Francis Bacon's *New Atlantis,* Charles Fourier's *Le Nouveau Monde Industriel,* Etienne Cabet's *Voyage en Icarie,* William Morris's "Valley of the Thames" in *News from Nowhere,* and H. G. Wells's *A Modern Utopia.*

The spirit of Geddes loomed large over the entire book, beginning with Mumford's discussion of Plato's *Republic* as an early precedent for the valley section.[163] Mumford was particularly excited over his discovery of Andreae's "Christianopolis." Andreae was a contemporary of Bacon, and Mumford ranked his seventeenth-century humanist utopia with Plato's for its enduring appeal.[164] Significantly, Andreae made provisions in his ideal community for both the study of nature and –

unlike Plato – of art, in buildings that anticipated the rise of nineteenth-century museums.[165]

Following his discussion of H. G. Wells in chapter nine, Mumford's format shifted from the history of utopias to an analysis of what he called "collective utopias."[166] These were contemporary social beliefs or myths held by society at large and manifested in towns and cities across the United States and Great Britain. He labeled these collective utopias the "Country House," "Coketown," and "Megalopolis." Mumford argued that modern society must reorient itself away from such artificial, and ultimately, inhumane environments.

Fresh from his contact in England with the aristocratic Branford, Mumford's description of the Country House was especially vivid. He used the term to describe not only the traditional estate, but its bourgeois imitations in suburbs everywhere. On economic grounds, he criticized the lack of connection between the consumption-oriented Country House and the labor that supported it. The arts themselves were among the chief goods that the Country House consumed. Moreover, Mumford believed that the revivalism that characterized Country House architecture was symbolic of what was wrong with the state of architecture in general:

> Observe the architecture of our Country House. If it has been built in England during the last three hundred years, the style is probably that bastard Greek or Roman which we call Renascence architecture; if the Country House was built in America during the last thirty years, it is as likely as not a Tudor residence with traces of castle fortification left here and there on the facade.[167]

In his view, the Country House fostered an appreciation of the arts rather than emphasizing the vital role which they play in the life of a community. Recalling his earlier piece on museums, he wrote:

> The effect of this gourmandism in the arts can be detected in every element of the Country House from cellar to roof; for the result has been to emphasize the collection of good things rather than their creation, and there is an aspect in which the Country House is little better than a robber's hoard or a hunter's cache – a miniature anticipation of the modern museums of natural history and art.[168]

Coketown, the second social myth that Mumford addressed in this chapter, was a term borrowed from Charles Dickens's novel *Hard Times* (1854). Mumford used it to describe the debased way of life he had witnessed in the industrial cities of England and America, particularly Pittsburgh. The economy of Coketown was based on factory production, and the city itself was planned on a monotonous grid that made no allowances for the natural topography of the area. Whereas the Country House was oriented toward consumption, Coketown was geared toward production. Obsolescence was built into products so that markets could keep expanding, resulting in giant rubbish heaps. According to Mumford, escape from this environment came through such outlets for mass entertainment as Broadway or even debased versions of Country Houses for the working classes themselves.

Megalopolis, the third of Mumford's collective utopias, was the bureaucratic center of the National State, controlling a large territory and obliterating regional competitors. Mumford's models for Megalopolis were clearly New York and London, whose impossible scale he saw as both seductive and destructive: "So the chief aim of every other city in the National Utopia is to become like Megalopolis; its chief hope is to grow as big as Megalopolis; its boast is that it is another Megalopolis."[169]

As an alternative to the ever-worsening quality of modern life under the Country House, Coketown, and Megalopolis, Mumford outlined his own eutopia in the last chapter of the book, a eutopia inspired, not surprisingly, by Patrick Geddes. The general format of *The Story of Utopias,* in fact, loosely followed Geddes's dictum "diagnosis before treatment." Thus, the review of utopian literature and collective utopias constituted Mumford's diagnosis of the past, while his treatment for the present was outlined in a general prescription for eutopian change. Mumford felt that a change in society's values must occur before the external world could be rectified. The inability to recognize this, he argued, was the chief failure of Marxism and other "partisan" utopias of the nineteenth century.[170]

Mumford's eutopia was predicated on the linkage of utopian ideals with the everyday world. New technologies would aid in this process, he argued, and the arts and sciences would work together for the general improvement of the community. The best means by which to accomplish this cooperation between disciplines, he believed, was the regional survey: "Regional survey, then, is the bridge by which the specialist whose face is turned towards the library and the laboratory, and the active worker in the field, whose face is turned towards the city and region in which he lives, may come into contact; and out of this contact our plans and our eutopias may be founded."[171]

Mumford only hinted as to what form eutopia should take, but it was clearly based on the garden city model of Ebenezer Howard that had already been realized in the English communities of Letchworth and Welwyn. Although Mumford had not visited either community while abroad in 1920, he had, as mentioned previously, met Raymond Unwin, one of Letchworth's town planners. In any case, from what Mumford had read about the garden city, he was convinced of its potential for success in America. Earlier in the book, he introduced the idea of the garden city to the reader:

> In 1898, Mr. Ebenezer Howard reconstructed [utopia] and set it forth in a persuasive little book called Tomorrow, and as a direct result of the plans advocated by Mr. Howard, a flourishing Garden City called Letchworth has come into existence; which in turn has propagated another garden city, called Wellwyn [sic]; and at the same time has, by example, paved the way for numerous other garden cities and garden suburbs in various parts of Europe and in America.[172]

In his conclusion, however, Mumford reemphasized that physical plans not accompanied by society's renewal were essentially futile: "Without the common background of eutopian idola, all our efforts at rehabilitation – the new architecture, the garden city movement, the electrification of industry, the organization of great industrial guilds . . . – without these common idola, I say, all our practical efforts are spotty and inconsecutive and incomplete."[173]

Mumford amplified his views on the garden city's role in eutopia in a 1923 article for the *Menorah Journal*, in which he discussed the utopian ideals of Theodore Herzl, a leading Zionist at the turn of the century. Herzl's *Alteneuland* (1904) had not been part of Mumford's survey in *The Story of Utopias*, and thus the article formed a sort of postscript to the book. Mumford suggested that rather than looking to Palestine for the reestablishment of an ideal community, Jewish leaders should look to other countries. He further proposed how a garden city might be planted near New York City:

> Suppose, now, that the principles so clearly outlined by Herzl for use in Palestine were applied to the creation of a Garden City on Long Island – a city in which the land would be owned in perpetuity by the community, in which appropriate culture institutes would be planted, in which the spiritual values which Zionism seeks to realize would be enshrined in the daily practices of the community.[174]

Significantly, this passage recalled Mumford's rejected essay for the *Journal of the American Institute of Architects*, in which he had proposed the establishment of a similar community in roughly the same location. In fact, construction would begin in 1924 on Sunnyside Gardens in Long Island City, Queens, the first community planned along garden city lines in America. Mumford's involvement with this project is discussed in chapter 4.

The Story of Utopias was well received in both Great Britain and the United States by critics who welcomed Mumford's fresh outlook on modern culture. Writing in the London-based *Literary Review*, Alfred Zimmern praised Mumford's critical faculty: "Mr. Mumford . . . treats his subject not merely descriptively but critically, so that what might seem, from a brief catalogue of its contents, a mere summary or compilation of other men's work turns out to be a work of real reflection and originality."[175] A. Emerson Palmer of the *New York Times Book Review* concurred: "A 'study' or 'survey' of utopias would almost certainly be a better fit as a title for Mr. Mumford's substantial and well-made book. Somehow 'story' does not seem adequate to describe the result of much reading and research, and not a little close reasoning and philosophizing."[176] Many of these favorable reviews were written by Mumford's colleagues at other literary journals, and this signaled Mumford's full acceptance into their ranks. For example, Robert Morss Lovett, Mumford's former editor at the *Dial*, wrote: "To bring both science and art to the service of mankind is Mr. Mumford's utopia; and if this seems a hard saying it is most persuasively and engagingly said."[177]

Perhaps the most welcome response to the book came from Victor Branford, who had helped to inspire it. Branford wrote to Mumford in November 1922: "I write now to send you most hearty congratulations on producing a work which will, I believe, mark a new departure in the literary attitude towards the subject. Your account[s] of Coketown and Megalopolis are certainly masterpieces that will live."[178] Curiously, Branford's use of the adjective "literary" rather than "sociological" seemed to anticipate the new path that Mumford's career was about to take.

At about the time *The Story of Utopias* was published, Mumford's contacts with the world of American letters had already begun to take precedence over his connections with Patrick Geddes, Branford, and the other members of the Sociological Society. Although Mumford was still acting as a reporter of Geddes's ideas, he was beginning to think more independently as a critic. Having successfully completed his first book, Mumford would apply what he had learned from his mentors to a new and largely undefined area: American culture. In his next four books, whose subjects ranged from American architecture to a biography of Herman Melville, Mumford would establish himself as a critic of considerable breadth and influence.

* * *

Before Mumford could break free from the ideological grip of Patrick Geddes, he first had to meet the energetic Scotsman. The two men had carried on a stimulating correspondence since 1918 that covered a vast range of issues, including the state of sociology, the potential role of motion pictures in education, and the political situation in Ireland. As early as December 1919, Geddes had raised the possibility of Mumford's collaboration, and it was only the Scotsman's sudden departure for India that prevented Mumford from joining him in England in 1920.[179] Geddes finally visited America in the spring of 1923, largely through Mumford's organizational efforts.[180] The trip was ostensibly planned around a series of lectures at the New School for Social Research in Manhattan, but uppermost in Geddes's mind must have been the possibility of persuading Mumford to work with him as an assistant.

Geddes's trip to America was an unmitigated disaster according to Mumford, primarily because of Geddes's notoriously difficult personality and the many false expectations raised by their correspondence. "Somehow, our companionship got off on the wrong foot," Mumford wrote in his autobiography, "and we never managed to fall in step afterward, though we tried more than once to begin all over again."[181] In a letter to Geddes written during the visit, Mumford made his resentment clear:

> In one sense, I have the feeling that we have yet to *meet*. We both have been aware of the obstacles to meeting: but it is rather hard to climb over them, partly because of the gap between our generations and our varieties of secular experi-

ence, and partly because my respect for you is so great that it reduces my mental reactions in your presence to those I used to feel in the presence of my teacher when I was twelve years old – that is, complete paralysis! Putting this last matter aside, there is a real barrier to understanding between us in the fact that you grew to manhood in a period of hope, when people looked forward with confidence to the "great world spinning forever down the ringing grooves of time"; whereas I spent my whole adolescence in the shadow of war and disappointment, growing up with a generation which, in large part, had no future.[182]

In a subsequent passage, Mumford tactfully indicated that a collaboration between the two could never work:

> You came over to America without, I suppose, any sufficient awareness of this change which, apart from any mere difference of age, separates a large part of the younger generation from the older: you came over, too, with a somewhat over-idealized portrait of me in your mind, as a vigorous young apprentice who might work at the same bench with you for a while, and keep on at the task when you had gone back from America. You are naturally disappointed to find me bound up with literary vocations, and to find that by natural bent and by training I am of the tribe of Euripides and Aristophanes rather than that of Pythagoras and Aristotle; a trait which is, possibly, a little obscured by the fact that mere necessity and convenience oblige me to get my living, from day to day, with the Sophists of journalism. . . .
>   . . . Eutopitects build in vain unless they prepare the mind as well as the ground for the New Jerusalem; and nothing you have said has shaken me in the belief that the best part of my work must be in the first field rather than in the second, although it may be true that I shall do the first task more sanely and adroitly if I have had a little direct experience of the second.[183]

Later that year, Geddes referred to the episode, with not a little of his characteristic irony:

> Write too, at leisure, yet before long, of how far you are *helped* & how far *discouraged*, by our active acquaintance of these past months, and of what sort of cooperation, if such you still think of in general ways, seems visible. You understand, do you not that I quite appreciate "*Utopias*" & as such very real cooperation. But I must stop now – & post – I hope Mrs. Mumford & you have found your country house?[184]

Although Geddes's apologetic response rekindled Mumford's admiration, the damage had been done. "Though we met briefly in 1925 and corresponded at irregular intervals up to the month of his death in 1932," Mumford wrote in his autobiography, "this parting was really our final one."[185] However frustrating this encounter proved to be, it ultimately had a liberating effect on the young man.

After Geddes's departure at the end of the summer of 1923, Mumford was finally

free to pursue his own intellectual interests. Nevertheless, Mumford would continue to acknowledge his debt to Geddes in numerous books and articles over the
course of his career. Mumford became Geddes's most effective spokesman, bringing
Geddes's ideas to a much wider audience than the Scotsman was ever able to reach
on his own. What Mumford came to value most about Geddes's life and work was
its "insurgency," a rebellious quality that prompted Geddes to reject the status quo
in favor of the fullest life imaginable. In a 1929 article in honor of Geddes's seventy-
fifth birthday, Mumford wrote: "Since men value the equanimity of Socrates or the
vision of Plato, they will come, I think, to treasure likewise the insurgence of
Patrick Geddes. He has shown the weakness of our customs, our mechanisms, our
automatisms; and in his own being he has demonstrated the impetus and the complete trajectory of life."[186]

Although the focus of Mumford's writings would shift toward the study of American culture during the mid to late 1920s, in his search for an ever larger cultural
synthesis and in his rebellion against the academic establishment, his intellectual
debt to Geddes endured. In 1925, Mumford named his first-born son Geddes after
the man who had loomed so large in his intellectual development.[187]

2

THE STUDY OF ARCHITECTURAL HISTORY

Between 1880 and 1895 the task and method of modern architecture were clarified through the example of a group of American architects whose consistent and united efforts in this line antedated, by at least a decade, the earliest similar innovations in Europe. Modern architecture had its beginning in this period.

— The Brown Decades: A Study of the Arts in America, 1865–1895

Although Lewis Mumford was not an architectural historian in a strictly academic sense, as an architectural critic, he made many important and enduring contributions to the study of the past, beginning with *The Story of Utopias* (1922).[1] During the mid to late 1920s, his focus narrowed from the broad tableau of Western civilization to the more specific study of American culture, only to widen again during the 1930s.[2] Architecture was not the only subject of Mumford's historical books, but, as the formal record of human development, architecture was integral to his larger cultural analysis.

From Patrick Geddes, Mumford had learned that the study of history was essential to understanding the present stage of a society's development and to formulating a plan for its future growth. Mumford's investigation led him first to the origins of American civilization in the seventeenth century, and, subsequently, to the nineteenth century, when America claimed its cultural independence from Western Europe. It was Mumford's greatest hope that his own contemporaries would be inspired to new heights of creativity once they had been reconnected spiritually to their past.

There were a number of reasons behind this intellectual shift. Mumford had carried the ideological torch of Geddes, Victor Branford, and the Sociological Society in America for several years, and he was anxious to make his own mark among his peers. Writing *The Story of Utopias* had freed him from his discipleship under Geddes. Moreover, by the mid-1920s, the issue of postwar reconstruction had lost its urgency in light of the nation's general economic prosperity. Van Wyck Brooks touched on Mumford's quandary in a 1922 letter, explaining the reservations that *Freeman* editor Albert J. Nock had with Mumford's sociological outlook:

> I am quite sure that it all goes back to the "sociological" question, and that there is nothing personal in it. Many and many a time I have heard [Nock] praise your work when it dealt with purely literary and artistic subjects. But he cannot abide, I think, the names of Veblen, Geddes, etc. or any of their words and ways.[3]

Consequently, Mumford began focusing on the type of writing that suited him best – literary, art, and architectural criticism – both to find an appropriate niche as a writer and to support his family.

Mumford's interest in American historiography stemmed largely from his association with Brooks, whom Mumford had met in the offices of the *Freeman* in 1920.[4] Brooks was a pivotal figure in the New York literary world and a leading authority on nineteenth-century American literature. He became an important mentor to Mumford, especially after the 1923 break with Geddes. Mumford soon joined Brooks in the quest to uncover America's "usable past." Brooks had coined this phrase in a 1918 article for the *Dial* in which he addressed what he perceived to be a malaise in American literary criticism. One way out of this malaise, according to Brooks, was for writers to probe into their own literary roots: "The spiritual past has no objective reality; it yields only what we are able to look for in it."[5] To Brooks, Mumford, and other critics during this period, it was essential that American artists and writers reconstruct their past as a foundation for their future creative endeavors. Before this could happen, however, American history had to be disentangled from that of Europe.

Mumford delved into America's usable past in his next four books: *Sticks and Stones: A Study of American Architecture and Civilization* (1924), *The Golden Day: A Study in American Experience and Culture* (1926), *Herman Melville* (1929), and *The Brown Decades: A Study of the Arts in America, 1865–1895* (1931). Of the four, *Sticks and Stones* and *The Brown Decades* were primarily critical histories of American architecture. Both books were extremely significant because they radically upset what was then a conservative field. Mumford eschewed the traditional, formalist approach in favor of analyzing the broad social movements that shaped the built environment. He was particularly interested in the interrelationship between America's architecture and its art, literature, philosophy, economics, and religion. During the course of his investigations, Mumford identified and celebrated a pantheon of distinguished American writers, artists, and architects that included Ralph Waldo Emerson, Thomas Eakins, and Louis Sullivan. Thus for Mumford, the nation's cultural heritage functioned as a wellspring from which his contemporaries might draw inspiration in the present.

* * *

Since Mumford had no academic background in architectural history, his extensive knowledge in this, as in other fields, was largely acquired through self-directed reading and observation. As a youth he had read the social and aesthetic criticism of William Morris and John Ruskin, and Mumford retained something of these critics' moral fervor in his own writings. While researching the cities of the eastern seaboard, Mumford also became familiar with many of the general and local histories of American architecture available to him at the New York Public Library. He supplemented his reading through direct observation of his surroundings, becoming a connoisseur of building materials and forms.

Mumford's earliest writings reveal a critic dissatisfied with his surroundings, but unsure of what steps architects might take to improve them. The romantic legacy of such nineteenth-century architects as Henry Hobson Richardson was nothing more than a jumble to Mumford's untutored eye. In a 1922 essay, Mumford wrote: "No one who has an eye for the fine incidence of beautiful architecture can avoid a shock at discovering a monumental Romanesque building at the foot of Pittsburgh's dingy 'Hump,' or the hardly less monstrous beauty of Trinity Church, Boston, as one approaches it from a waste of railroad yards that lie on one side of it."[6]

Over the next several years, Mumford worked diligently to master the field of American architectural history, mainly by writing book reviews and short essays on the subject. His opinions reached a wide audience of both professionals and laypeople, since in addition to being a regular contributor to the *Journal of the American Institute of Architects* and the *Freeman,* he was beginning to write with some frequency in the pages of the *New Republic,* the *American Mercury,* and other general-interest magazines.

Robert Littell, the book review editor at the *New Republic,* recognized in Mumford a budding young talent with an unusual grasp of a broad range of subjects. More often than not, Mumford was assigned to review books on art and architecture, if only because there were no other staff members with the requisite expertise. This caused Mumford some concern, however, since he adamantly refused to be pigeonholed into a single field. Littell reassured Mumford that this would not be the case: "Don't think that I am trying to crystallize you into an architectural expert. You are an expert in a lot of things – or better, let's say you are not an expert at all, but merely a member of our regular reviewing batting order. I know that you can hit curves as well as straight balls shoulder high."[7]

The few books on American architecture that appeared during the early 1920s were primarily concerned with the colonial period through the Greek revival. The later nineteenth century, if discussed at all, was usually treated as a digression into eclectic bad taste that was not redeemed until the 1893 World's Columbian Exposition returned neoclassicism to the public's favor. Mumford took issue with this biased view of the past, especially since it was used by historians to validate the work of contemporary architects in the neoclassical mode.

Although Mumford's criticism was always balanced and not prone to personal attack, his more controversial pieces continued to appear in the nonprofessional magazines. In March 1922, for example, he reviewed Talbot Hamlin's *Enjoyment of Architecture* in the *Freeman,* criticizing the author's defense of a modern style based upon historical forms:

> Mr. Hamlin is perhaps a little too ready to defend archaeological detail against the criticism of those who seek more functional modes which shall arise out of modern necessities of building, and accentuate what is peculiar and fine in modern civilization.... Mr. Hamlin apparently does not discriminate between adapting a live tradition and copying a dead form.[8]

The following year Mumford intensified his attack against historical revivalism in a lengthy review of Fiske Kimball's *Domestic Architecture of the American Colonies and of the Early Republic.* At the time, Kimball was the doyen of American architectural history and the chief advocate of an American neoclassicism.[9] While Mumford praised the book for its wealth of information regarding Georgian and Federal architecture, he criticized Kimball's conclusion that neoclassicism was the only appropriate national style for the United States:

> It is precisely because we are no longer dealing with our ancestors' problems and solutions, but with our own, that the relation of the classic style to function becomes a highly important question today; and it is because of the elephantine inadaptability of the classic mode, in pure or Renaissance design, that we feel a sense of biting futility when we contemplate the pious and elegant stylicism to which we are nowadays being treated.[10]

Yet, in certain cases, Mumford believed that revival architecture was acceptable in a historic setting. In a 1923 article, he advocated such a contextual approach when and where appropriate: "Piety and originality, tradition and innovation, are each good in their place; and they are altogether pathetic and ludicrous when they are out of it. It is equally vain to deny the past where it exists, or to attempt to live by it where it does not exist."[11] But in the same piece, Mumford argued that architects might learn more from emulating the spirit of the past than by copying it outright: "Instead of going back nowadays to Tudor and Elizabethan models in a desperate effort to bring to light a 'usable past' we might have preserved a little of the flair of Elizabethan workmanship in direct succession."[12] What Mumford disliked most about the formalist approach of historians like Kimball was that it presented the past as a succession of tasteful styles to be imitated. Whereas architecture had once served the needs and purposes of American communities without any pretensions toward style, the surrender to taste had led to modern architecture's downfall. "The more one understands the past, the more one sees how impossible it is to recover it by any external device, except as a masquerade," Mumford concluded in a 1924 essay.[13]

Mumford soon found an alternative approach in the writings of Louis Sullivan. Beginning in 1922, Charles Harris Whitaker serialized Sullivan's *Autobiography of an Idea* in the pages of the *Journal of the American Institute of Architects,* returning the architect to prominence just before his death in 1924. Although not yet familiar with Sullivan's architecture, Mumford was deeply affected by his prose. When *The Autobiography of an Idea* was published as a book in 1924, Mumford reviewed it in the *New Republic,* praising Sullivan's "logical and straightforward" treatment of design problems and his rejection of historical revivalism in favor of fresh design solutions.[14] Mumford ascribed a democratic spirit of creativity to Sullivan and his Chicago colleagues that distinguished their work from the rampant eclecticism of the late nineteenth century. Although, according to Mumford, this spirit had died in America, it had been successfully transplanted in Europe: "If one looks for Sullivan's architecture [today], one must go to Finland and examine the works of Eliel Saarinen, or to the Netherlands and witness the creations of a whole school."[15]

By the time that Mumford began researching *Sticks and Stones* in 1923, he was well prepared to undertake an architectural history of the United States. He had read widely in the field, he had published several short reviews and essays, and most important, he had the encouragement of colleagues like Whitaker and Van Wyck Brooks. As the book progressed, Claude Bragdon lent his support. In a July 1924 letter, Bragdon reassured the young writer: "I see that though [you] may lack some of the technical insight into architecture that only an architectural education can give . . . you have the insight, the vision, the sense of values which make you far more important than some of the saxophones and bass drums of the architectural orchestra."[16] As a critic of the contemporary scene, Mumford was still uncertain about the direction modern architecture should take, but he was adamant in his belief that a truly modern architecture could only arise from a society in touch with its region, its culture, and its history. This was to be the guiding theme of *Sticks and Stones.*

* * *

Mumford's second book was the direct result of his first teaching stint. His numerous essays and book reviews on architecture had attracted the notice of Alvin Johnson, an editor at the *New Republic* who was also the director of the New School for Social Research. In the spring of 1923, Johnson invited Mumford to participate in a lecture series on contemporary architecture.[17] Mumford seized this opportunity to make his academic debut, and he even managed to convince Johnson that he could teach the entire course and that it should cover the whole history of American architecture. As Mumford recalled in his autobiography: "Viewed in any light, this was a dubious adventure, both in Johnson's first conception and even more in my overconfident response: for the historical and critical analysis of post-Colonial American architecture was only beginning."[18] Over the summer, Mumford immersed himself in reading and research for the course, but unfortunately it was canceled when only a handful of auditors attended the first lecture that autumn.[19] Despite this setback, Johnson again asked Mumford to lecture at the school the following autumn, and this time there were enough students in attendance for the course to be given.[20]

Mumford's notes for the course survive, and they offer an interesting insight into the organizing themes that he would subsequently develop in *Sticks and Stones*. He divided American architectural history into distinct periods, devoting a lecture apiece to what he called the "Colonial," the "Early Republican," and the "Eclectic."[21] The Eclectic period included Mumford's discussion of "Richardson, the last of the masons, versus Roebling, the first of the steel builders."[22] Still, Mumford did not grasp fully the pivotal role of Richardson in American architecture. In a surviving notebook for the course, he wrote: "A great artist, such as Richardson really was, can make a fashion; but he cannot create a style; he can produce an aetelier of minor Richardsons but not a school."[23] Nevertheless, Mumford was already making informed observations about shingle-style architecture:

> In the 80's, there developed something like a free style in country house architecture; even McKim & White broke with precedent and produced very good looking low, rambling houses, with round turrets & long steep roofs; sometimes entirely of wood, sometimes with a heavy stone base.... Richardson did well with wood in the Stoughton's cottage, Cambridge, Mass.[24]

These early periods, predating the Columbian Exposition, were in turn followed by the "Classic Revival" and the "New Vernacular." The latter was Mumford's name for the nonrevivalist architecture that he had come to favor, and it included the works of Louis Sullivan and Claude Bragdon. Subsequent lectures dealt with city, suburban, and regional planning.

Following Patrick Geddes's lead, Mumford organized his lectures in gridded charts under the headings of place, work, and folk.[25] Mumford also collected visual materials for the course from the various places he had visited, including postcards of New York City; Philadelphia; Stockbridge, Massachusetts; and Peterborough, New Hampshire, where he had once worked as a tutor.[26] He assembled architectural sketches from his past outings, and he copied drawings from books.

Not surprisingly, Mumford developed his lectures with an eye toward publication. Soon after the cancellation of his course in the autumn of 1923, he began rewriting his notes into a series of articles on American architecture for the *Freeman* and the *Journal of the American Institute of Architects,* which in turn formed the nucleus of *Sticks and Stones.*[27] True to form, early drafts for an unused introduction to the book reveal Mumford's continued intellectual allegiance to Geddes, Branford, and the regional survey. One such passage explored the simile of architecture as the stage setting for life, an idea that Mumford had already developed in his plays:

> What I purpose to do is to describe the setting, to enumerate the properties, and to throw a little light, perhaps, upon the designers and hands, that made up the stage upon which the drama of each American community was played.
>
> ... regional sociology ... begins with the perception that all the world's just such a stage, and that history, as distinguished from statistics and dates, is the unravelling of the significant threads in the regional drama.[28]

The underlying impetus for *Sticks and Stones,* however, was Brooks's call for an American usable past. In another passage from the introduction, Mumford explained how the usable past could bring one to a fuller understanding of contemporary architecture:

> The past is ours to the extent that we are affected by it: the future is ours to the extent that we affect it. Neither the past nor the future, in architecture or in anything else, are determined completely for us by external forces: they exist, they play a part in our conduct, to the extent that, in the broadest sense, we take them in.[29]

In fact, both Brooks and Whitaker advised Mumford on the writing of *Sticks and Stones.* Brooks evidently served as an informal reader on at least one chapter, while surviving notations on the actual manuscript indicate that Whitaker was a reader for the book's publishers, Boni and Liveright.[30]

Although inspired by Mumford's mentors, *Sticks and Stones* in its final form was clearly the product of his own thinking. The ponderous introduction was eliminated and the book was divided into eight tersely written chapters, roughly corresponding to the lectures he had written for the New School. Plans to include illustrations were dropped before the book's publication.[31] In the acknowledgments, Mumford explained that an unillustrated text would compel the reader to explore his own environment, one of the chief tenets of Geddes's regional survey:

> Lest my purpose be misunderstood, I have left out illustrations; for a building is not merely a sight; it is an experience: and one who knows architecture only by photographs does not know it at all. If the omission of pictures lead the reader occasionally to break away from the orbit of his daily walks, and examine our development in cities and buildings for himself, it will be sufficiently justified.[32]

In *Sticks and Stones,* Mumford moved beyond the formal analysis of buildings and the application of stylistic labels that had been the organizing structure of most books on architectural history up until that time. He made the unorthodox structure of the book immediately apparent through his choice of a title. Originally, he was going to title the book "Architecture in America," but he soon changed it to *Sticks and Stones: A Study of American Architecture and Civilization.*[33] The title was, of course, derived from the popular children's retort: "Sticks and stones may break my bones, but names will never hurt me." Simple and unpretentious in its reference to two of the most common building materials, wood and masonry, the title was at the same time a response to contemporary architectural historiography. Mumford's implication was that names, or style terms alone, cannot explain the historical development of architecture. Instead, he presented a broad, cultural study that related American architectural history to the nation's climate, economy, politics, arts, and literature.

Before the publication of *Sticks and Stones,* American architectural history was viewed by most scholars within the larger context of European architectural history. In his study, Mumford sought to recover American architecture from the usable past, and to place it within its proper context on its own soil. The book opened with Mumford's somewhat utopian analysis of the New England village in the seventeenth century. He identified the New England village as one of the last vestiges of medieval culture, a place where the land was apportioned fairly among the residents, with some of it held in common. Mumford particularly admired the New England practice of establishing satellite communities when the original settlements grew too large, and he saw this as an American precursor of garden city planning. He urged architects and city planners to utilize this solid, medieval tradition for more than stylistic models: "If we wish to tie up with our colonial tradition, we must recover more than architectural forms: we must recover the interests, the standards, the institutions that gave to the villages and buildings of early times their appropriate shapes."[34]

In the second chapter, Mumford argued that this medieval unity began to disintegrate in the eighteenth century, as the focus of American civilization shifted from agricultural to maritime pursuits. Although these economic forces greatly affected American building practices, Mumford believed that it was the availability of treatises and pattern books that actually severed architecture's organic roots into the land:

> Victor Hugo said in Notre Dame that the printing-press destroyed architecture, which had hitherto been the stone record of mankind. The real misdemeanor of the printing-press, however, was not that it took literary values away from architecture, but that it caused architecture to derive its value from literature.[35]

To Mumford, this bookish imitation was the chief defect of the Georgian period and of all revivalism, since one had only to consult a dead written past rather than a living local tradition for solutions. Furthermore, he argued that the aesthetic tastes of the eighteenth century should not be perpetuated in the twentieth:

> We must not make the mistake of the modern revivalists, like Mr. Fiske Kimball, who urge the acceptance of the classic tradition in America as a foundation for a general modern style. Form and function are too far divorced in the classic mode to permit the growth of an architecture which will proceed on all fours in houses and public buildings, and factories and barns.[36]

Even though Mumford found much to admire in the architecture and planning of the late eighteenth century, including Charles Pierre L'Enfant's plan for Washington (1791) and Thomas Jefferson's design for the University of Virginia (1817–1826), his overall opinion was that "a great deal of the architecture of the early republic is tedious and banal."[37]

Mumford's view of the nineteenth century in chapter three was even more pessimistic. The process of disintegration that had begun in the eighteenth century was essentially completed in the nineteenth by the relentless assault of the pioneer on the landscape. Once stripped of its beauty and resources, the land was then prepared for subdivision on the gridiron model. The architecture of the period was eclectic, and although numerous advances had been made in engineering, the two fields had yet to join their creative forces. He used the careers of Henry Hobson Richardson and John and Washington Roebling to flesh out this discussion. Significantly, Mumford's admiration for Richardson had grown in just a few short months. Mumford praised the design of Trinity Church, for example, linking its Romanesque detailing to the structural rationalism of Eugene-Emmanuel Viollet-le-Duc.[38] Yet, Mumford still saw Richardson's work as the last phase of romanticism, rather than the birth of something new:

> Richardson was a mason, and masonry was being driven out by steel; he was an original artist, and original art was being thrust into the background by connoisseurship and collection; he was a builder, and architecture was committing itself more and more to the paper plan; he insisted upon building foursquare, and building was doomed more and more to *façaderie.*[39]

Mumford's assessment of the Roeblings' careers and of their masterwork, the Brooklyn Bridge, was more positive. To Mumford, the bridge was the pinnacle of nineteenth-century engineering. He had, of course, admired the bridge since his youth; in the sweep of its cables, the solidity of its masonry, and the human tragedy associated with its construction, he saw a true work of art revealed. "Beyond any other aspect of New York, I think, the Brooklyn Bridge has been a source of joy and inspiration to the artist," Mumford concluded.[40] He closed the chapter with only a brief mention of Louis Sullivan and John Wellborn Root.

Mumford's analysis of the "Imperial Age" was drawn largely from his earlier magazine articles that had criticized neoclassical architecture and City Beautiful planning. He compared the modern American metropolis to imperial Rome, with its monumental public buildings masking the vastly overcrowded slums behind them. While Mumford found much to fault in the "Machine Age" that followed, including the building of subways and skyscrapers, he saw reason for optimism in the stripped-down utilitarian forms of contemporary architecture. Nevertheless, he discarded the viewpoint that a modern style could be based exclusively on zoning ordinances or the machine, as much as he admired factories and grain elevators:

> The error with regard to these new forms of building is the attempt to univer-salize the mere process or form, instead of attempting to universalize the scientific spirit in which they have been conceived. The design for a dwelling-house which ignores everything but the physical necessities of the occupants is the product of a limited conception of science which stops short at physics and mechanics, and neglects biology, psychology, and sociology.[41]

As proof that such a comprehensive approach to design existed in America, Mumford cited the work of Frank Lloyd Wright. Yet, Mumford recognized that the most advanced architecture was being built overseas: "In Europe, particularly in Finland, Germany, and the Netherlands, the best American work has been appreciated and followed up."[42]

In the final chapter of *Sticks and Stones,* Mumford introduced some familiar Geddesian themes, including the sociological divisions of place, work, and folk. To this he added references to the garden cities of Ebenezer Howard, the democratic outlook of Sullivan, and the ecological writings of George Perkins Marsh. Mumford's call at the end of the book for institutional reform, comprehensive regional planning, and garden cities was a predictable one, given the similar conclusions he had articulated in *The Story of Utopias.* In moving from the abstract world of utopia to the very real world of architecture and planning, however, Mumford's call for social and institutional change had gained in potency. In the envoi to the book, he wrote: *"The prospects for our architecture are bound up with a new orientation towards the things that are symbolized in the home, the garden, and the temple; for architecture sums up the civilization it enshrines, and the mass of our buildings can never be better or worse than the institutions that have shaped them."*[43]

At the end of *Sticks and Stones,* Mumford appended an annotated bibliography that reveals the depth of his source material. The bibliography includes guidebooks and histories of architecture, biographies of prominent architects, and critical and theoretical works. He urged the reader to consult the writings of Eugene-Emmanuel Viollet-le-Duc, John Ruskin, W. R. Lethaby, Geoffrey Scott, and Claude Bragdon. Mumford referred to Le Corbusier's *Vers une architecture* as "an able exposition of the absolutist, mechanical point of view."[44] For a sociological perspective on architecture and planning, Mumford recommended the writings of Patrick

Geddes, Victor Branford, Ebenezer Howard, and the Regional Planning Association of America, a group with which Mumford was affiliated.

Sticks and Stones quickly established Mumford as a prominent authority on American architecture. The book appealed to a much broader audience than *The Story of Utopias,* but its critical reception was decidedly mixed since its content was more controversial. Percy A. Hutchison faulted Mumford for seeking refuge from the present in the study of the past: "Like many another intrigued by the past, Mr. Mumford fails to realize that the world of today differs more radically from the world of 300 years ago than the world of 300 years ago differed from the age of the Roman emperors."[45] Yet, architects who reviewed the book noted that Mumford brought a fresh perspective to the criticism of their field since he was an outsider. "No practicing architect could possibly write the truths that Mr. Mumford has written about our efforts without subconsciously endeavoring to excuse our faults," concluded Aymar Embury II.[46]

Sticks and Stones made its strongest impact, both negative and positive, among architectural historians, the group of academics to which Mumford's criticism was primarily directed. As might be expected, Fiske Kimball gave Mumford's book a scathing review in the *New York Herald Tribune.* Kimball was especially appalled by what he saw as Mumford's distorted picture of seventeenth-century New England:

> Then, ah, then was the Golden Age. At least it was the golden afterglow of that hey-day of human freedom, the Middle Ages, when agriculture was the mainstay of life. The medieval serf, rotting in his fleas under the exactions of a feudal landlord, might not recognize his environment, to be sure, in Mr. Mumford's "community of freemen, living the good life."[47]

Kimball's review so outraged Mumford that he wrote a response to the editor of the *Herald Tribune* the very next day.[48] *Sticks and Stones* had the opposite effect on historian Talbot Hamlin. In fact, Hamlin seems to have been the only reviewer to recognize the "gentle sarcasm in the title itself."[49] Although Hamlin did not reverse his own position regarding revivalism, he did recognize the validity of Mumford's central thesis: "The 'style' is an accident, a mere vocabulary; wherever true beauty has entered, now or generations ago, it is because the creative spirit has brooded over the creation, which is raised at once to a new plane; the true art of architecture is timeless and without bounds of geography or dates."[50] Over the course of the next two decades, Mumford and Hamlin would draw closer together both in friendship and in their views on architecture.

* * *

Seven years separated the publication of *The Brown Decades,* Mumford's second book on American architecture, and *Sticks and Stones.* During this interval, Mumford's interests shifted toward literary criticism. He belonged to a circle of writers and critics instrumental in legitimizing American cultural studies as a scholarly discipline. This group, which included Van Wyck Brooks, Waldo Frank, Constance Rourke, and Paul Rosenfeld, rejected the traditional, academic view that American culture was merely an offshoot of that of Western Europe. They instead sought to rehabilitate and elevate nineteenth-century American writers to a place of preeminence in the public's mind.

Mumford's next book after *Sticks and Stones* was an investigation of nineteenth-century American literature, metaphorically titled *The Golden Day*. This book continued a line of inquiry initiated three years earlier by the British writer D. H. Lawrence in *Studies in Classic American Literature* (1923), which Mumford acknowledged as a source.[51] In *The Golden Day*, Mumford celebrated the literary flowering that occurred at midcentury in New York and New England, regions of the country passed over in the pioneers' greedy rush toward the Pacific.

Mumford identified a pantheon of five writers at the center of this efflorescence: Ralph Waldo Emerson, Henry David Thoreau, Walt Whitman, Nathaniel Hawthorne, and Herman Melville. Emerson, the "Morning Star," was in Mumford's view, the first American writer to rethink life afresh and to face the challenges of the industrial age. Thoreau, following Emerson's path, was the "Dawn," a pioneer who, rather than exploiting nature, discovered the roots of American culture there instead. Whitman was the "High Noon" of the "Golden Day," the poet who wrote candidly of the American experience in its most exhilarating aspects. Hawthorne and Melville represented the "Twilight" and the "Night," respectively, the tragic side of the same American experience.[52] According to Mumford, this extraordinary period of creativity came to a close later in the nineteenth century, as writers abandoned their idealism in the wake of the Civil War and as society embraced the materialistic excesses of the Gilded Age. Pragmatism replaced transcendentalism as the guiding philosophy of the day, and culture was pillaged from Europe by such wealthy socialites as Isabella Stewart Gardner.

Although *The Golden Day* was essentially a literary companion to *Sticks and Stones*, Mumford would not complete his analysis of American culture until the writing of *The Brown Decades* in 1931. The seeds for this later study were already in place, however, buried deep in the fifth chapter of *The Golden Day*:

> A genuine culture was beginning again to struggle upwards in the seventies: a Peirce, a Shaler, a Marsh, a Gibbs, a Ryder, a Roebling, a Thomas Eakins, a Richardson, a Sullivan, an Adams, a La Farge were men that any age might proudly exhibit and make use of. But the procession of American civilization divided and walked around these men.[53]

This passage was, in fact, used by Mumford to open *The Brown Decades*.

Mumford's architectural criticism was deeply rooted in his literary criticism, and this was a natural outcome of his desire to understand American culture in its totality. It was his research for *The Golden Day*, in fact, that would later prompt him to create a complementary pantheon of artists and architects. Mumford continued to write literary criticism until the end of the 1920s. In 1929, he published a revisionist biography of Herman Melville, and he also served as an editor on *The American Caravan: A Yearbook of American Literature* (1927–1936).

* * *

During this period of involvement with American literature, Mumford continued to keep abreast of architectural developments by writing articles and book reviews. American architectural history was a burgeoning field, owing in part to the original and provocative argument of *Sticks and Stones*. Mumford's criticism began to focus primarily on the coverage of the late nineteenth century, the period that had been neglected most by scholars, including Mumford himself. Talbot Hamlin's encyclopedic survey *The American Spirit in Architecture* (1926) was one of the first books to take a more inclusive approach. In a review of the book, Mumford praised Hamlin's revised analysis, particularly of the contributions of Chicago architects: "Mr. Hamlin . . . for the first time gives something like their public due to Richardson, Halsey Wood, Louis Sullivan, and Frank Lloyd Wright, a continuous succession of American architects whose buildings expressed the first originality in design, apart from plan and purely functional elements, that had appeared in American architecture."[54] Mumford reviewed Suzanne La Follette's book *Art in America* in 1930, praising her overall analysis of American architectural history, but faulting her for missing "the historic importance of Richardson."[55] Mumford also used this review to launch a direct attack on Fiske Kimball's *American Architecture* (1928): "[La Follette] upsets Mr. Fiske Kimball's perverse interpretation of the progress of modern architecture and demolishes his silly attempt to supplant the virile modern design initiated by Sullivan and Mr. Frank Lloyd Wright by the feeble classicism of his favorite Fifth Avenue apartment house."[56]

Mumford also began to travel more widely, in part to broaden his knowledge of American architecture. Of particular importance was Mumford's trip to Chicago in January 1927, the first time he had visited the Midwestern city. The trip was prompted by glowing reports Mumford had received earlier from European architects like Eric Mendelsohn, whose friendship with Mumford is discussed in chapter 3.[57] Chicago was a revelation to Mumford since his knowledge of American architecture had been confined primarily to the eastern seaboard.

During his visit, Mumford met several notable American architects, including Henry Klaber and Ernest Grunsfeld, partners in a Chicago firm.[58] Grunsfeld led Mumford around the city's suburbs, showing him several residences designed by Frank Lloyd Wright, including the Cheney House in Oak Park (1904).[59] Wright and Mumford did not meet on this trip, however. Mumford's guide to Chicago was Barry Byrne, a Prairie school architect who had once worked for Wright and whose work Mumford had admired previously.[60] On his tour of the city, Mumford was particularly taken with Richardson's Marshall Field Warehouse (1885–1887), Adler and Sullivan's Auditorium Building (1887–1889), Burnham and Root's Monadnock Building (1889–1891), and Wright's Midway Gardens (1914).

Mumford evidently impressed a selected Chicago audience as well. In a letter to Mumford later that spring, Ernest Grunsfeld's wife, Mary-Jane wrote:

> From a few gatherings we've been peeking in on lately, I should say that you did a good thing for Chicago's lesser intelligentsia. They are discussing Frank Lloyd Wright, the issues of sociology and the aesthetics of the skyscraper, and are still hauling the architect mercilessly over the coals or excusing him on the grounds that he's impotent to "do his stuff" in an altogether bad economic and social situation. Bravo, Lewis, for a topic of conversation!![61]

Ultimately, the trip to Chicago convinced Mumford of the creative genius of Richardson, Sullivan, Root, and Wright. Mumford also realized that his discussion of this group in *Sticks and Stones,* and especially of Wright, had been grossly inadequate.

In November 1927, Mumford reported on his findings in the journal *Architecture.* Chicago, he wrote, was home to "a great school of architects" in the nineteenth century.[62] Moreover, Chicago, and not New York, was the chief source of inspiration for modern European architecture:

> The Americans who look to-day at the work of Gropius and Mendelssohn [sic] and Taut in Germany, of Oudt [sic] in Holland, of Garnier and Le Corbusier and Mallet-Stevens in France, do not perhaps realize that the inspiration of this work came largely from America, and in particular from Chicago. The place to study the development of American architecture from the foundation laid down in the eighties and the early nineties is – Europe. The men who continued this line of development in America, Louis Sullivan and Frank Lloyd Wright, had a hard, up-hill time of it; for architecture in America lost its native bias in the nineties.[63]

Someday, Mumford concluded, New York architects might catch up with their "original exemplars in Chicago."[64]

Mumford's admiration for Wright in particular had grown substantially, even before the Chicago trip.[65] The 1920s were a period, paradoxically, in which the architect's reputation was in serious decline in the United States. When Mumford was writing *Sticks and Stones,* he knew Wright's work only through published photographs and illustrations. Nevertheless, the book's success attracted the attention of Hendricus Wijdeveld, editor of the Dutch journal *Wendingen,* who invited Mumford to contribute an essay to a special issue of the journal dedicated to Wright in 1925.[66] Mumford rose to the challenge, in a glowing essay that compared the architecture of Wright with the poetry of Carl Sandburg: "Both [Wright and Sandburg] have faced our age, have absorbed the broken rhythm of the machine, feel the jagged geometry of our new adventure in space: they have something to express in plastic or literary form that an earlier age was not aware of."[67] Despite Wright's neglect by his American colleagues, Mumford considered the architect to be both a living link to the creative spirit of nineteenth-century Chicago and the most vital force on the contemporary scene. As a result of this favorable appreciation, Wright initiated a correspondence with Mumford in 1926 that continued, with several stormy interruptions, until the architect's death in 1959.

By the late 1920s, Mumford had become one of Wright's chief supporters. Wright's name appeared frequently in Mumford's essays and reviews as an example of an architect in touch with modern life and the machine. Mumford stood almost alone in his assessment of Wright, however. Traditionalist critics found the architect's work to be too radical in its break with historical precedent, while more progressive critics found it wanting in comparison with European modernism. Mumford, in fact, soon found himself in disagreement about Wright with Henry-Russell Hitchcock Jr., a rising young enthusiast of the new architecture just emerging from Europe.[68] This disagreement was to have profound implications concerning the critical reception of modernism in America.

The Hitchcock–Mumford relationship began on rather friendly terms. In 1927, Hitchcock, then still in graduate school at Harvard University, sent Mumford the premiere issue of *The Hound and the Horn,* a student publication, with the following inscription: "For America's leading critic of modern architecture."[69] Mumford in turn praised Hitchcock's article, "The Decline of Architecture," and the two men began a regular correspondence.[70] For the first few years of their acquaintance, the two men actively encouraged each other in their architectural endeavors. Hitchcock was especially concerned that Mumford would abandon architectural criticism for the world of letters in the period following the publication of *The Golden Day.* In a 1927 letter to Mumford, Hitchcock wrote: "I trust your later books on more literary subjects do not imply that you have given up the position which America needs so much of architectural critic. Your Harper's article ["American Taste"] hopefully means you still have an iron in the fire."[71] In the same letter, Hitchcock voiced his own frustration in gathering information and illustrations of American architecture:

> I should like very much to have the opportunity of talking with you sometime and seeing if you have ... the documentation on late xix century architecture which you used in Sticks and Stones – or bibliographic suggestions. My own collection of books and photos I find on the whole adequate for the xx century – despite lack of American factories – but for the xix century I am in poorer case.[72]

Mumford recalled in his autobiography that Hitchcock was "baffled by my admission that it was on my urban and rural rambles, not in libraries, that I had mostly encountered the buildings I had written about."[73] Nevertheless, Hitchcock held

Mumford in considerable esteem, calling *Sticks and Stones* "one of the two great books of the twentieth century on architecture in our language."[74]

Later, however, when Hitchcock asked Mumford to read a draft of his manuscript for *Modern Architecture: Romanticism and Reintegration* (1929), it became apparent that the two men were in fundamental disagreement over the course that modern architecture was taking by the late 1920s. Mumford objected primarily to Hitchcock's proposed stylistic categories of "New Traditionalists" and "New Pioneers" to describe the work of contemporary architects.[75] According to Hitchcock, the former category included Peter Behrens in Germany, Eliel Saarinen in Finland, and Bertram Grosvenor Goodhue and Frank Lloyd Wright in America since these architects designed primarily in an updated idiom of past styles using traditional materials. Conversely, those in the latter category, such as Le Corbusier in France and Walter Gropius and Ludwig Mies van der Rohe in Germany, utilized new materials and embraced a machine-inspired aesthetic.

In particular, Mumford and Hitchcock diverged in their views on Wright's position vis-à-vis modern architecture. Mumford believed that by the late 1920s, Wright had surpassed the achievements of the New Pioneers, whereas Hitchcock felt that the architect had reached a standstill in his development. Mumford first ushered this disagreement into print in a 1929 review of a brief monograph that Hitchcock had written on Wright: "In failing to grasp the inevitability of this humanization of the machine, this addition of feeling to form, or of poetry to mathematics as we become more and more the master of it, Mr. Hitchcock has, it seems to me, lost the central clue in Mr. Wright's career."[76] Hitchcock, however, sought to minimize these differences. After the review appeared, Hitchcock wrote to Mumford: "We have more in common than you are willing to admit – our chief difference being that it pleases me to look for a warming – if that is the word I want – or enriching of architecture – au delà de Le Corbusier and not before him chez Wright."[77]

Modern Architecture was published in 1929, and it immediately established Hitchcock as the leading advocate of European modernism in the United States. Mumford, who had labored for almost a decade to establish the field of American architectural history, was dismayed by what he viewed as Hitchcock's unfair treatment of the native tradition. In a 1930 review for the *New Republic,* Mumford criticized Hitchcock for creating arbitrary distinctions: "One suspects that terms like the New Traditionalist and the New Pioneer describe stable aspects of the modern spirit, rather than schools of thought that follow in succession."[78] In general, however, he praised Hitchcock's scholarship for its breadth and soundness. "Your review swelled my head considerably," Hitchcock wrote to Mumford soon after it was published. "Particularly as there is between the lines of my last chapter more accord with your contentions than your feelings read there."[79] Still, the disagreement between

Hitchcock and Mumford was not over, and their views on modern architecture and on Wright would continue to diverge over the next few years.

* * *

In the period following the publication of *Sticks and Stones,* Mumford had been nagged by the inadequacies of the book, particularly by his treatment of the architecture of the late nineteenth century. As early as 1927 he began making notes for the book that eventually became *The Brown Decades,* but he did not begin planning the book in earnest until two years later, when he had completed his biography of Herman Melville. Henry-Russell Hitchcock Jr. expressed his delight at the possibility of Mumford's return to the architectural history fold in a letter from August 1928:

> If you can be drawn back into writing on architecture I shall feel I have done a general service. There is not the slightest danger of rehashing things [in your proposed book] and the clarification of the *leniencies* as you call them of Sticks & Stones would I think even these few years later be of immense importance. If you would extend your study of the nineteenth century in America to its arts I feel that you would provide a book of the utmost importance. Notably the Brown Eighties but the preceding decades of the mid century require such handling as you almost alone could give them.[80]

Hitchcock was not the only one urging Mumford to return to the study of American architecture. A few months earlier, Barry Byrne, the Chicago architect, urged Mumford to consider writing a history of more recent developments:

> Don't you think something might be done about an article summarizing the scattered independent architectural work that was done in the United States over the last twenty-five years – when it was not a popular idea as it now threatens to be. This might offset the insularity of New York writers (you see I do not so classify *you*) who think only in terms of [Frank] Lloyd Wright whom they regard as a discovery and in all other ways have their view on the European modernists.[81]

In such a survey, Byrne proposed for inclusion Irving Gill, Charles and Henry Greene, and Louis Christian Mullgardt from the West Coast and George Elmslie, Bruce Goff, William E. Drummond, and Walter Burley Griffin from the Midwest. "Others might be brought in but their names escape me at the moment," Byrne continued. "Why don't *you* do it? Europe again threatens us."[82] Although Mumford did not take up Byrne's suggestion directly, the growing "threat" of European ascendancy in modern architecture was a major impetus behind the writing of *The Brown Decades.*

As indicated in Hitchcock's letter, the color brown was to become the organizing theme of Mumford's book. Mumford had been fascinated by this color since his youthful surveys of Manhattan's architecture, and he had already explored many of its metaphorical possibilities in his play "The Brownstone Front." His use of the color brown also allowed him to avoid referring to style terms in his discussion. To Mumford, the works of architects such as Henry Hobson Richardson, Louis Sullivan, and Frank Lloyd Wright were essentially styleless, since they were a functional response to the demands of the modern age. In making such a distinction, moreover, Mumford used the architecture of the "Brown Decades" as a foil to the characteristically "white" neoclassicism that prevailed after the 1893 World's Columbian Exposition.

In December 1929, Mumford was invited to Dartmouth College to deliver the Guernsey Center Moore Foundation lectures, and he chose as his topic "The Arts in America since 1870."[83] Like *Sticks and Stones, The Brown Decades* thus developed out of lecture notes, and the thematic organization and polemical thrust of the latter book reflected its origins in the classroom. In his surviving lecture notes, Mumford distinguished between the "Brown Decades" and the period that followed: "The positive ugliness of 1870 – born of a certain confidence & conviction vs. tepid connoisseurship & imitation of 1890–1920."[84] This statement foreshadows one of the book's overriding themes. The art and architecture of the "Brown Decades," while lacking in so-called good taste, were in accord with the spirit of the society that produced them. This period of original creativity was succeeded by a period of disintegration in the arts as they returned to established academic canons at the end of the century. In a 1927 article for *Harper's,* Mumford discussed this shift in taste:

> During the nineties American taste was faced with a critical alternative. It could either have accepted the forces of its own age, and sought to humanize them and turn them to aesthetic ends, as Richardson, Sullivan, and Frank Lloyd Wright were doing in architecture; or it could shirk the problem of contemporary taste altogether, neglecting the lessons to be drawn from engineering and the sciences, neglecting all the vital impulses of the American scene itself – and take refuge in the taste and products of other periods and other cultures, no matter how remote or dissimilar they were.[85]

As was the case with *Sticks and Stones,* Mumford submitted whole sections of his work in progress as individual articles to *Scribner's* magazine and the *American Mercury.*[86] Mumford's articles caught the attention of George Elmslie, an architect who was a former associate of Louis Sullivan. After reading the section on nineteenth-century architecture, Elmslie wrote several lengthy letters to Mumford in an attempt to clarify Sullivan's position in modern architecture. Elmslie was particularly worried that Sullivan had been unfairly cast by Mumford as a transitional figure between Richardson and Wright. In a letter to Mumford from April 1931, Elmslie wrote: "Your idea of Sullivan being merely a link between Richardson (who did not create a significant form) and Wright (who has created many) – basing all Sullivan's work on a Richardson foundation, is too much for me."[87] Although Mumford did not waiver from his proposed lineage, he did incorporate a number of Elmslie's suggested corrections into the text, with the result that Sullivan was portrayed more sympathetically.

Mumford also consulted with Wright when preparing the manuscript for *The Brown Decades*. In July 1930, Mumford wrote to the architect: "The first rough draft of my book is done, and, since the chapter on Building more or less leads up to you, I have one or two questions to ask you. How far were you hindered by Sullivan's example? How much of him did you have to throw overboard? Did you do this consciously or unconsciously?"[88] A few days later, Wright responded: "[I was h]elped rather than hindered by Sullivan – because – though pupil, I think I was never his disciple. (It is the disciple who is hindered by his master.) Sullivan is on record as gratefully acknowledging this."[89] Concerning his own work, Wright added: "Perhaps my delight in the square-cut and the rectilinear were, in some small degree, reaction from too sensuous fluctuation and flutter of surface – Sullivan's ebullient efflorescence."[90]

The publication in 1931 of *The Brown Decades* was the culmination of more than a decade of Mumford's critical observations, scholarly research, and personal contacts. At a time when colonial studies still predominated, *The Brown Decades* broke new ground in late-nineteenth-century American architectural history. Although architecture lay at the center of the book's argument, Mumford also covered American literature and painting in separate chapters, using the color metaphor of the title, rather than style, to delineate unifying themes that cut across the various arts. Thus, earth tones link the buildings of Henry Hobson Richardson, the paintings of Albert Pinkham Ryder, and the verse of Walt Whitman. Even the book's binding was brown. Mumford urged his readers to look beyond the muddiness on the period's surface:

> The Brown Decades, with all their sordidness, their weaknesses, their monstrosities, are not without their contribution to our "usable past." Through all the dun colours of that period the work of its creative minds gleams – vivid, complex, harmonious, contradicting or enriching the sober prevalent browns. The treasure has long been buried. It is time to open it up.[91]

The Brown Decades was divided into four main chapters. Mumford opened the book with a revised look at American literature, giving particular attention to the writings of Emily Dickinson and Whitman. Individual chapters on the American landscape and on architecture followed, and the last chapter covered American painting. As in *The Golden Day,* Mumford identified a pantheon of creative individuals, this time composed of artists and architects, whose achievements, he believed, had been largely overlooked in the twentieth century. This pantheon included John and Washington Roebling in the field of engineering; Frederick Law Olmsted in landscape architecture; Henry Hobson Richardson, John Wellborn Root, Louis Sullivan, and Frank Lloyd Wright in architecture; and Thomas Eakins and Albert Pinkham Ryder in painting. Mumford claimed that this group was the first to make a decisive break with the European tradition and to build something wholly and originally American. This pantheon would, in fact, become a "usable" reference point in Mumford's criticism, a standard of excellence by which he would judge his contemporaries.

The core of Mumford's analysis in *The Brown Decades* is found in the chapter on architecture. Significantly, he titled it "Towards Modern Architecture," perhaps in response to Le Corbusier's *Vers une architecture* (1923), the most famous architectural polemic of the period. In any case, Mumford's chief goal was to connect late-nineteenth-century American architecture to twentieth-century European architecture. He focused on the group of Midwestern architects now commonly referred to as the "Chicago school," although this was not a term he used at the time.[92] According to Mumford's analysis, the transplanted Richardson was the progenitor of modern form, and he was followed by Sullivan and Root, under whom this form matured. When the Columbian Exposition interrupted this period of original expression, it was left to Frank Lloyd Wright to carry it into the twentieth century. Mumford was actually not the first to recognize this group of Midwesterners since scholars as diverse as Montgomery Schuyler, Henry-Russell Hitchcock Jr., and Fiske Kimball had all treated the Chicago school as a distinct phase in American architecture. Mumford, however, was the first to claim its position at the headwaters of modern architecture.

In comparison with *Sticks and Stones,* Mumford's discussion of late-nineteenth-century architecture in *The Brown Decades* was much more thorough and balanced. His views on Richardson in particular had changed dramatically. Mumford now described Richardson as "an architect who almost single-handed created out of a confusion which was actually worse than a mere void the beginnings of a new architecture."[93] In the development of Richardson's plans, the massing of his forms, and the placement of his windows, Mumford discerned the emergence of a truly functional approach. Richardson's work in Chicago, Mumford argued further, inspired the next generation of the city's architects to lay "the basis of modern architecture throughout the world."[94] Mumford only briefly touched on the early work of Richardson's erstwhile pupils, Charles Follen McKim and Stanford White, including their First Methodist Church in Baltimore, designed before the two embraced neoclassicism.

Following the discussion of Richardson, Mumford next turned to the career of Root. As with the older architect, Root's career was cut short by an untimely death, but Mumford found the younger architect to be even more attuned to the demands of an emerging modernism. As evidence of this, Mumford quoted directly from

Root's own writings: "A new spirit of beauty is being developed and perfected, and even now its first achievements are beginning to delight us. This is not the old thing made over; it is new. It springs out of the past, but it is not tied to it; it studies the traditions, but is not enslaved by them."[95] Not surprisingly, Mumford virtually ignored Root's partnership with Daniel H. Burnham. Mumford identified Burnham almost exclusively with the return to neoclassicism heralded by the Columbian Exposition. Having thus fallen from grace, Burnham was ineligible for Mumford's discussion, or, for that matter, for membership in Mumford's pantheon.

Mumford devoted a substantial section of the chapter to Louis Sullivan, whose broad powers of thinking Mumford had admired since reading *The Autobiography of an Idea*. Whereas Richardson had provided the form for modern architecture, Sullivan defined its rules:

> Sullivan saw that the business of the architect was to organize the forces of modern society, discipline them for humane ends, express them in the plastic-utilitarian form of building. To achieve this purpose, the architect must abandon the tedious and unmeaning symbolism of older cultural forms: a modern building could no more wear the dress of the classic than the architect could wear a peruke and sword.[96]

Yet, Mumford was not as completely satisfied with Sullivan's architecture on a number of different levels. Mumford admired Sullivan's functional solution to the modern office building but in general disliked skyscrapers. In fact, Mumford reserved his greatest praise for the largely horizontal form of Sullivan's Schlesinger and Mayer Building (1899–1904). Mumford was also critical of Sullivan's ornament, calling it "restless and assertive, without being in a sculptural sense entertaining."[97] At this point in time, Mumford was himself struggling with the role that ornament would play in contemporary architecture, and his negative criticism of Sullivan on this point indicated Mumford's emerging predilection for the clean surfaces of European modernism. Despite Elmslie's plea, Mumford persisted in his argument that Sullivan was the "link" between Richardson and Wright. Mumford strengthened Sullivan's position, however, by assigning to him the origins of the "organic" in modern architecture. "On Richardson's solid foundations, [Sullivan] laid the cornerstone of the new organic architecture," Mumford concluded.[98]

Mumford included a brief discussion of Wright in this chapter, keeping the primary focus on the architect's early career. In Wright's architecture, Mumford saw not only the continued search for new expression initiated during the "Brown Decades," but also an intelligent response to the demands of the Machine Age that followed. Mumford indirectly linked Wright to Patrick Geddes in his analysis, reading into the architect's work the same concern for environmental equilibrium:

[Wright's] architecture, though he has pioneered with modern methods of construction and delighted in mechanical techniques, is not merely a passive adaptation to the machine age: it is a reaching toward a more biotechnic economy, better grounded in the permanent realities of birth, growth, reproduction, and the natural environment than is the dominant order of paper values and merely mechanical efficiencies.[99]

In Mumford's view, Wright was still the most significant force in modern American architecture.

In the chapter titled "The Renewal of the Landscape," Mumford discussed the careers of Frederick Law Olmsted and John and Washington Roebling, the leading figures in their respective fields of landscape architecture and engineering. At the heart of the chapter was a discussion of the planning and development of Olmsted's Central Park. Mumford, who had admired the park since his childhood, praised Olmsted's ability to manipulate the landscape in an artistic manner. "By making nature urbane [Olmsted] naturalized the city," Mumford wrote.[100] Mumford was particularly impressed by Olmsted's careful separation of pedestrian and vehicular traffic in the park, noting that this was a feature widely emulated by town planners in Europe and America.

Just as Mumford viewed Central Park as a direct ancestor of modern town planning, he saw the Brooklyn Bridge as a forerunner of the Machine Age. On an aesthetic level, Mumford considered the bridge to be an unparalleled triumph, a synthesis of the organic and the technic. This dialectic was fundamental to his later studies of technology and culture, and it will be discussed at greater length in chapter 3. Mumford described the bridge in almost lyrical terms: "The stone plays against the steel: the granite mass in compression, the spidery steel in tension. In this structure, the architecture of the past, massive and protective, meets the architecture of the future, light, aerial, open to sunlight, an architecture of voids rather than solids."[101] As a youth, of course, Mumford had been profoundly moved by the bridge, and in 1927, he was inspired to write a play about the span while he and his wife lived in Brooklyn Heights, not far from Washington Roebling's former home.[102] Mumford's protagonist was, once again, a semiautobiographical creation.

In contrast to *Sticks and Stones*, *The Brown Decades* was illustrated with notable works by Richardson, Root, and Sullivan that emphasized the somber yet solid qualities of their buildings. The annotated bibliography at the end of the book reflected Mumford's extensive knowledge of the field, and it included works by Fiske Kimball, Talbot Hamlin, Thomas Tallmadge, Montgomery Schuyler, and Louis Sullivan. Mumford also indicated that he had gathered additional material from Charles Harris Whitaker, George Elmslie, Frank Lloyd Wright, Alfred Stieglitz, and William B. Bigelow, the architect whom Mumford had met years before in Cambridge.

Ultimately, by awakening his contemporaries to this tradition in architecture, landscape architecture, and engineering, Mumford hoped to spark a period of creativity equal to that of the "Brown Decades" at a moment when European ascendancy seemed imminent. Mumford expressed this desire at the book's conclusion:

> When the creative artists are reckoned with – an Olmsted, a Roebling, a Richardson, a Ryder – the Brown Decades become in the arts what the Golden Day was in literature: a fulfillment of the past and a starting point for the future. Does this work lead toward our own generation? In a measure, at least, yes. Toward even more solid achievements beyond our own? Let us hope so.[103]

The Brown Decades was a greater critical success than *Sticks and Stones,* in part because Mumford no longer seemed the young radical bent on changing the direction of American architectural history. His foray into literary criticism had also enriched his prose to the extent that *The Brown Decades* transcended the limitations of historical narrative to become a genuine work of American letters. Critics praised both the richness of the book's content and the writing style of its author. "This book about the arts is written in the spirit of a true artist," Albert Guerard remarked.[104] Henry Hazlitt agreed: "[Mumford's] criticisms are always shrewd, and illuminating even when not entirely just, for behind them lies not only a well-considered philosophy of criticism, but a remarkably well-articulated philosophy of life. His style, too, is a worthy medium for his thought."[105] Other critics, however, were dissatisfied by the depth of Mumford's analysis. As Matthew Josephson wrote in the *New Republic:*

> We owe much to Lewis Mumford for having championed the great architects of the "brown decades" long ago, and for having sensed their vital connection with our own time. One might have wished, however, that his critique presented them less as insurgent or idealistic individuals, and more explicitly drew the inferences of their concerted program, their answer to the cultural dilemma.[106]

Still, the degree to which Mumford's views on nineteenth-century architecture had already been accepted was confirmed by the book's reception in the architectural press. "Whether or not one is willing to accept such a positive classification of the last century's architects, one is sure to find something of mental digestibility in what [Mumford] says," the *Architectural Forum* concluded.[107]

The Brown Decades made its most profound impact in the field of American architectural history. Mumford's book opened the territory for more in-depth studies of the late nineteenth century, and it was also pivotal in the critical reevaluation of Frank Lloyd Wright. Although Wright himself did not entirely agree with Mumford's analysis, the architect sent his congratulations to the author anyway in December 1931: "I've read 'The Brown Decades' you so kindly sent me and it is a useful work in your splendid style. I didn't agree in toto but admire and respect [it]."[108]

Henry-Russell Hitchcock Jr.'s response was much more enthusiastic. The previous month he wrote to Mumford: "[*The Brown Decades*] seems to me the finest thing ever written on American architecture and indeed one of the finest things written on the architecture of the last fifty years – for few fine things have I fear been written on American architecture."[109] Referring to his own analysis in *Modern Architecture,* Hitchcock added: "You convert me positively to Sullivan. You see him justly, I have not."[110] Still, Mumford was unable to alter Hitchcock's opinion of Wright. As Hitchcock concluded: "When the discipline begins to bind, and the imitators of L[e] C[orbusier] to flourish doubtless I will return with gusto to Wright but now I am for reintegration, socialization, international style, to the founding of which the American Brown Decades surely led the way."[111] Hitchcock's letter proved to be prophetic since he did eventually "return" to Wright in the 1942 monograph *In the Nature of Materials.*

Gradually, to Mumford's delight, other scholars filled the historical gaps in the study of American architecture over the next decade. When Hugh Morrison's biography of Sullivan and Hitchcock's biography of Richardson were both published in the mid-1930s, Mumford felt vindicated in writing: "These two biographies bear witness to the fact that the day of pleading for a usable past is now over."[112] Sigfried Giedion's *Space, Time and Architecture* (1941) contained an extended discussion of Wright and the architects of the Chicago school, linking them to modern developments in Europe. When Carl Condit wrote his definitive survey, *The Rise of the Skyscraper* (1952), he gratefully acknowledged Mumford's contribution to the historiography of American architecture: "Perhaps the first to [rediscover the Chicago school] . . . was Lewis Mumford, whose sensitive and discerning chapter on the school in *The Brown Decades* . . . awakened interest on the part of those prepared to appreciate it."[113] Similarly, other scholars have credited Mumford with rekindling interest in John and Washington Roebling and Frederick Law Olmsted.[114]

Mumford's pantheon of American architects was his most significant and enduring contribution to the historiography of the field; Richardson, Root, Sullivan, and Wright have figured prominently in almost every textbook on American architecture since the publication of *The Brown Decades.* In identifying and glorifying such a group, Mumford followed in a long historical tradition that began with Giorgio Vasari in the Renaissance and flourished under the Romantic critics of the nineteenth century. Nevertheless, the pantheon can also be viewed as the book's greatest weakness. In identifying this hallowed group, Mumford delved only so far into the usable past as was necessary to suit his somewhat narrowly defined polemical purpose. He passed over the significant achievements of other, lesser-known architects, and he left most of the vast territory outside of New York and Chicago unexplored.

Several years after Mumford's study was published, its limitations were recognized by historian Robert Anderson, who questioned the role of the creative individual in a profession that relied so heavily on collaboration with others. Paraphrasing Mumford's analysis of Richardson in *The Brown Decades,* Anderson wrote: "Great men do not create out of a void. They merely fuse and synthesize the product of the labor of their fellow men. If they be geniuses, they are the geniuses of the finishing room, the masters of the final stage of a vast and complicated production-assembly line."[115] Recent revisionist studies have since provided a much more balanced view of American architecture both before and after the World's Columbian Exposition.[116]

Yet, despite such objections, the members of Mumford's pantheon continue to be admired for their creativity and originality, even as they have been joined by new members nominated in later years by other scholars. This is an ongoing process to which Mumford was not opposed, since he realized that such was the arbitrary and cyclical nature of criticism. In a 1929 review of Walter Pach's *Ananias, or the False Artist,* Mumford described what he viewed as an almost hagiographic process in the creation of the larger pantheon of Western art: "The standard is not, of course, 'absolute' in the sense that it is registered in heaven for all time; but it varies in slow movement and cycles. El Greco may drop out for a while or Raphael may be over-valued; but in the end a steady process of canonization goes on."[117]

In Mumford's writings after *The Brown Decades,* the members of his American pantheon appeared both as a group and separately, with sustained regularity and without extensive explanation. While this presupposed that the reader was familiar with the author's earlier works, it was also through constant repetition that Mumford validated the pantheon that he had created. Contemporary architects, artists, philosophers, writers, or even personal friends could earn no greater critical acclaim from Mumford than to be compared or grouped with the pantheon. In his later works, the American pantheon was eventually merged with the larger pantheon of Western civilization. Mumford placed Sullivan, for example, in an international league of thinkers, both past and present and from all disciplines in *The Condition of Man* (1944), Mumford's historical survey of religious and philosophical thought: "From Goethe to Louis Sullivan, from Claude Bernard to Osler, from Emerson to Whitehead, from Ebenezer Howard to Henry Wright, from Whitman to Stieglitz this new sense of the organic has made its way steadily into every sphere of creative activity."[118] In essence, Mumford mixed hagiography with historiography in his writings, using the names of the pantheon's members in a kind of litany that gained in authority through repetition over time.

* * *

Although *The Brown Decades* was Mumford's last major book on American culture, he returned intermittently to the field, polishing and refining his study of the usable past. During the mid to late 1930s, Mumford became immersed in an ambitious four-volume survey of Western civilization, *The Renewal of Life* (1934, 1938, 1944, and 1951), which is discussed in chapters 3 and 4. At the same time, Mumford became a more politically active writer, warning his American readers of the mounting crisis in Europe. With the outbreak of World War II, Mumford became an ardent interventionist on behalf of the Allies, accusing the nation's liberal leaders of shirking their moral responsibilities because of their reluctance to become involved in the conflict.

Politics would initially seem to have little to do with architectural history, but in Mumford's view the link was incontrovertible. The destruction of architecture in wars fueled by nationalist motives was perhaps the most visible symbol of the destruction of a region's culture accumulated over centuries. Mumford viewed the fight against Fascism and Nazism as nothing less than the fight to save European, American, and, by extension, world culture. When in 1941 Mumford was invited to deliver the Dancy lectures at Alabama College, he chose as his topic a comparative study of the architecture of Thomas Jefferson and Henry Hobson Richardson.[119] These lectures, subsequently published as *The South in Architecture,* applied the lessons of the usable past to contemporary world events.

To longtime Mumford readers, the book reworked familiar ideas, but with a political edge that was new. In the first lecture, "The Basis of American Form," Mumford reviewed themes from his earlier works: the role of the book in architecture, the primacy of the region, and the futility of historical revivalism. "Our task is not to imitate the past, but to understand it," Mumford wrote, "so that we may face the opportunities of our own day and deal with them in an equally creative spirit."[120]

Mumford's analysis of Jefferson in the second lecture was his first reevaluation of the gentleman architect since *Sticks and Stones.* In general, Mumford praised Jefferson, calling him "one of the last true figures of the Renaissance."[121] Mumford particularly admired the functional plan of Monticello and the village-like layout of the University of Virginia. Only in the design of the University's Rotunda did Mumford feel that Jefferson erred, because its monumental scale overwhelmed the rest of the campus buildings. Yet, Mumford ultimately could not forgive Jefferson for discarding regional, American elements in the search for universal values in architecture, a search that led Jefferson to the model of ancient Roman classicism.

In the third lecture, Mumford found himself in the ticklish situation of fitting the gargantuan square peg of Richardson into the limited round hole of Southern regionalism. Mumford reminded his audience that Richardson was born and raised in Louisiana, and that he was truly "a Southern architect in whose achievements every American has a special cause for pride."[122] As unconvincing as this statement was, considering that Richardson practiced almost exclusively in the Northeast and Midwest, Mumford effectively pleaded the case for Richardson's regionalism. In Mumford's view, this regionalism was born directly out of Richardson's "adopted" New England landscape:[123]

[Richardson] interpreted that New England to itself and gave it a better sense of its own identity: he modified its Puritanic austerities: he gave to its buildings a color that they lacked: a color derived from its native granites and sandstones, from weathered shingles and from the autumnal tints of sumach and red oak that linger longer in the countryside of the North than any other colors.[124]

Mumford cited Richardson's shingle-style houses in New England as among the finest examples of this regionalism.

In the final lecture, Mumford valiantly attempted to reconcile the dialectical forces of universalism and regionalism, classicism and romanticism in architecture. He identified the beginnings of a synthesis in the buildings of Richardson, which in turn inspired the architects of the Chicago school. Furthermore, Mumford argued once again that the fullest expression of this synthesis in the twentieth century was to be found in the architecture of Frank Lloyd Wright: "In Wright's domestic architecture the gap between the universal and the local was closed up; for he created a truly organic form in which both elements were steadily brought into play."[125]

At the beginning of this last lecture, Mumford called upon his audience to rise to the challenge of universalism if Western civilization was to survive another world war. He attacked those isolationists who believed otherwise:

That problem has been sharpened for us today, because large groups of people have arisen who deny they have any allegiance to the universal, or any obligation to live under common rule, obey a common moral law, act in terms of a common light and a common understanding. The practical outcome of this gospel of isolation is that millions of such people in Europe have already fallen the victims to the more dynamic kind of tribalism that the totalitarian countries practice.[126]

Returning to the main subject of his lecture, Mumford reminded his audience that it was "not by accident that the Nazis singled out modern architecture, with its emphasis upon the rational and universal elements introduced through modern technics, as the embodiment of all that they hated."[127] It is the study of history, Mumford concluded, that gives humankind the resolve to press forward:

We are interested in the South's contribution to architecture, I take it, precisely because we believe that this civilization is worth saving, precisely because we believe in human continuity; and we must therefore consider . . . what has been happening to our civilization as a whole, in order to safeguard that future, that destiny, that free play of the human spirit, in which we emphatically believe.[128]

Mumford's strongly moralistic tone was soon justified by the Japanese attack on Pearl Harbor in December 1941.

Ironically, it was Wright, the hero of Mumford's last Dancy lecture and a confirmed isolationist, who most vociferously opposed Mumford's interventionist message. In a review for the *Saturday Review of Literature,* Wright attacked *The South in Architecture* for both its distorted historical analysis and its political thrust:

> I am mildly mortified to learn from Mr. Mumford's final lecture that I "widened and carried along the Richardson principles" because I never believed Mr. Richardson had any "principles."
>
> No Lewis! While I am hardly looking, you can't bring this man Richardson up on me from behind, slip in a coupling pin, and ask me to take him along! Moreover, can't you see Lewis, that according to your view of me you are only turning him over to the Japanese?[129]

In this review, Wright ushered into the public's eye a disagreement that the two men had already been conducting privately in their correspondence about the war. This rift went to the core of each man's basic philosophy of life: Wright opposed violence at any cost, but Mumford believed that some causes were worth human sacrifice. Mumford lost many friends because of his political views, but the rift with Wright was particularly painful since each man had respected and supported each other's work for so long. Mumford was particularly upset by an isolationist broadside that Wright had sent to the critic. Mumford wrote back in May 1941:

> You shrink into your selfish ego and urge America to follow you; you are willing to abandon to their terrible fate the conquered, the helpless, the humiliated, the suffering: you carefully refrain from offending, if only by a passing reference, those Nazi overlords to whom in your heart you, like [Charles] Lindbergh, have already freely given the fruits of victory. In short: you have become a living corpse: a spreader of active corruption. You dishonor all the generous impulses you once ennobled. Be silent! lest you bring upon yourself some greater shame.[130]

Wright responded in an equally harsh tone:

> You prate of culture, Lewis. Organic character is the basis of true greatness in that or in any individual or in any nation. War is the negation of all these potentialities now as ever and forever.... Christ! Lewis, is it possible that you are unable to see your own hypocrisy? Why do you try to hide behind what you call mine?[131]

This exchange of letters led to a painful silence between the two men that lasted for a decade.

* * *

After World War II, as the European-based International Style gained a stronger footing in America, Mumford became increasingly troubled that in the rush to discard the old Beaux-Arts method of training, architecture schools were also eliminating the study of history from their revamped curricula. At the time, Mumford held a visiting professorship at the North Carolina State College, and he was concerned about the inaccessibility of many primary sources in American architectural history. He remedied this situation by editing a collection of essays by various nineteenth- and twentieth-century authors, which, significantly, he titled, *Roots of Contemporary American Architecture* (1952).

This curious compilation reveals a great deal about Mumford's own development as an architectural critic. In it, he codified the writings and achievements of the members of his architectural pantheon, while connecting them in spirit to a select group of his contemporaries. The texts that he included were unusually diverse. From the usable past he exhumed the writings of Horatio Greenough and Joseph Warren Yost, grouping them with well-known essays by Louis Sullivan, Henry David Thoreau, Mariana Griswold Van Rensselaer, and Montgomery Schuyler. To this nineteenth-century foundation, Mumford added some of his own writings, including excerpts from *The Brown Decades* and *The South in Architecture,* and essays by his contemporaries, such as Claude Bragdon, Charles Harris Whitaker, Sigfried Giedion, and Henry-Russell Hitchcock Jr. By this time, Mumford and Frank Lloyd Wright had reconciled, and Mumford included the architect's seminal address at Chicago's Hull House, "The Art and Craft of the Machine" (1901). Out of this disparate group of texts, Mumford forged a critical history of the origins and development of American architecture that was documentary in its sources but somewhat arbitrary in its selection.

Although Mumford ostensibly collected this group of essays for the benefit of architecture students, he had an ulterior motive as well. At the end of the book's introductory essay, he discussed how an America that was informed about its architectural past might participate more fully in rebuilding efforts around the world in the postwar period:

> On such foundations, the modern tradition in American architecture can never be reduced to any of the current forms of know-nothingism or isolationism; for though the roots of an organic architecture will lie deep in our soil, our occupations, our people, our institutions, the atmosphere that surrounds it will, by the mere turning of the earth, carry freshening currents from every other country on earth, and in turn spread further what is universal and viable in our own tradition. Our inner strength and our potential service to humanity rest on this fact.[132]

Despite its idiosyncrasies, *Roots of Contemporary American Architecture* became a popular textbook that helped to establish a distinctly American foundation for European modernism.

Soon after the publication of *Roots of Contemporary American Architecture,* Mumford prepared new editions of both *Sticks and Stones* and *The Brown Decades.* The 1955 edition of *Sticks and Stones* was illustrated for the first time, and its text was revised slightly. In the new preface to the book, Mumford recounted his early contributions to the study of American culture, and although he recognized that the book had become somewhat dated, he argued for its "unity as a work of art" and its importance as a work of history:[133]

> From the standpoint of American architectural history *Sticks and Stones* has perforce become just another document. If I have any abiding satisfactions over this work of my youth, it is in the pioneer's secret pride that scholarly buildings are now being built, in distant historic territory, over the buried ashes of a hasty campfire I once lighted, near a spring from whose waters I was the first explorer to drink.[134]

Mumford was less self-congratulatory in his new preface to *The Brown Decades* (1955), reflecting his uncertainty about the toll exacted by the nation's urban renewal programs of the 1940s and 1950s: "*The Brown Decades* had perhaps more influence than *Sticks and Stones* in promoting a revaluation of American architectural history. Much has been uncovered since 1931; but much belated exploration remains to be done before the neglected buildings of this period become dilapidated or are demolished."[135] A third edition of *The Brown Decades* was published in 1971, a testament to its continued popularity and relevance in American architectural history.

* * *

As Mumford advanced in years, he turned to writing autobiographical works. He began to come to terms with his own place in history and with the absorption of his writings into the usable past. With the publication of *Architecture as a Home for Man* on the occasion of his eightieth birthday in 1975, Mumford's own position in the history of American architectural criticism was celebrated. This collection of essays from the *Architectural Record,* however, is just a sampling of the voluminous writings that form Mumford's legacy as an architectural critic, a legacy discussed in chapter 3.

Mumford's books and articles on American architectural history, although thoroughly grounded in scholarly research, stand outside the academic mainstream. Lacking footnotes and a systematic presentation of names, places, and dates, his writings were not directed to the specialist but to the general reader seeking a deeper understanding of the role of architecture in civilization. Mumford wrote history with a polemical intent, and even if his colleagues failed to understand the creative possibilities that history offered, he could at least take solace in having uncovered a wealth of important material from the past for future generations to mine. *Sticks and Stones* and *The Brown Decades* have since been surpassed by later surveys and monographs, but Mumford's analysis of the cultural forces that have shaped the built environment remains remarkably up to date, even in a period of postmodern revisionism.

Mumford was a key figure in the recovery of America's usable past, but he wrote with an eye turned continually toward the future. As he wrote to his daughter Alison in 1954: "Some day some sedulous Ph.D. will go through my literary remains and compose a really brilliant dinner out of what was left in the garbage pail: thus raising the embarrassing question of what I thought I was doing when I cooked the original dinner itself."[136]

It is not surprising that he would eventually hold a spot open for himself in the larger pantheon of Western civilization. In a letter of recommendation for the Polish artist Jan Le Witt that Mumford wrote to Metropolitan Museum of Art Director Thomas Hoving, he made his desired place in the pantheon explicit: "While Le Witt paints in the language of abstraction, he is close to Blake and Ryder in spirit, as he is likewise to Emerson, Thoreau, and – if I may dare to add! – myself."[137]

3

TOWARD AN ORGANIC
ARCHITECTURAL
CRITICISM

Architecture is bound up with the social transition; and it is
the singular demerit of a large part of architectural theory and
practice that it has no living relation with the society that produces it.

– "Form in Modern Architecture"

Lewis Mumford was the first American architectural critic to have a national and
international impact.[1] He began his writing career as a journalist, and his most
insightful observations about the architectural scene are found in the hundreds of
articles and book reviews that he wrote from the early 1920s through the early
1960s. From his base in New York City, Mumford first rose to national prominence
in the pages of the *Journal of the American Institute of Architects,* the *Freeman,* the *New
Republic,* the *American Mercury,* and other national magazines. In 1931, he became
the regular architectural critic for the *New Yorker* and began reaching a broad audience composed of both architects and laypeople. For more than thirty years, Mumford's "Sky Line" column in the *New Yorker* was one of the most controversial and
closely followed outlets for architectural criticism in the United States. This position, moreover, allowed him to keep pace with the contemporary architectural
scene, even after he became absorbed by the larger social and cultural issues affecting
Western civilization.

In his criticism, Mumford promoted the concept of an "organic" modern architecture, one that eschewed issues of form and style in favor of sociological and
functional concerns. According to Mumford, a building was successful if it was
connected to its region, if it was oriented for maximum light and ventilation, if it
functioned efficiently according to its program, if it eliminated useless and costly
decoration, and, most important, if it served human needs properly. Although he
appreciated the practical and aesthetic potential of such modern materials as steel,

plate glass, and concrete, he was not opposed to the continued use of such tradi-tional materials as brick, stone, or wood. Thus, Mumford's organic definition of modern architecture was as broad as the various cultures and regions that it served.

The main difficulty in analyzing Mumford's organic ideal is that in his writings he only hinted at how modern buildings should look. It is, in fact, easier to deter-mine how he believed modern buildings should *not* look. Mumford was decidedly against historical revivalism of any sort, but at the same time he was opposed to technological obeisance in design. In his early writings, therefore, Mumford steered a middle course between Henry-Russell Hitchcock Jr.'s "New Traditionalists" and "New Pioneers," believing that each camp had much to teach the other in the development of modern architecture.

Mumford developed most of his ideas about modern architecture independently. Unlike Hitchcock, Mumford did not have close ties to any of the European mod-ernists. Mumford's closest American friends in the architectural profession – Clar-ence Stein, Henry Wright, and Frederick Ackerman – designed in a rather conser-vative idiom, and they influenced Mumford primarily in planning matters. Together with Mumford, they made up the core of the Regional Planning Association of America, a group whose activities are discussed at length in chapter 4. The one architect whose works best demonstrated Mumford's ideals was Frank Lloyd Wright, and although the two men did not develop their ideas jointly, they were in regular contact during this period. The salient points of Mumford's organic archi-tecture did not coalesce in his criticism until the close of the 1920s. This was a decade of enormous and dramatic change, as the conservative legacy of the Ecole des Beaux-Arts in the American profession was being challenged by new ideas from Europe.

* * *

Before World War I, architectural criticism was a specialized craft, confined mostly to the pages of the professional magazines.[2] Only a few critics of real stature had preceded Mumford in this role around the turn of the century, most notably Mont-gomery Schuyler, Russell Sturgis, Mariana Griswold Van Rensselaer, Herbert Croly, and Claude Bragdon. By the time Mumford made his initial foray into architectural criticism in the early 1920s, only Bragdon was still practicing his craft. As Mumford would later complain, the field of architectural criticism was essentially "dead": "In the architectural magazines, [architects] have been treated, not to criticism, but to flattery, appreciation, 'publicity': and in the case of the more successful practitioners, their own sense of self-importance is increased by the swelling size of their in-come."[3] Mumford was only too happy to step into this critical void, using his socio-logically based standards and an often irreverent writing style to cut through the usual journalistic platitudes.

In developing his own style of criticism, Mumford was well aware of the contributions of his predecessors, whom he freely acknowledged in his autobiography and other accounts. Van Rensselaer had written on a variety of topics, but it was undoubtedly her monograph on Henry Hobson Richardson (1888) that influenced Mumford most.[4] Schuyler's effect on Mumford was more pronounced, and, in fact, Schuyler's career paralleled Mumford's in many ways.[5] Like Mumford, Schuyler had a deeply cultivated interest in literature that enriched his prose considerably. Schuyler wrote both architectural and literary criticism for a number of newspapers and journals, including the *New York World,* the *New York Sun,* the *New York Times,* the *Architectural Record,* and the *New York Sketch-book of Architecture.* Many of his articles were collected and published as *American Architecture* (1892).

Herbert Croly, who had been Schuyler's associate at the *Architectural Record,* had a more professional impact on Mumford's career.[6] Croly left the field of architectural criticism in 1914 when he became the editor of the *New Republic.* Indirectly, he encouraged Mumford to contribute essays and reviews on architecture and city planning to the magazine after Mumford joined the staff in 1920. Under Croly's leadership, the *New Republic* became one of the first general-interest magazines to print architectural criticism on a fairly regular basis at a time when the professional journals shrank from evaluating buildings in print.

Of the group, Claude Bragdon had the most direct and lasting influence on Mumford's intellectual development. Bragdon's *Architecture and Democracy* (1918) was strikingly similar in tone to the work of Patrick Geddes, particularly in its discussion of the evolutionary development of architectural forms. Toward the end of the book, for example, Bragdon wrote: "After the war we are likely to witness an art evolution which will not be restricted to statues and pictures and insincere essays in dry-as-dust architectural styles, but one which will permeate the whole social fabric, and make it palpitate with the rhythm of a younger, a more abundant life."[7] Bragdon's words must have excited Mumford at a time when he was thickly involved in reconstructionist ferment. As discussed previously, *Architecture and Democracy* led Mumford to the writings of Louis Sullivan and, eventually, to the achievements of the Chicago school.

Mumford also appropriated Bragdon's use of the term "organic" to describe contemporary architecture that broke free of the past and responded more closely to human needs in the present. According to Bragdon's recapitulation of Sullivan's famous dictum, "a building is an organism and should follow the law of organisms, which decrees that the form must everywhere follow and express the function, the function determining and creating its appropriate form."[8] Mumford applied the label "organic" to designs that he believed accommodated human need and growth within a healthy environment. Yet, he believed that modern architecture often fell short of this goal or, at its worst, even thwarted it. Thus, he sought to redirect architecture and technology toward more positive, organic ends. With Bragdon's encouragement and with Charles Harris Whitaker's support as editor of the *Journal of the American Institute of Architects,* Mumford's success as a young critic of architecture was virtually assured.

The most important of Mumford's contemporaries in the field of architectural criticism included Talbot Hamlin, Henry-Russell Hitchcock Jr., and Douglas Haskell. Whereas the first two were primarily architectural historians who wrote criticism, Haskell was closer to Mumford in both outlook and circumstance.[9] Haskell's criticism had a strong social basis, and he argued repeatedly for an inclusive modern architecture unhampered by stylistic dogmatism. A journalist by profession, Haskell contributed to many of the same periodicals as Mumford, including *Creative Art, Architecture,* the *Architectural Record,* and the *New Republic.* Between 1930 and 1942, a period that corresponds with Mumford's most prolific years at the *New Yorker,* he was the architectural critic of the *Nation.* Mumford's influence has been much greater than Haskell's, however, because of the enduring appeal of Mumford's books.

It was Mumford himself who was most instrumental in piecing together the history of American architectural criticism and establishing his own place within its ranks. In his 1952 collection of essays, *Roots of Contemporary American Architecture,* Mumford wrote brief biographies of Schuyler, Van Rensselaer, Bragdon, and Whitaker in addition to an autobiographical piece describing his own involvement in the field.[10] Mumford reinforced his connection to Schuyler in the foreword to *Architecture as a Home for Man* (1975), a collection of essays that Mumford had written for the *Architectural Record* over the course of four decades: "Though my active work in other fields kept me from enjoying the close and constant professional association that Schuyler had, I find satisfaction not only in having carried on his studies in contemporary building but in having had a hand in replenishing his critical reputation."[11]

On a broader level, Mumford's architectural criticism was rooted in the British Arts and Crafts movement of the nineteenth century and, specifically, the ideas of John Ruskin and William Morris. This tradition was conveyed to Mumford via their writings but also through Patrick Geddes, who, although a peripheral figure in the Arts and Crafts movement, had as a young man crossed paths with Morris.[12] With the older critics, Geddes shared a concern for the changing role of the community in modern life and the social, if not socialistic, underpinnings of aesthetic production. Yet, Geddes was much more receptive to the potential benefits of modern technology in what he dubbed the "neotechnic" era. Subsequently, it was primarily through Geddes that Mumford would develop his ideas about handicraft and machine production.

Mumford shared Ruskin's view that architecture was the record of civilization and that the critic must interpret his environment through its cultural context. However, Mumford rejected what he viewed as Ruskin's arbitrary distinction between "architecture" and mere "building." In a 1926 pamphlet, Mumford noted that Ruskin's division "is a great error. A building may be plastered with decoration and still be hideous or absurd; on the other hand, a structure may be as lean and stark as a corn elevator, and still have some of the massive grandeur of an Egyptian tomb."[13] By embracing such utilitarian forms as corn elevators, Mumford's architectural criticism asserted its place in the twentieth century even as it looked to the nineteenth century for its authority. Like Ruskin, Mumford also believed that the critic bore a moral responsibility to his public. He demonstrated a fervency for his subject that was rarely matched in the twentieth century.

The writings of the British architect and historian W. R. Lethaby also exerted a formative influence on Mumford. Lethaby was a key figure in the second generation of the Arts and Crafts movement, and his approach to history was based on what he believed were cultural myths rooted in nature. When Lethaby published *Form in Civilization* in 1922, its impact on Mumford was clearly discernible. "Architecture properly understood is largely civilization itself," Lethaby wrote. Mumford abridged this statement slightly and used it to open *Sticks and Stones* (1924).[14] Moreover, Mumford applied many of Lethaby's observations to the American scene in subsequent chapters of the book: the overemphasis on architectural styles in general and the classical revival in particular, the new challenges posed by engineering, and the continued relevance of the handicraft tradition. Soon after *Sticks and Stones* was published, the book editor of the *Dial* sent Lethaby a copy. "I have been reading it with deep interest and *agreement,* and I should be very glad to express this," Lethaby responded, but added that he did not have the time to review the book.[15] Nevertheless, such a favorable response must have boosted Mumford's confidence considerably.

Conversely, Mumford reacted strongly against the ideas of another British historian and critic, Geoffrey Scott. Mumford spurned Scott's landmark study, *The Architecture of Humanism* (1914), because of its narrow, formalist interpretation of the history of architecture, which Scott ultimately used to justify the contemporary revival of neoclassicism. In a 1929 essay, Mumford discussed what he viewed as the major flaw of Scott's book:

> Indeed, Mr. Scott himself seems to believe that success in architecture depends chiefly upon the architect's skill in composition, in handling mass and line and interval, without respect to the means he may use or all the other relationships of function. On examination, one sees that Mr. Scott is in fact talking about pictures and not about buildings in their entirety.[16]

Ironically, Geddes, whose progressive views on technology had influenced Mumford in so many ways, adhered to a somewhat narrow view of architecture that Mumford eventually rejected. Geddes continued to prefer the informal Arts and Crafts vernacular, especially the work of British architects C. R. Ashbee and Charles Rennie Mackintosh, even after it had been challenged in the 1920s by new currents from the European continent. After reading the Museum of Modern Art's catalog, *Modern Architecture: International Exhibition* (1932), that Mumford had sent, Geddes responded: "I don't quite accept that [style?] of particular architecture & esp[ecially] without reference to real origins! If you could come or go by *Glasgow* & see Charles Mackintosh's *G[lasgo]w School of Art,* you'd have this new movement thereafter in better perspective than as of all from Le Corbusier." [17] Although Geddes's ideas concerning architecture, technology, and the regional environment would remain at the core of Mumford's criticism, Mumford had to rely on his own taste in analyzing the outward form of buildings.

* * *

Mumford first attempted to express his views on modern architecture in a 1921 article for the *New Republic,* aptly titled "Machinery and the Modern Style." In this piece, Mumford argued that a truly modern architecture would only emerge when society was ready to embrace practical and utilitarian forms for modern living. He found his anonymous models in New York City's lunchrooms and subway stations, the successful design of which, he believed, was due to their lowly place in the scale of building types. To apply this functional standard to other types, Mumford urged the architect to become the master of the machine:

> We have yet to see what humane fulfillments the machine may bring about when we finally come to grips with it, and neither allow ourselves to be overridden by a crude and boisterous utilitarianism nor turn a repugnant, ineffectual face completely away from the instrument which promises – at least promises! – to liberate the community. [18]

The following year in an essay simply titled "The City," Mumford continued his exploration of the state of contemporary American architecture. He found the best examples of modern design to be the anonymous buildings of the industrial age, which, like the lunchroom and the subway station, were based upon the machine:

> A grain elevator here, a warehouse there, an office building, a garage – there has been the promise of a stripped, athletic, classical style of architecture in these buildings which shall embody all that is good in the Machine Age: its precision, its cleanliness, its hard illuminations, its unflinching logic. [19]

For Mumford then, modern architecture was inextricably bound together with technology in the evolution of new forms, but he soon began to voice his ambivalence about what was popularly referred to as the "Machine Age." [20] He could not deny the machine's powerful attraction, aesthetic potential, and economic efficiency, but he could not accept it as a design panacea. Furthermore, he was alarmed at America's insatiable appetite for new technological products whose actual value as labor-saving devices was low, but whose status as luxury goods was high. Mumford's hope was that new products would be designed to fit changes in the modern lifestyle, rather than dictating those changes. In his view, American architecture was subject to many of the same market forces, as land values and technological innovations threatened to push human requirements into the background.

Several of Mumford's early essays addressed the ongoing conflict between handicraft and the machine. He believed that good industrial design could provide aesthetic delight to the user, but he criticized those products that imitated handicraft:

> It is ... futile and perverse to imitate in a mechanical age the objects that were created during the period of handicraft. Our pathetic servility to the past is due to the fact that we have been slow in perceiving that, once we refuse to accept the norms of handicraft as absolute, there is a new kind of beauty to be achieved *in* and *through* the machine.[21]

Mumford noted, furthermore, that in the modern house, only the kitchen and the bathroom reflected this new industrial aesthetic. Whether it could be spread to the other rooms of the house, he added, depends "upon our ability to humanize our mechanical culture."[22]

Mumford did not completely exclude handicraft from modern architecture. Used sparingly instead of lavishly, he believed that the various crafts would be dramatically offset by a neutral background:

> Handicraft, original art, must again enter our architecture; and it will tend to have the same relation to the broad frame of building, as the trees and flowers do among the walks, balustrades, fountains, and terraces of a formal garden. What will save us from foolish profusion is the fact that original handicraft costs money; and most of us will have to use it sparingly, jealously.[23]

Mumford challenged his readers to "live barely" and to resist collecting "mercenary knick-knacks, like our fathers before us."[24] To those who protested such rigid asceticism, he boldly proclaimed in a subsequent article that "we must either find some new outlet for snobbery and caste-assertion, or we must experience a spiritual conversion, and accept the values introduced with the machine."[25]

Mumford did not escape criticism for such heavy-handed, moral pronouncements on modern technology. In a playful debate published in the socialist magazine the *New Masses* in 1927, he sparred with writer Genevieve Taggard over the "bourgeois comforts" that American industry had produced in abundance for its consumers.[26] Mumford, of course, took the ascetic's point of view, but Taggard would not submit to such idealism. Noting that she had also read the works of Thorstein Veblen and John Ruskin, Taggard reproached Mumford for his elitist position on modern technology: "I [don't] think that the Machine Age is good or perfect, but . . . I know we like it. And it is false and literary to go on pretending that we don't."[27] Mumford, for his part, responded that some machines were not beneficial at all, and he decried their worship:

> It takes a little thought to separate what is humanly helpful in the Machine Age from what is futile, dreary, antagonistic to life; and when people are in the mood of worship – when they must adore something, if it be nothing more than a noise-less water-closet or glass rent-barracks – they prefer to accept things-as-they-are in one large complacent gulp.[28]

In the theory and practice of architecture during the 1920s, Mumford was particularly disturbed by the emerging implication that buildings in general, and skyscrapers in particular, were nothing more than machines themselves. Mumford voiced his pessimism about this in *Sticks and Stones:* "The end of a civilization that considers buildings as mere machines is that it considers human beings as mere machine-tenders: it therefore frustrates or diverts the more vital impulses which would lead to the culture of the earth or the intelligent care of the young."[29] Mumford reserved his harshest criticism for the new skyscrapers that were springing up in Manhattan because of rising land values. This race to the skies culminated in the dueling spires of William Van Alen's Chrysler Building (1929) at 1,048 feet and Shreve, Lamb, and Harmon's Empire State Building at 1,250 feet (1931). "Heaven help the person who critically looks at this building without the help of distance and heavy mists," Mumford wrote of the Chrysler Building in the *New Republic*.[30] Of its cross-town rival then under construction, he concluded that "the building looks as if it would be respectable but dull. It shows no real advance."[31]

Although Mumford admitted to the skyscraper's occasional aesthetic appeal, he repeatedly attacked it for its lack of human scale and its tendency to foster congestion on the ground. He often sketched the New York skyline, and on one occasion he used one of his drawings to underscore this point. In 1925, the *Survey* published his satirical cartoon of two figures dwarfed by an imaginary group of setback skyscrapers. Mumford's caption read:

> Yes, sir, that's the city of the future! Two-hundred-story skyscrapers! Air pumped in from the country. Every cubic foot of space used day and night. Mechanically perfect!
>
> Magnificent! Will anyone live there?[32]

Unlike many architects and critics of the period, Mumford did not particularly like the 1916 New York City zoning ordinance, which required that tall buildings have setbacks at their upper levels in order to allow light to penetrate to the street. From this ordinance developed the characteristic ziggurat skyscraper of the 1920s, whose setbacks were determined by the maximum density that its site allowed. Although to many architects the ordinance seemed to hold innumerable creative possibilities, Mumford viewed the end result as nearly the same: more buildings and congestion, and less sunlight and air. Furthermore, he refused to be seduced by artists' dramatic renderings of the new zoning envelopes, particularly those by the well-known draftsman Hugh Ferriss: "The setback skyscraper is rapidly turning out to be the great booby prize in American architecture; and by now it has become pretty plain that building ordinances and ideal schemes by Mr. Hugh Ferriss cannot take the place of a genuine aesthetic command over the materials, structure, and site."[33] Several years later, Mumford harshly criticized Ferriss's *The Metropolis of Tomorrow,* comparing its deceptively illuminated renderings of setback skyscrapers to Dante's *Inferno.* Mumford was not immune to the beauty of Ferris's drawings, which "softened, sometimes almost smudged" the hard lines of American architecture.[34] Nevertheless, Mumford concluded that "the very method [Ferriss] uses to portray the dream persuades us that the reality which would correspond to it would be a nightmare."[35]

Despite this antipathy toward the skyscraper, Mumford did admire several tall buildings in Manhattan, especially those that could be viewed in their entirety. These included Cass Gilbert's Woolworth Building (1913), Raymond Hood's Radiator Building (1924), and Harvey Corbett's Bush Tower (1918), although the view of this last building was subsequently obscured by yet more skyscrapers, as was the view of Arthur L. Harmon's Shelton Hotel (1924), also a favorite of Mumford's.[36] In a 1927 essay, Mumford complained: "A sufficiently large site, a sufficiently long approach, and a sufficient interval between skyscrapers – these are the basic conditions [for a skyscraper's success]. Without them, the skyscraper becomes a ridiculous and impotent architectural form, of no esthetic value."[37]

Mumford lavished his most enthusiastic praise on Ralph Walker's Barclay-Vesey Building (1926) in Lower Manhattan, calling it "one of the few skyscrapers that will bear close inspection."[38] He particularly liked the sober, largely unornamented mass of its exterior, but he also admired the "gay efflourescence" of its lobby decoration.[39] Still, Mumford was perturbed by the building's cramped downtown site. "The Barclay–Vesey Building is about as good as the architect can do today – business permitting," he concluded. "In a congested city, this freedom doesn't take the architect very far."[40] Yet, by the beginning of the next decade, as Mumford became more sympathetic to European modernism, he began to view the ornamental exuberance of the Art Deco skyscraper as outmoded: "To be modern is in fact to be at the opposite pole from being 'modernist.' The latter represents the esthetic collywobbles of the pusher, the advertiser, the booster; . . . and it is, if anything, an even lower and deader stage of architecture than the archaism of the past generation."[41]

Mumford's outspokenness occasionally provoked the wrath of his colleagues in the architectural profession. In a letter to the *New Republic* decrying this last essay, one reader undoubtedly summarized the feelings of many fellow architects:

> In the interest of American culture, will you please see to it the plans, interior and exterior, of all important buildings, be submitted to Mr. Lewis Mumford before erection begins. It is such a pity that all our modern architecture should be chaotic, stupid, non-integral, nuisancic, inane, respectable, dull, New Yorkish, egoistic, silly, sorry, mistaken, nastily tricky, indecent, unsatisfactory, pasted on, funny, riotous, wrong, grievous, bad, modernistic mish-mashy, restless, egregious, ecclesiastical, Chicago moviesque, meaninglessly voluptuous, weakly conceived, sorriest, stultifying, deplorable, gew-gawish, mistaken, lower, deader, feeble and finally frantic, when we have with us a person like Mr. Mumford, who knows the opposites of all these adjectives, and who, therefore, undoubtedly could erect a building to which not even he could apply one of them.[42]

To this written onslaught, Mumford responded with characteristic aplomb: "I am not at all won over to Mr. Cavendish's notion that the fact that I cannot design a building disables me from passing upon the results. I am not able to lay an egg, either, but I can tell by testing it whether it is good or bad."[43]

Despite Mumford's warnings, skyscrapers continued to be built in New York City and elsewhere, and this high-rise building boom did not abate until the depression. When the real estate market collapsed after 1930, Mumford felt vindicated. In June of 1931, he wrote gleefully to Frank Lloyd Wright: "The bottom is dropping out of the skyscraper business: there is nothing to keep up the inflation. It will be a fine time for those of us who have kept close to the ground."[44]

* * *

Mumford formed many of his views about architecture and technology during the mid-1920s in direct response to the ideas promulgated by European architects and designers, particularly in Germany.[45] Mumford expressed the same ambivalence about the *neue Sachlichkeit* that he had about technology in general. He found much to admire about the Europeans and their architecture – their manipulation of new materials, their new modes of construction, their geometric purity of form, their command of interior volumes, and their eschewal of ornament – but he was deeply concerned that they had lost sight of the human factor in their wholesale acceptance of modern technology.

Mumford kept abreast of new architectural developments in Europe through American, British, and German periodicals, at the same time that his own writings were becoming known abroad. For readers in Great Britain, Mumford continued to contribute an occasional article to the *Sociological Review,* although not specifically on architectural subjects. Although there was no British edition of *Sticks and Stones,* many of the leading architects and planners involved in the Garden City movement read the book because it was brought to their attention by either Mumford or one of his friends. Barry Parker, who along with Raymond Unwin had planned Letchworth Garden City, wrote to Mumford in June 1925 to express his praise for the book.[46] Somewhat earlier, Charles B. Purdom, another prominent English town planner, wrote an enthusiastic letter about *Sticks and Stones* to Mumford's friend Clarence Stein.[47] Ebenezer Howard, to whom Mumford was so deeply indebted for his ideas, called *Sticks and Stones* "a truly wonderful book."[48] In April of 1925, Howard wrote to Stein:

> If I understood architecture a little I should more readily follow some of [Mumford's] criticisms [in *Sticks and Stones*]. But he has wonderful powers of observation; very keen and sound reasoning powers; great imagination; a perfect mastery of English, together with a remarkable insight into the great and pressing problems of the day, and above all he is possessed of the spirit of service which is the great key to their solution.[49]

Mumford's reputation was also growing outside of Great Britain. Through Charles Harris Whitaker, Mumford met Walter Curt Behrendt, who was the newly appointed editor of *Die Form,* the journal of the Deutscher Werkbund.[50] Behrendt subsequently arranged to have *Sticks and Stones* translated and published in German in 1925 with the title *Vom Blockhaus zum Wolkenkratzer: Eine Studie über Amerikanische Architektur und Zivilisation* (From log cabin to skyscraper: A study of American architecture and civilization).[51] Despite what Behrendt called its "journalistic" tone, the new title was chosen to capitalize on German perceptions about American building types.[52] In contrast to the American edition, *Vom Blockhaus zum Wolkenkratzer* was illustrated throughout with black-and-white plates depicting such well-known American landmarks as the Brooklyn Bridge and the Woolworth Building. In the book's new foreword, Mumford explained that he included these photographs for the benefit of those German readers who would be unfamiliar with the American scene:

> For the present edition, however, I have resolved to get illustrations of some of the best or most characteristic examples of each period, not to furnish exhaustive study materials, but to guide the imagination of the reader into the right channels; unfortunately, along with it, this method forces [one] to overlook the great mass of crude and degenerate architecture that the first industrial cities filled up with, and the reader himself must always keep an inner equilibrium against these deficiencies before his eyes.[53]

Following the book's translation, Mumford became widely known in Germany as a leading American architectural critic. Behrendt actively sought articles from Mumford, and during the next five years, Mumford contributed more than a dozen essays on architecture and design to *Die Form, Innen-dekoration,* and other German-language periodicals. Some of these articles were excerpted or adapted from *Vom Blockhaus zum Wolkenkratzer,* but others were translations of essays that he had written for American magazines. Mumford's pieces seem to have been selected for their distinctly American perspective. For example, in a 1925 article written for the *American Mercury* and subsequently translated into German for *Die Form,* Mumford wrote:

> In architecture, we are not Romans or Greeks or Florentines; and worst of all, we are not even Americans. Or rather, we *are* Americans; and we are only too ready to exhibit our snobbishness, our timorousness, our haste, and our distrust of the imagination. We are not yet convinced that art is a good business risk; whereas everyone knows that gentility pays.[54]

Conversely, Mumford learned about new architectural developments on the continent through German periodicals prior to visiting these works in person.

Even before this exposure in *Vom Blockhaus zum Wolkenkratzer,* Mumford had become a chief contact for German architects who were traveling to America. Mumford met Eric Mendelsohn in 1924 when Mendelsohn was visiting the United States, the first such trip made by a German avant-garde architect after World War I. From New York, Mendelsohn traveled to the Midwest, where he toured Chicago with Barry Byrne and visited Frank Lloyd Wright at Taliesin in Wisconsin.[55] Mumford's whole awareness of Midwestern architecture was heightened by Mendelsohn's reports, although it would be three more years before Mumford traveled to that part of the country.

As a token of friendship, Mumford provided Mendelsohn with copies of *Sticks and Stones* and *The Story of Utopias* to take back to Germany. Mendelsohn responded:

> After my return to Europe I want to tell you once more what a pleasure it was to me to make your acquaintance and what a joy your "Stocks [sic] and Stones" gave me. I have read it right away on board ship, regretting all the time, not to have had it on my way over. It opens a number of vistas, unaccessable [sic] for us about influences and reasons in the American architecture and is so closely related to all the social problems which closely touch our life, that it seemed to me like a friend.[56]

Mendelsohn even offered to translate *Sticks and Stones* into German, but it was Behrendt's offer that Mumford eventually accepted. The following month, Mendelsohn brought Mumford's work to the attention of Hendricus Wijdeveld, the editor of *Wendingen.*[57] Mumford was subsequently invited to contribute an essay to the special issue on Frank Lloyd Wright, and this was widely circulated among European architects and planners.

In December 1925, Mendelsohn reciprocated Mumford's gift of *Sticks and Stones* by sending the critic a copy of *Amerika,* the book of photographs that Mendelsohn had assembled from his trip to the United States.[58] Evidently, Mendelsohn had shared these photographs with Mumford even before returning to Germany, since it was undoubtedly Mendelsohn to whom Mumford was referring in a September 1925 essay, "The Poison of Good Taste": "The final comment on our genteel [revivalist] tradition was expressed by a German architect who showed me the snapshots he had taken on his travels about the country: except for a few grain elevators and warehouses, they were all photographs of the backs – the unornamented parts – of our buildings!"[59] Although never close, Mumford and Mendelsohn continued their friendship for many years, exchanging letters and even book illustrations.[60]

In a trip that followed Mendelsohn's by a few months, the German architect and planner Ernst May traveled to America with his wife, stopping to visit Mumford in New York and to view Wright's work in Oak Park.[61] Mumford likewise presented May with a copy of *Sticks and Stones* to read on the return trip across the Atlantic. May praised the book as well: "We read your book while crossing the ocean and found it excellent. We made an extract which I intend to publish in a German journal, as I think that many people should get acquainted with your description of the development of American architecture."[62]

In 1928, when Walter Gropius traveled to America, he also visited Mumford, bringing with him a letter of introduction from Mendelsohn.[63] The meeting must have been amicable, since Gropius's name began to appear more frequently in Mumford's articles. Indeed, through his articles and his personal contacts, Mumford played a pivotal role in the exchange of information about modern architecture across the Atlantic.

Although Mumford developed rather close ties to British and German architects, he maintained his distance from the Swiss-born architect Le Corbusier, the leading avant-garde figure in France. Mumford had read Le Corbusier's polemical tract *Vers une architecture* soon after it was published, and he was wary of the architect's technological bias. Nevertheless, Mumford was clearly intrigued by Le Corbusier's vision of a modern dwelling efficiently designed to suit modern purposes. In a 1930 essay, for example, he recommended that the hygienic standards of hospital design be applied to the interior of the modern house, reducing the labor put into unnecessary cleaning. Yet, in Mumford's view, the modern house was no mere machine for living:

> With the background stripped clean of every piece of meaningless ornament, the foreground will become more prominent: the body, the face, the dress of each inhabitant of the room will not be absorbed by the furnishings, but will stand out in fine relief. The chief forms of decoration in the modern house will be living things: flowers, pictures, people.[64]

Significantly, Mumford disliked the only Corbusian interior that he visited in person during this period. In 1925, following a lecturing stint at the International

Summer School in Geneva, Mumford stopped at the Exposition of Modern Decorative and Industrial Arts in Paris, the birthplace of the Art Deco movement in architecture and design. He deplored the architecture of the exposition in general, but he especially derided Le Corbusier's Pavillon de L'Espirit Nouveau, calling it "fanatically barren."[65]

To many architects visiting from abroad, American cities seemed dynamic and modern with their soaring buildings, bustling factories, and clanging streetcars, especially when compared to the older cities of war-ravaged Europe. Mumford, however, was keenly aware that their impressions of the American scene were highly romanticized, and he sought to correct them:

> Foreign critics have sometimes hailed the triumph of engineering over architecture in America as an aesthetic achievement; but when one examines the matter a little one discovers that a good part of the aesthetic achievement is the result of excellent photographs, snapped in unusual positions, and so the triumphs turn out to be not quite so brave and formidable as enthusiasts make them out.[66]

Such remarks forecast an emerging trend in European publishing toward generously photographed books about American architecture. These included the German edition of *Sticks and Stones* (1925), Gropius's *Internationale Architektur* (1925), and Mendelsohn's *Amerika* (1926) and *Russland: Europa: Amerika* (1929).

In Mumford's estimation, no European architect came close to Frank Lloyd Wright in adapting the machine to humane purposes. Wright's attitude toward the machine was more "modern" than that of the European modernists, and furthermore, Wright's architecture pointed toward a higher synthesis of art and technology. Mumford underscored this point in reviewing Henry-Russell Hitchcock Jr.'s monograph on Wright:

> Mr. Wright is not the forerunner of Le Corbusier but, in a real sense, his successor. He has passed that painful step in learning when one is conscious of one's movements and one's instruments, and has reached that period in pure mechanical design when he can play with it; in short, the engineer has given way to the artist, and despite a hundred efforts to prove either that the engineer *is* the artist, or that engineering is the only possible type of art in the modern world, Mr. Wright's work exists as a living refutation of this notion.[67]

Nevertheless, by the end of the decade, Mumford had come to the somewhat reluctant conclusion that the architecture of Le Corbusier, Gropius, and the other European modernists was far superior to anything being built in America, except for the work of Wright. Mumford discussed their accomplishments in Veblenian terms:

> Much as I may differ with particular items in their creed, or dislike some particular manifestation in design, the exposition of the principle of conspicuous economy in the work of Le Corbusier and Walter Gropius seems to me to be one of the

great contributions that has been made to modern esthetics. . . . If they sometimes err, as I think they do, in treating the machine as a pattern rather than as a means, their attitude is nevertheless sound: they are for conspicuous economy and against conspicuous waste.[68]

Mumford's acceptance of the *neue Sachlichkeit* was due not only to his personal contacts with the visiting Europeans, but also to his friendship with the writer and critic Catherine Bauer. Mumford met Bauer in 1929 in the offices of his publisher, Harcourt, Brace and Company, and their friendship soon blossomed into a romantic affair that lasted for several years.[69] Bauer was admitted to Mumford's circle of friends in New York, and she quickly developed an interest in architecture and planning. When Bauer traveled to Europe in 1930 to view the new architecture in person, she corresponded with Mumford almost daily, recounting her meetings with various architects and her impressions of their buildings. That July, for example, Bauer wrote to Mumford from Stuttgart after having visited the Weissenhof Siedlung, the 1927 international exhibition of modern housing, which had by then been turned into a residential neighborhood:

> Even if van der Rohe's roofs *do* leak in winter – even if it *does* break dishes in a Le Corbusier basement when a man drops his shoe on the top floor – I don't give a damn – nobody ought to drop shoes anyway & it's a serious reflection on the human race if members of it can't live comfortably in those swell houses.[70]

Such glowing reports by Bauer certainly reinforced what Mumford had already come to believe on his own. In a June 1930 article for *Die Form,* Mumford wrote optimistically of "the victory which has been achieved in architecture by Wright, Gropius, Le Corbusier, and Mies van der Rohe, and which has been the product of a hundred almost anonymous designers in the industrial arts."[71] To Mumford, this victory was perhaps the most visible indication of a new world zeitgeist. Although he arrived at this conclusion only after a considerable ideological struggle, to many conservative architects and laymen in America, his European bias was all too painfully clear. In 1931, one disgruntled reader of the *T-Square Club Journal* called Mumford "the high priest of the Saarinen, Neutra, Le Corbusier, Frank Lloyd Wright – lovely names all of them – group of despairers."[72]

* * *

Mumford's architectural criticism was more practical than theoretical in nature. Since the early 1920s, he had been the chief advocate of a sociologically based method, in which the merits of a given building were judged by how well it served human needs. As discussed previously, he embraced the ideal of an organic architecture, one rooted in nineteenth-century evolutionary theory as manifested variously in the writings of Claude Bragdon, Louis Sullivan, Patrick Geddes, and perhaps, even earlier, Samuel Taylor Coleridge.[73] Mumford enriched this ideal through his study of America's "usable past," finding particular inspiration in the transcendentalist writings of Ralph Waldo Emerson and Henry David Thoreau and in the bucolic New England region that Mumford celebrated in *The Golden Day.*

By the end of the 1920s, Mumford forged a personal philosophy that developed out of his longstanding criticism of the Machine Age's materialistic excesses and impoverished values. He outlined his beliefs in a 1930 essay titled "Towards an Organic Humanism." This was the concluding essay in *The Critique of Humanism,* a volume edited by C. Hartley Grattan that featured the contributions of several prominent American writers, including Edmund Wilson, Malcolm Cowley, Henry Hazlitt, and Henry-Russell Hitchcock Jr., among others. Mumford, in his essay, proposed a union between two contemporary rival schools of philosophy: the "New Mechanism" and its attendant faith in the positive value of science and technology and the "New Humanism" and its belief in the primacy of the personality and individual creativity. Out of this union, Mumford argued, there would develop an "organic humanism," which would enrich all aspects of modern life. Near the end of his essay, he summarized the basic tenets of this personal philosophy:

> The real problem of life, both for men and societies, is to keep the organism and the environment, the inner world and the outer, the personality and its creative sources, in the state of tension wherein growth and renewal may continually take place. That balance is always a precarious one; and it was badly upset for the western world by the industrial revolution. It is for us to restore it. An organic attitude towards life can truly be called humanism; for it will reconcile by its superior comprehension the one-sided philosophies which men have formulated out of a raw and imperfect experience. In our new bed, Romanticist and Classicist, "Humanist" and Mechanist, naturalist and idealist will lie down happily together; but they must cast off, before they do so, the soiled and tattered philosophical clothes in which they now parade.[74]

This self-professed organic humanism guided Mumford for the rest of his career, providing the theoretical and moral underpinning for his architectural and urban criticism.

Mumford never wrote a general survey or theoretical study of modern architecture. The closest he came to this was a five-part series of articles written in 1929–1930 for the magazine *Architecture.* The series title, "Form in Modern Architecture," clearly alluded to W. R. Lethaby's *Form in Civilization.*[75] Not surprisingly, Mumford's main thesis was that sociology rather than aesthetics should be the primary basis for architectural criticism. In the first article of the series, he wrote: "Architecture is building; and building is an organic expression of social life. The architect who understands his society, though inferior in imagination and design, may have more to contribute to modern architecture than the brilliant artist who misinter-prets his functions and relationships."[76]

The three intermediate articles in the series addressed such practical issues as the role of new materials in modern architecture, the evolution of various building functions, and comprehensive community planning; the final article, "The Wavy Line versus the Cube," was Mumford's meditation upon style in modern architec-ture. In lieu of Henry-Russell Hitchcock Jr.'s two categories of New Traditionalists and New Pioneers, Mumford proposed two of his own: the "school of the wavy line" and the "school of the cube." The first category represented the Art Nouveau movement while the second included *de Stijl* and the *neue Sachlichkeit*. Mumford castigated the school of the wavy line for being too decorative and luxurious, but he also recognized the weaknesses of the school of the cube:

> If L'Art Nouveau was marked by a meaningless stylistic exuberance, the Neue Sachlichkeit, as it is called in Germany, or the work of the New Pioneers, as Mr. H. R. Hitchcock has called it in America, is marked at first by an equally meaning-less sense of restriction. . . . The building not only becomes rationally simple, which is all to the good; it becomes rationally simplified too, by reason of considerations which have nothing whatever to do with functional requirements.[77]

Nevertheless, Mumford concluded the article, and the series, on a profoundly opti-mistic note. The rigid, stylistic tenets of the two schools were being modified in both Europe and America, he argued, and a truly modern architecture was at last free to emerge. Its progenitor was, not surprisingly, Frank Lloyd Wright.

Both Mumford and Wright sought an organic basis for modern architecture that was part of a more general philosophy of life rooted in nineteenth-century transcendentalism. In their remarkably similar visions, men and women everywhere would live in harmony with nature, and the machine would be at their service. "Frank Lloyd Wright has used some of the words I have used and perhaps has, in the depths of his mind, similar intuitions [about the organic]," Mumford confided to Catherine Bauer in 1933.[78] Yet, Mumford steadfastly avoided discussing such matters in his correspondence with Wright, perhaps fearing that the architect was too strong-willed to debate such theoretical ideas.

Mumford's apprehension about his friendship with Wright became evident when, in February 1932, Mumford declined Wright's invitation to teach at the newly formed Taliesin Fellowship at the architect's estate in southern Wisconsin. Mumford replied:

> I am warmed by the honor and confidence and all that they imply . . . but much as I would like to be near you and to work with you, the job is outside my range and powers. I am now in the midst of a book: there are four or five other books inside of me, kicking around and waiting for their chance to be born: and, as you

know, though we both are men, gestation is a good large job in itself, and necessarily everything else must take second place to it.[79]

Up until this point the two men had conducted a warm and mutually supportive
correspondence, meeting intermittently when Wright was in New York to conduct
business. Afterward, their friendship cooled somewhat. Mumford was always reluctant to break into his writing routine, and in later years he repeatedly resisted
Wright's periodic summons to Taliesin. In fact, Mumford never visited Wright at
Taliesin or Taliesin West in Arizona.[80]

* * *

Mumford was most comfortable with the new machine aesthetic in architecture
when it was applied economically and salubriously in the European Siedlungen; his
investigations into modern housing are examined at length in chapter 4. He was
not convinced, however, that the New Pioneers held the design solutions to all
building types, and in his criticism, he looked for a synthesis of their work with
that of the New Traditionalists. Moreover, Mumford believed strongly in a regional
rather than an international basis for modern architecture, and he looked to
America rather than to Europe for its origins.

Consequently, Mumford found himself in a somewhat awkward situation when
he was asked to write an essay on modern housing for the Museum of Modern
Art's landmark "International Style" exhibition held in 1932.[81] He agreed to participate in the exhibition because he was anxious to promote the positive aspects of
modern architecture regardless of its country of origin. Nevertheless, despite his
association with Henry-Russell Hitchcock Jr and Philip Johnson, the exhibition's
curators, and Alfred H. Barr Jr., the museum's director, Mumford remained uncom-
mitted to the concept of an international style defined by a standard set of aesthetic
criteria. Guilty by association, Mumford spent a good part of his later career de-
bunking the cult of the International Style as its influence grew within the American architectural profession.

During the 1920s, Mumford had eschewed the use of "style" as the sole visual
organizing concept in the history of architecture. To Mumford, architecture was a
multidimensional index of the society that built it, and style terms such as "medieval" or "Renaissance" were meaningless once forms were detached from their
historical and geographical context. Logically, he was opposed to the various revival
styles favored by American architects in the late nineteenth and early twentieth
centuries, believing that these styles cloaked the realities of the modern age. Except
for a brief period in the early 1920s, Mumford was also opposed to the artificial
creation of a new style of architecture since he believed that a truly modern architecture would emerge organically and functionally from the requirements of site,

climate, and human need. In both *Sticks and Stones* and *The Brown Decades,* he argued persuasively for a sociological approach to understanding architecture, and furthermore, neither book used style terms as an organizing rubric.

As the "International Style" exhibition began to take shape in the winter of 1930–1931, Mumford was confronted with the distinct possibility that the new architecture, which had shown such evolutionary potential over the course of the previous decade, was now threatened with stylistic arrest. Whereas modern architecture in Europe and America had been the separate accomplishment of individuals responding to local needs, it was now being forced by Hitchcock and Johnson into a stylistic straightjacket.

Johnson first approached Mumford about participating in the "International Style" exhibition in January 1931.[82] Mumford evidently agreed, although he was skeptical of the museum's exhibition proposal from the very start. The following month, Mumford confided his doubts to Catherine Bauer:

> I sweetly suggested in a letter to [Philip Johnson] that he give a section to the history of modern architecture, so that no one would think it was invented by Norman Bel Geddes and the Bowman Brothers ... the day before yesterday. ...
> [A]ll in all, I am afraid it will be a typical Museum of Modern Art modern exhibition – and that's pretty, pretty bad – Barrbarous in fact.[83]

Despite his punning, Mumford seems genuinely to have been vexed by the exhibition's ideological thrust. Several months later, he again expressed his misgivings to Bauer, but this time in a far more serious tone:

> What I don't like about the New Pioneers – aside from their personalities – is their decoration, and their willingness to sacrifice more important things to decoration. For what is the cantilever and concrete ... but decoration: if it's there, it's the new architecture, and if it isn't, it's just new traditionalism. That's too easy both as architecture and as criticism.[84]

Mumford was also uneasy about the exhibition's European bias because of his friendship with Frank Lloyd Wright. Wright's architecture was to be included in the show, but Hitchcock and Johnson interpreted it merely as preliminary to the work of the European modernists.

Consequently, Mumford decided to ignore the aesthetic issues promulgated by the curators. In his essay, he concentrated instead on the functional, economic, and social requirements of modern housing, using such European examples as Ernst May's Frankfurt-Römerstadt and such American examples as Clarence Stein and Henry Wright's Radburn, New Jersey. Mumford's only concession to matters of style was an indirect endorsement of the unornamented terrace blocks of the European Siedlungen:

Modern architecture, with its strong lines, its disdain for the "quaint" and the "pretty," its communal unity, its submergence of the individual unit in the design of the whole, is not a poor substitute for our abandoned heaven of the individual romantic house, built according to the heart's desire; on the contrary, it is far superior, superior not only to the speculative builder's pathetic caricature but likewise to such nearer approximations as one finds in the upper class suburbs today.[85]

Meanwhile, the inevitable controversy erupted over Frank Lloyd Wright. For some time Wright had bristled over his exclusion from Hitchcock and Johnson's inner circle of acceptable modernists, yet simultaneously, Wright's strong individualism prevented him from wanting his work grouped with the work of others, or from having it placed under the International Style label at all. Mumford was subsequently forced into the difficult role of mediator between the museum and Wright in the months prior to the exhibition's opening.

Wright principally objected to the inclusion of foreign-born architects in the American section, including William Lescaze, who was Swiss by birth, and Richard Neutra, who was a native of Vienna. The selection of Neutra in particular irked Wright. Neutra had once worked for him, but they had not parted company amicably. In addition, for personal reasons Wright disapproved of the selection of the American architect Raymond Hood as inappropriate despite his nationality:[86]

Neutra is the eclectic "up to date," copying the living.

Hood was the eclectic copying the dead, is now the improved eclectic, copying the living. I do not propose to "take the road" in fellowship with eclecticism in any form![87]

Wright threatened to pull out of the show and to organize his own in retaliation for the museum's treatment of him, but with great diplomatic skill, Mumford managed to persuade the architect to remain. By this time, Mumford had put aside most of his doubts about the exhibition in the interest of advancing modern architecture, an issue that he saw as separate from the International Style itself. Mumford cabled Wright immediately:

YOUR ABSENCE FROM MODERN MUSEUMS ARCHITECTURAL SHOW WOULD BE CALAMITY PLEASE RECONSIDER YOUR REFUSAL I HAVE NO CONCERN WHATEVER ON BEHALF OF MUSEUM BUT AM INTERESTED IN YOUR OWN PLACE AND INFLUENCE STOP WE NEED YOU AND CANNOT DO WITHOUT YOU STOP YOUR WITHDRAWAL WILL BE USED BY THAT LOW RASCAL HOOD TO HIS OWN GLORY AND ADVANTAGE STOP AS FOR COMPANY THERE IS NO MORE HONORABLE POSITION THAN TO BE CRUCIFIED BETWEEN TWO THIEVES PLEASE WIRE YOUR OKAY[88]

Wright cabled his acquiescence to Mumford that same day.[89] Eager to define his own role in the planning of the show and to soothe Wright's ruffled ego, Mumford wrote to the architect a few days later: "I have written the introduction to the Housing Section of the show: but have scrupulously kept out of suggesting items even for that tiny piece of it: the whole thing represents Johnson and Hitchcock. No matter what its errors of omission and commission, I think the show will be worth while having and worth while being in."[90] A few days before the exhibition was to open, Mumford again wrote to clarify his position further:

> As for the so-called International Style: it is a dreadful phrase, since architecture is architecture and never, except in a bastard form, a style: so I share your irritation over it, and I sympathize with your disgust over the numerous neurotic and gutless young men, who have seized on the cliches and externalities of the new architecture, and made them their own. But the work itself is often much better than the words that are used about it: I have never thought seriously of Le Corbusier's talents as an architect, for his designs are as weak as his soul itself is arid: but both Van der Rohe and Oud seem to me to have some of the heart of the matter in them, and the fact that the Modern Museum show is a mixed one, with both good and bad stuff in it, seems to me almost inevitable, given the actual state of taste and knowledge and the limitations that dog even the best selection: I don't see how the good work can possibly suffer by juxtapposition [sic] with the insincere and the second-rate. But while the phrase international style emphasizes all the wrong things architecturally, I think it is a fine sign that men o[f] good will all over the world are beginning to face life in the same way, and to seek similar means of expressing it and focussing it: without such consciousness, your own work would not have been such a powerful influence in Europe. I am all for that common spirit, although I reject any little box of tags and labels that the pedants may construct for themselves and affix to the architecture.[91]

Whatever lingering apprehensions Mumford had about the International Style he initially kept to himself. He was unable to attend the late January preview of the exhibition, which officially opened in early February.[92] Mumford was present, however, at a related symposium held at the museum in the middle of February. In an essay that accompanied the published proceedings of the symposium, Hitchcock somewhat surprisingly referred to Mumford as an "older critic than myself whose point of view corresponds fairly closely with my own."[93] Mumford confined his own remarks at the symposium to the sociological and economic challenges of modern housing, perhaps shocking many architects in the audience by his admonition that "you must plan [new housing] as though you were working for a communist government."[94] This statement was not so much a profession of Mumford's radical political views, as it was an indication of his support for government-funded housing initiatives, to be discussed in chapter 4.

Mumford was not silent on the International Style for long, however. He reviewed the exhibition for the *New Yorker* at the end of February, and although the piece was generally favorable, his conclusions ultimately undermined the exhibition's premise. Mumford called the show "a great triumph" for Frank Lloyd Wright and suggested that European architects were showing signs of Wright's influence.[95] Furthermore, as a confirmed regionalist, Mumford expressed his dissatisfaction with the implications of the term "International Style," and he suggested that the label be dropped altogether:

> In discussing the forms of architecture which integrate both the practical and the ideal elements in modern civilization, I prefer Mr. Wright's term, "organic," to the more current adjectives, "modern" or "international"; and this organic architecture is not merely a matter of using new materials and techniques or of conceiving new forms for their effective employment; it is a matter of relating air, sunlight, space, gardens, outlook, social intercourse, economic activity, in such a fashion as to form a concrete whole.[96]

Mumford was not the only critic to express his reservations about the exhibition. "Nothing is established yet, except possibly the common victory over copying the periods and adapting ancient methods," Douglas Haskell wrote in the *Nation*. "We are at the beginning, not the end, of modern imagination."[97] Ironically, Mumford found himself at odds over the exhibition with Catherine Bauer, who had by this point moved toward a more aesthetic appreciation of the new architecture. In a review of the exhibition for *Creative Art,* Bauer made her own position clear: "This exhibition has style. . . . And the proof of it is (1) that the exhibition makes sense when considered as a whole, and (2) that some of the least successful designs achieve a degree of sense merely by being related to the rest of the show."[98]

Bauer, of course, had the advantage of actually having seen the new architecture in person during her 1930 trip to Europe, but Mumford soon remedied this deficiency in his own background. He left for Europe in the spring of 1932, ostensibly to conduct research for a new survey of technology that he was planning to write, but also to examine recent architectural developments, and in particular, the new Siedlungen. Mumford's travels were extensive, taking him to England, Scotland, France, the Netherlands, Germany, and Austria.

During the course of his journey, Mumford met Oskar Stonorov, the German-born architect who had emigrated to America a few years earlier, and Mumford also renewed his acquaintance with Eric Mendelsohn.[99] Mumford, however, was still wary of meeting many of the more prominent European modernists. Philip Johnson provided Mumford with the addresses of Le Corbusier, Walter Gropius, Marcel Breuer, Ludwig Mies van der Rohe, J. J. P. Oud, and others, but Mumford evidently did not bother to contact them.[100] "I haven't yet got courage enough to try my stumbling sentences [in French] & embarrassed silences on Le Corbusier," Mumford wrote half-heartedly to his wife Sophia from Paris in June.[101] Moreover, although Catherine Bauer joined him for part of the journey, the two quarreled, and their investigation of modern housing did not proceed as smoothly as planned.[102]

At this point, Mumford was evidently weary of the International Style. Although he admired Eric Mendelsohn's Metal Workers' Union Hall in Berlin and the new Siedlungen on the outskirts of several German cities, much of the new architecture left Mumford cold.[103] In July, he wrote to Douglas Haskell, who had earlier visited many of the same sites: "The good work I found in unexpected places: in German post-offices, in subways, in one or two Siedlungen, Neubuehl and Roemerstadt, particularly: and much of the architecture which Johnson and Hitchcock have been so loud in praise of seemed a little seedy, or at least, incompletely thought out."[104] Significantly, Mumford's sketches from this trip reveal a growing fascination with medieval architecture and town planning, rather than an abiding interest in modern architecture.

After his return to America, Mumford put aside his reservations about the International Style for several years, since he realized that, Hitchcock and Johnson's formalist pronouncements notwithstanding, the modern movement had yet to mature. Nevertheless, Mumford's reluctance to embrace European modernism as a template for American modernism isolated him ideologically from Hitchcock, Johnson, and, ultimately, the avant-garde whose work Mumford had helped to publicize in the 1920s.

* * *

By 1932, Mumford had reached a crossroads in his career. He had established himself as an internationally renowned critic of architecture and as a writer of short, pithy books on American culture. Nevertheless, he was dissatisfied, for he had yet to write the landmark cultural study for which he had been preparing himself since his student days. Mumford fulfilled his ambition by writing *The Renewal of Life,* an exhaustive four-volume study of Western civilization that built upon the ideas regarding social change that he had first articulated in *The Story of Utopias.*[105]

As early as 1929, Mumford had begun to rework and expand his previous articles on architecture and planning into a more general work about society.[106] He wrote several drafts of a manuscript variously named "Form and Personality" and "Form and Civilization," titles that once again alluded to W. R. Lethaby's *Form in Civilization.* Mumford's book was to include chapters on "machines," "buildings," "cities," and "regions." Yet, rather than concentrating on the technological, architectural, or urban forms themselves, the focus of the manuscript was on the social forces that shaped them. In one of the surviving drafts for the introduction, for example, Mumford contended that it was futile to study the "practical arts" of architecture and planning in isolation from the human personality:

> It is impossible to have an intelligent theory of architecture or the landscape with-
> out also hav[ing] a philosophy of life, a sense of the human forces and impulses
> that tend to objectify themselves in such concrete terms. To seek the basis of
> these arts in technique or in an abstract esthetic judgement is merely to cut the
> problem short at the point where it becomes interesting: namely, out of what
> human sentiments and impulses does the technique or the judgement spring[?][107]

The chapter on buildings was drawn mainly from Mumford's previously published articles, but linked together in one text, they formed a more coherent re-
statement of his ideas. He identified three guiding principles at the basis of modern
design: the economical use of materials, the neutral background, and the integration
of the building to its site. In writing this section, Mumford drew upon the ideas of
several leading European modernists, including J. J. P. Oud and Le Corbusier.
Oud's writings especially appealed to Mumford because they argued for an organic
basis for modern architecture. In one section of the chapter, Mumford quoted from
Oud directly:

> Architectural evolution ... will lead us toward a style that will appear liberated
> from matter, although it is joined to it more completely than ever. Disengaged
> from all impressionistic sentimentality; dependent on clear proportions, frank col-
> ours, plainly organic forms; divested of all that is superfluous; the new architecture
> will be able to outvie even classic limpidity.[108]

In an earlier passage, Mumford alluded to the writings of Le Corbusier: "Though
the conception of the house as a machine is too limited to cover all its functions, it
is preferable to the conception of a house as an expression of the patron's or the
architect's personality. The place to express personality is in manners, in morals, in
the arts of communication; but not in building."[109]

Mumford next introduced the work of Frank Lloyd Wright, but carefully skirted
the "personality" issue that he criticized in the passage just quoted. Wright's buildings, he said,

> show not gingerly care, prudence, restraint, but the exuberance and joy of a great
> spirit, gathering up for itself all the riches of sense and experience and leaving its
> human individuality upon everything it touches. . . . The need for architecture to-
> day is to begin again from the point at which Wright began, and to find a collective
> scientifically grounded solution for those problems which he, single handed,
> solved by brilliant improvisation for other individuals.[110]

This statement underscored one of the fundamental paradoxes of Mumford's architectural criticism. His ideas concerning creative individuality, exemplified by
Wright and the pantheon of American architectural genius, could not easily coexist
with the straightforward, utilitarian architecture that he advocated for modern soci-

ety. Catherine Bauer confronted Mumford about this point after reading over this part of the manuscript:

> As long as people live closer together than two to the square mile and retain their capacity for involuntary sensory stimulation, their public manners – and their architecture – must be modified, limited, ritualized, de-individualized. What is good architecture but a crystallization, a clarification, of this communal ritual? . . .
>
> Fine individual expressions as Frank Lloyd Wright's best houses are – and extremely important in their incidental qualities, fresh use of material, plan, imaginative fitness to terrain, etc., particularly in this fluctuant age – still, they are somehow out of the current. I couldn't possibly live in one – and you would damned well rather live in a severe white farmhouse yourself.[111]

Mumford subsequently struck his praise for Wright's individualistic architecture from the manuscript, and eventually the whole section on architecture was dropped altogether.

Had Mumford published "Form and Civilization" in 1932, it might well have become a standard book on modern architecture and planning. Instead, he expanded the remaining chapters on machines, cities, regions, and personality into *The Renewal of Life,* a multivolume work that was to preoccupy him for nearly twenty years. The lingering influence of Patrick Geddes can be discerned in Mumford's choice of topics for the individual volumes in the series – technology (*Technics and Civilization*), regionalism (*The Culture of Cities*), and the human personality (*The Condition of Man* and *The Conduct of Life*) – which roughly correspond to Geddes's sociological categories of work, place, and folk, respectively. Although architecture figures prominently in the background of all the books in the series, Mumford's failure to include a separate volume on the subject is the series' most glaring omission.

In a letter to Van Wyck Brooks in June 1933, Mumford discussed the magnified scope that his project had taken:

> By now my book has expanded into three books: one on machines, which covers incidentally the major problems of economics, and of politics and morals as related to that: the second on cities, which will cover politics, and to no small degree include also culture and art; and the third on the Personality, which will bring everything together, but which will mainly be concerned with philosophy and education and marriage and what not.[112]

Although Mumford admitted to Brooks that "to even imagine such a series is a piece of unmitigated and unpardonable impudence," he was determined to complete this enormous undertaking on which he believed his reputation would ultimately rest.[113]

Mumford began his study of Western civilization by analyzing the technological forces that had enabled its expansion, but that, left unchecked, could lead to its demise. He soon realized that he lacked the proper background for writing such an in-depth historical study and that American libraries were deficient in this area. In the spring of 1932, he applied for and received a $1,600 Guggenheim fellowship that enabled him to visit Germany and other European countries in order to pursue his research.[114] As noted previously, it was during this same trip that Mumford initially encountered many works of modern architecture. He spent much of his time in the library of the Museum of Natural Sciences and Technics in Munich, reading obscure works in French and German, and he returned to the United States at the end of the summer with a far deeper knowledge of his subject.[115]

Lurking in the back of Mumford's mind as he prepared his study was Oswald Spengler's *The Decline of the West* (2 vols., 1926, 1928), one of the most influential books of the early twentieth century. Although Mumford admired the breadth of Spengler's scholarship, Mumford ultimately rejected Spengler's bleak forecast for modern civilization. Specifically, Spengler made no allowance for what Patrick Geddes had termed "insurgency," the human capacity for renewal. Mumford reviewed the first volume of *The Decline of the West* in 1926, refuting Spengler's main thesis: "May we not, perhaps for the first time, make the transposition consciously, from a finished civilization to a new and budding culture? May we not retain a little of our painfully acquired technique whilst we renew the life, without which that technique is so empty and sterile?"[116] Spengler's subsequent study, *Man and Technics* (1932), alienated Mumford even further. In his review of the book, Mumford refuted Spengler's prediction that the "machine technic will come to an end with Faustian civilization itself, and one day will lie in ruins, forgotten."[117]

Technics and Civilization, published in 1934, was Mumford's response to Spengler, European modernists, and American industrialists. In format, the book is remarkably similar to *The Story of Utopias:* both begin with a sweeping historical survey, and both conclude with a general call for the reorientation of society's values. The program Mumford outlined in the second part of *Technics and Civilization,* however, was the first full-scale application of his organic humanism to society's ills.

Mumford's survey began during the Middle Ages when the rituals of the monastery and the invention of the clock led to mechanical standardization in daily life. He divided the history of technology into distinct periods, just as Geddes had done in *Cities in Evolution,* but with one significant addition. According to Mumford, there was a somewhat idyllic "eotechnic" period that lasted roughly from A.D. 1000 to 1750, and it produced such important naturally powered inventions as the crane and the windmill. The eotechnic period was followed by an era of great economic and social upheaval, commonly known as the Industrial Revolution but called the "paleotechnic" period by Geddes. Founded on a mining economy, this period was one of remarkable mechanical invention, environmental destruction, and human degradation. Yet, this period also produced new forms of technical and artistic delight such as the Brooklyn Bridge and the modern steamship.

The third phase, which Geddes termed the "neotechnic" period, had its roots in the nineteenth century, but it did not gather strength until the turn of the twentieth century. Mumford defined its inventions as being cleanly powered by electricity or gasoline, and they included the lightbulb, the moving picture, and the airplane. World War I had interrupted the neotechnic period, but Mumford was confident that it would ultimately triumph over the destructive tendencies of the paleotechnic period. Once again, he emphasized that society would have to transform itself if this feat was to be accomplished:

> Though the instruments of a neotechnic civilization are now at hand, and though many definite signs of an integration are not lacking, one cannot say confidently that a single region, much less our Western Civilization as a whole, has entirely embraced the neotechnic complex: for the necessary social institutions and the explicit social purposes requisite even for complete technological fulfillment are lacking.[118]

The first step toward this reorientation, according to Mumford, would be to end the wholesale worship of the machine for its own sake and to redirect the machine toward more organic purposes. At the foundation of his thesis was a dialectical analysis of the organic and the technic, whose synthesis he saw as essential to society's future survival. Once under control, the machine could enhance the daily activities of modern life rather than burden them further, and at the same time it could bring about a greater aesthetic fulfillment. To illustrate this point, Mumford juxtaposed a photograph of a grain elevator by Eric Mendelsohn with a sculpture by Constantin Brancusi and paintings by Ferdinand Léger and Thomas Hart Benton.[119] Advances in the design of common household objects were illustrated by photographs from the Museum of Modern Art's "Machine Art" exhibition, which Mumford had reviewed favorably in the spring of 1934.[120] As historian Stanislaus von Moos has noted, Mumford's choice of illustrations for the book betrays his cultural rather than aesthetic bias: "The magnifying glass of the art critic is replaced by the binoculars of the cultural historian."[121]

Mumford devoted the last three chapters of the book to his neotechnic vision for the future. Rejecting the capitalistic belief in mechanical progress, he instead called for a "basic communism" that owed more to Edward Bellamy than to Karl Marx.[122] Under Mumford's proposed system, the state would control industrial production, guaranteeing an improved standard of living for all members of society. Ultimately, he believed that the key to society's betterment lay in harnessing the enormous potential of the machine. Mumford stated this point succinctly at the end of chapter 7: "*Our capacity to go beyond the machine rests upon our power to assimilate the machine. Until we have absorbed the lessons of objectivity, impersonality, neutrality, the lessons of the mechanical realm, we cannot go further in our development toward the more richly organic, the more profoundly human."*[123]

* * *

Although Mumford focused his energies primarily on *The Renewal of Life* during the 1930s, he was thrust into greater prominence as an architectural critic when he began writing for the *New Yorker*. In 1931, Mumford joined the magazine's staff, inheriting a regular feature called "The Sky Line."[124] The column had been controversial virtually from its inception. Mumford's predecessor, George Sheppard Chappell, had become embroiled in a lawsuit because of a highly critical review of H. Craig Severance's Delmonico Building in Midtown Manhattan (1926); eventually, the magazine was forced to print a retraction.[125]

Harold Ross, the founder and editor of the *New Yorker*, ambitiously sought prominent writers for the magazine's regular departments. Evidently, he was first drawn to Mumford's work in such rival publications as the *New Republic* and the *American Mercury*. Certainly, Mumford's often irreverent outlook was in keeping with the *New Yorker*'s general tone. Ross also may have been eager to have a critic more sympathetic toward modern architecture, since Chappell was somewhat conservative in his views.[126] Encouraged by Ross, Mumford transformed "The Sky Line" into a controversial, national forum oriented primarily to the educated layman, but read avidly by architects as well.

As a trial submission, Mumford wrote a particularly biting review in June 1931 of the new plans for Radio City, the original name for the entire Rockefeller Center complex in the heart of Midtown Manhattan.[127] Mumford had already indicated his dissatisfaction with the project in the *New Republic* several months earlier, and his feelings had only intensified in the intervening period.[128] He was especially perturbed by the project's high density, owing to the height of many of its buildings. "If Radio City, as now forecast, is the best that could be done, there is not the faintest reason for anyone to attempt to assemble a big site," he concluded. "Chaos does not have to be planned."[129]

Harsh but essentially fair, Mumford's review of Rockefeller Center set the pace for his tenure at the magazine. To ward off possible lawsuits, it was carefully scrutinized by the magazine's fact checkers.[130] In his autobiography, Mumford speculated further that "perhaps my knowledge of literary law, thanks to two brothers-in-law . . . who had specialized in this field, reassured Ross."[131] Fortunately, the review did not provoke any new legal action against the magazine, and Ross gave Mumford "The Sky Line" to write on a regular basis. The critic's star rose quickly at the magazine. "Your Sky Line is my favorite feature," Ross confided to Mumford in April 1933.[132]

Mumford's criticism for the *New Yorker* reached a much broader audience than his highly polemical books and his articles for the architectural journals. The *New Yorker's* focus was primarily literary, and Mumford was free to indulge in prose that was richer in its use of metaphor and historical references, devices that would have been out of place in a journal like the *Architectural Record*. Furthermore, during Mumford's tenure, the magazine rarely published photographs or illustrations with its articles, placing an unusual restriction on a department so visually and spatially oriented. Only small vignettes of buildings occasionally appeared near the headline, less a visual aid than a characteristic graphic feature of the magazine's layout. In any case, this nonvisual approach suited his writing well, considering his aversion to formal analysis.

Mumford was never a central figure among the *New Yorker's* colorful circle of writers, but he was actively involved in the magazine beyond his duties as its architectural critic. From 1932 to 1937, he served as the *New Yorker's* art critic, writing "The Art Galleries" on a regular basis. Mumford edited part of the magazine's "Goings On about Town" listings, and, on occasion, he would contribute suggestions to the "Talk of the Town."[133] Two of Mumford's earliest and most successful attempts at autobiography also appeared in the magazine under the headings "A New York Childhood" and "A New York Adolescence."[134] For the first few years of his association with the magazine, Mumford wrote columns and other assorted pieces on an almost weekly basis, with only an extended break during the summer months. The relatively generous salary he earned in this position, moreover, enabled him to support his family during the leanest years of the depression.

Since the real estate market in New York was stagnant during the 1930s, Mumford devoted "The Sky Line" to a variety of topics, including store and restaurant remodelings, museum exhibitions, and book reviews. As he wrote in his autobiography of his shorter "Sky Line" pieces: "They tested my critical competence: if I could make a discriminating esthetic judgement about the design of a modern lunchroom, I could perhaps handle Michelangelo or Le Corbusier!"[135] No project was too mundane for Mumford to overlook. Of the new Trufood Restaurant in Midtown Manhattan, for example, he wrote in 1934:

> I recommend that little job, on purely esthetic grounds for the following reasons. Glass brick is used very intelligently as a frame for the transparent window. The color of the brick is carried into the interior walls in a lighter tone of green, and that is a welcome relief from the blaring poster colors of sandwich-shop modernism.... As it is, the whole thing is a modest triumph, from which much more expensive places could learn a lesson.[136]

It should be noted that Mumford, whose tastes were modest, was a habitué of lunchrooms, coffee shops, and inexpensive restaurants.

Rockefeller Center was the one large group of buildings to be constructed in

Manhattan during the depression, mainly because of the immense wealth of its principal backer, John D. Rockefeller Jr. After having lambasted the project when it was first unveiled, Mumford devoted several, more favorable columns to its progress over the course of the decade. Mumford was still opposed to the height and density of Rockefeller Center's skyscrapers, but he praised other aspects of the collaborative design by the Associated Architects led by Raymond Hood. In 1933, Mumford described the Radio City Music Hall and the R.K.O. Roxy Theater as "so far above the Hollywood-Grauman-Paramount-Albee tradition that it is scarcely fair to couple them in the same breath."[137] He found the Music Hall to be "positive and dashing," and he especially liked the "stunning" telescoping effect of the auditorium's interior.[138]

In another column, Mumford joined the controversy over Diego Rivera's infamous mural, "Man at the Crossroads," commissioned for the main lobby of the Center's R.C.A. Building.[139] Rivera's inclusion of a portrait of Nicolai Lenin in the mural led to the artist's well-publicized dismissal, and the mural was eventually overpainted by José Maria Sert, the artist who had received the commission for the lobby's side walls. With more than a touch of sarcasm, Mumford commented on this politically charged incident when it was at its height: "The guardians of Rockefeller Center have wisely chosen to hide [Diego Rivera's] painting and to display [Sert's] wallpaper. One says 'wisely' because the unity of the building was threatened by Rivera's painting – an imaginative work which would have redeemed its colossal and unfaltering inanity."[140]

Nine years into the design and construction of Rockefeller Center, Mumford reconsidered his earlier, harsh judgment of the complex, recognizing that with effective planning even skyscrapers could coexist harmoniously: "Rockefeller Center has turned into an impressive collection of structures, they form a composition in which unity and coherence have to a considerable degree diminished the fault of overemphasis."[141] Still, Mumford would not soften his opposition to skyscrapers, no matter how soundly designed or planned, if they were at the center of densely built cities without sufficient room to view them. "Once we lay out parks and ribbons of open space around such units . . . they will form a new kind of urban organism," Mumford concluded, sounding suspiciously like Le Corbusier.[142]

That Mumford was able to challenge John D. Rockefeller Jr.'s patronage of architecture was not only an indication of the critic's independent resolve, but also a testament to Harold Ross's unswerving confidence in Mumford's opinions. Yet, when the citizens of New York stood to benefit from Rockefeller's efforts, Mumford was equally generous with his praise for the philanthropist. Such was the case with the Cloisters Museum (1934–1938) in Fort Tryon Park at the northern tip of Manhattan, a project underwritten by Rockefeller and designed by the firm of Allen, Collens and Willis.[143] The neomedieval design of the museum incorporated parts of four cloisters, two chapels, a chapter house, and assorted architectural frag-

ments, seamlessly bound together by new construction. Although Mumford generally disdained historical revivalism in modern architecture, in this case, he recognized the special mission of the museum in providing a suitable context for its
collection of medieval objects. Moreover, his review of the museum for the *New
Yorker* was emblematic of how his criticism often moved the reader beyond formal
issues into the realms of history, literature, politics, religion, and the imagination.

Mumford carefully led the reader around the site, analyzing the exterior first and
then the interior. He admired the building particularly for what he called its "au-
thentic disharmonies": "The designers have not only skillfully incorporated the
window openings of various periods, they have even added a Gothic chapel which
looks as uncomfortably new in relation to the rest as such an addition might well
have looked in the thirteenth century."[144] Never an admirer of the vertical line in
architecture, Mumford disapproved of only the central tower, which contained the
museum's administrative offices. He praised the simplicity of the interior and its
cross-axial plan, which supplied "the eye's need for an occasional glimpse of a garden,
a sunlit space, or a patch of sky."[145] The gardens were similar to "those Giotto or St.
Francis might have looked on."[146] He also praised the use of modern interior fittings,
which did not attempt to mimic the style of the actual architectural fragments.

Mumford viewed the design of the Cloisters as a successful solution to housing
a unique collection, but on a broader level, he found in this unusual museum a
temporary solution to the larger, more immediate problems that beset New York
City and the world at large in 1938. "A little of that ancient peace still broods over
this museum," he wrote near the end of the review; "you can walk around one of
these quiet gardens and even discover whether or not you have a soul."[147] Mumford
concluded on a particularly ominous note:

> One remembers how people went in for the collective security of these retreats
> when the power of Rome was dwindling and the proud stones of Rome had
> become a mockery.... [H]ow close the barbarian has already crept up on us
> today. Maybe Mr. Rockefeller hasn't given us just a museum. Maybe this is an ex-
> perimental model to help us face more cheerfully the Dark Ages.[148]

Mumford's writings had increasingly assumed a political tone in the late 1930s, and
this review was a thinly veiled statement of his anti-Nazi and anti-Fascist beliefs.
The title of the piece, "Pax in Urbe," although probably not written by Mumford
himself, was nevertheless his plea for "pax in orbe," or peace in the world. Thus,
he challenged his readers to assess for themselves what specific meaning the Cloisters held for modern American society, and in broader terms, what general purpose
modern architecture served in a civilization gone awry.

A more universal design solution for museums presented itself in 1939 when the
new building of the Museum of Modern Art opened to the public. Designed by
Philip L. Goodwin and Edward Durrell Stone, the museum was one of Manhattan's

first buildings in the International Style. Yet, in Mumford's eyes, the building succeeded not because it adhered to the tenets of a preordained style, but because it
was truly modern and functional. In a review of the new building for the *New
Yorker,* Mumford praised its overall design, from its flexible gallery spaces to its
rooftop terrace and rear garden. "As an exhibition museum, the present building
seems to me a pretty complete success," Mumford concluded.[149]

Despite the ideological differences that had arisen from the "International Style"
exhibition, Mumford remained one of the staunchest supporters of the museum
and its mission of presenting modern design to an often unreceptive American
public. For this, the museum's director, Alfred H. Barr Jr., was openly grateful to
the critic. When, for example, Mumford wrote a glowing review of the museum's
Bauhaus exhibition in December 1938, Barr responded appreciatively:

> We don't often write critics to thank them for their interest in our exhibitions,
> but your recent review of the Bauhaus exhibition in the *New Yorker* was friendly
> and so understanding that I feel that we are much in your debt – especially as a
> great many of the newspaper art critics did not approve of the exhibition.... So
> far as I know, your column in the *New Yorker* is the only regular channel for archi-
> tectural criticism in the United States.[150]

Barr's letter underscored Mumford's almost solitary position in the field of American
architectural criticism in the late 1930s. It also pointed to Mumford's enormous
influence on the general public on matters of architecture and design, an influence
that extended well beyond the New York metropolitan area. At this point in his
career, he was thrust into the international spotlight with the success of his book
The Culture of Cities (1938), the second volume of his *Renewal of Life,* which is
discussed in chapter 4. In April 1938, *Time* featured Mumford on its cover, calling
"The Sky Line" "the most perceptive, severe and expert column of architectural
criticism in the U.S."[151]

* * *

Mumford's output as an architectural critic dropped considerably around 1940, as
he devoted increasing attention to political subjects. With the outbreak of war in
Europe, he became one of the first American intellectuals to advocate participation
in the Allied effort. He pleaded his case eloquently and persuasively in *Men Must
Act* (1939) and *Faith for Living* (1940), books written in rapid succession. When the
United States finally joined the Allies after the Japanese attack on Pearl Harbor,
Mumford felt that his efforts had been vindicated. This turn of events, however,
eventually resulted in a great personal loss for Mumford: the death of his son Geddes
in 1944 while serving on the front line in Italy.[152]

The following year, when the United States dropped atomic bombs on Hiro-
shima and Nagasaki, Mumford's worst fears about the destructive capabilities of

modern technology were confirmed. Despite his son's untimely death, Mumford did not regret his earlier interventionist position. Nevertheless, he began to campaign actively for peace during the cold war, alerting the public to the threat of nuclear annihilation. The resulting arms race of the 1950s filled Mumford with apprehension, which left him far less optimistic about the possibilities for global reconstruction than he had been in the years following World War I.

In part because of his wartime activities, Mumford did not finish the third volume of *The Renewal of Life, The Condition of Man,* until 1944. In it, he was finally able to explore the human personality, a subject that had intrigued him since the drafting of the original "Form and Personality" manuscript. *The Condition of Man* was a history of religious, philosophical, and political thought that in its structure paralleled the first two volumes of the series. The book opened with ancient Greece, moved to the rise and decline of Christianity, and closed with the cultural barbarism of the twentieth century. With World War II in the immediate background of the text, Mumford argued for a wholesale transformation of values at the individual level: "The inner crisis in our civilization must be resolved before the outer crisis can be effectively met. Our first duty is to revamp our ideas and values and to reorganize the human personality around its highest and most central needs."[153] Mumford called this newly reorganized personality the "organic person."[154] Although not stated explicitly by Mumford, the organic person presumably would also become the model resident of the regional city he had outlined in *The Culture of Cities.* Close to nature while stimulated by moderately dense urban surroundings and carefully nurtured social networks, the organic person would find his or her fulfillment in the routine of everyday living. In *The Conduct of Life* (1951), the fourth and final volume of *The Renewal of Life,* Mumford developed his ideas about the reorientation of human values further with a distinct affirmation of traditional Judeo-Christian ethics. However, he also included other world religions in his discussion, believing that they made a vital contribution to a complete and balanced humanism.

If *Technics and Civilization* was partly formulated in response to philosopher Oswald Spengler, the subsequent volumes of *The Renewal of Life* revealed Mumford's debt to historian Arnold Toynbee. The first three volumes of Toynbee's monumental *A Study of History* had appeared in the mid-1930s, and Mumford immediately recognized the similarity in their beliefs. Although Toynbee and Mumford were pessimistic about the state of modern civilization, unlike Spengler they believed that cultural disintegration was not inevitable and that positive change was possible if only society willed it. In a 1935 review of *A Study of History,* Mumford praised Toynbee's acknowledgment of man's "regenerative character":

> How do civilizations develop? Beyond all the special factors that enter into the process of change, Toynbee is conscious of the possibility of some inner rhythm that may abet the process: rest and motion, God and Devil, Love and Hate, Yin

and Yang – these are some of the names various societies have given to the primordial go of things.[155]

As the subsequent volumes of *A Study of History* appeared, Mumford became less enthusiastic about Toynbee's ideas. Nevertheless, Mumford was convinced that Toynbee's contribution to the understanding of the historical process would be lasting. In a 1954 review of the last four volumes of the series, Mumford concluded: "This *Study of History,* then, is at bottom of a great act: an assertion, against the materialism and nihilism of our time, of the dignity of human life and the importance of history itself."[156] Mumford could have applied this statement equally to his own *Renewal of Life*.

* * *

Between 1943 and 1946 Mumford had taken a hiatus from "The Sky Line" because of his political activities and various academic appointments. One measure of his stature as an architectural critic and his drawing power for the *New Yorker* was the persistence with which Harold Ross tried to cajole him into returning. In January 1947, Ross wrote to Mumford: "I want to argue with you once more before giving up the 'Skyline' project. I think we'll have to give it up if you don't follow through. There is no one else. I'm sure of that. The new generation is a collapse. It has produced no talent of any kind whatever to speak of."[157] Mumford eventually acquiesced, resuming his duties later that year.

In the years following World War II, Mumford concentrated on shedding the column's metropolitan New York bias, and he began to review buildings of national and international importance. He republished many of these columns in *From the Ground Up* (1956) and *The Highway and the City* (1963), bringing his criticism of contemporary architecture to a wider readership in the United States. Although, for the most part, he remained an advocate of modern architecture during the postwar period, he continued to urge his colleagues to adopt a more organic approach to modern design.

At this point in his career, however, the middle-aged critic was beginning to sound old-fashioned to architects and critics who came of age after World War II, when modernism no longer seemed to be a strange intruder from Europe. Architect Peter Blake perhaps summarized the feelings of many: "We thought that people like Lewis Mumford (who challenged much of our dogma in the name of humanism) and a few surviving classicists were sweet and sentimental holdovers from an earlier time – and obviously out of touch."[158] This was in part Mumford's fault, for he remained somewhat aloof from the architectural profession. Of the German architects who were fleeing Nazi oppression and resettling in the United States during the 1930s, Mumford forged closer ties only with Walter Curt Behrendt; Walter Gropius, Marcel Breuer, and Ludwig Mies van der Rohe all remained outside of Mumford's circle of friends.[159] Mumford and Le Corbusier had virtually no contact with each other during the postwar years, and any possibility of a rapprochement between the two was dashed by Mumford's scathing review of the architect's Unité d'Habitation in Marseilles (1946–1952).[160]

Mumford and Frank Lloyd Wright mended their differences over World War II around 1950, but their friendship never again regained its former intimacy.[161] A rather telling episode involving the two men was recounted by Mumford in his autobiography. In 1953, when the Guggenheim Museum mounted a retrospective exhibition of the architect's work in a temporary building on upper Fifth Avenue, Wright acted as Mumford's guide. "In seeing his life, so to say, spread before me, with his voice as a persistent undertone, I realized as never before how the insolence of his genius sometimes repelled me," Mumford wrote.[162] A few years later when Wright unveiled his proposal for a "mile-high" skyscraper, Mumford was further appalled by what appeared to be the architect's complete abandonment of the human element in design.[163] Yet, when Wright died in 1959, Mumford was extraordinarily saddened. "One of our giant redwoods has fallen, and left a space we cannot fill by any quick plantation of lesser trees," Mumford wrote.[164]

The one close friendship that Mumford did form with a younger architect ended in tragedy. While a visiting professor at the North Carolina State College's School of Design in 1948, Mumford had become acquainted with the Polish-born architect Matthew Nowicki. Before joining the school's faculty, Nowicki had been a member of the United Nations Planning Commission, and at the time of his death, he was an assistant to Albert Mayer on the design of the provincial capital of Chandigarh, India.

Mumford greatly admired Nowicki's work, because it moved beyond what Mumford viewed as the formal clichés of the International Style toward a truly functional modern architecture that effectively served human needs. Nowicki's best-known work, the North Carolina State Fair Arena in Raleigh (1948–1953), was a tour de force of engineering that utilized intersecting parabolic arches to support the clear span of its roof. To Mumford, Nowicki's unbuilt designs for Chandigarh demonstrated the architect's ability to create novel forms within a radically different climate and culture that were at the same time infused with the spirit of traditional Indian architecture. It was on a return trip to the United States from Chandigarh in 1950 that Nowicki died in a plane crash. Mumford evaluated Nowicki's life and work extensively in a series of articles for the *Architectural Record* in 1954.[165] In Nowicki's work at Chandigarh, Mumford wrote, one could discern an emerging synthesis: "It was a union of Le Corbusier and Frank Lloyd Wright, the two opposite poles of the modern spirit, one formal, cartesian, rational, mechanistic, cubist and classicist; the other vital, full-blooded, constructively inventive, organic and romantic."[166]

* * *

Mumford continued to hammer away at the notion of a monolithic International Style as it became more widely accepted by architects in the United States during the postwar period. Although historians such as Hugh Morrison had begun to question the direction of the International Style as early as 1940, it was a controversial "Sky Line" that Mumford wrote in 1947 about the so-called Bay Region Style that spurred the first major reassessment of the 1932 exhibition.[167] In the piece, Mumford heartily endorsed the spread of this regional movement on the West Coast, since its design principles revolved around the California terrain, climate, and lifestyle, rather than a set of aesthetic criteria. His definition of the Bay Region Style was broad enough to admit both the work of Bernard Maybeck in the first quarter of the twentieth century and the work of William Wurster a generation later. Most important, Mumford believed that modern architecture was finally showing signs of maturity: "The change that is now going on in both Europe and America means only that modern architecture is past its adolescent period, with its quixotic purities, its awkward self-consciousness, its assertive dogmatism."[168]

The resulting brouhaha in the architectural community was so great that the Museum of Modern Art organized a symposium to reassess the importance of the International Style the following spring, almost sixteen years to the date of the exhibition's opening. Although the title of the symposium posed the seemingly simple question "What Is Happening to Modern Architecture?" no definitive answers were reached by the diverse panel, which included the organizers of the original exhibition – Mumford, Henry-Russell Hitchcock Jr., Philip Johnson, and Alfred H. Barr Jr. – and several prominent architects and critics, among them Walter Gropius, Marcel Breuer, Eero Saarinen, Ralph Walker, Talbot Hamlin, and Peter Blake. Mumford moderated the lively discussion that evening, but he held fast to his views about the Bay Region Style and its potential for adaptation in other areas of the United States. At the symposium's conclusion, he asked the audience:

> What is the Bay Region Style? Nothing but an example of a form of modern architecture which came into existence with our growth and which is so native that people, when they ask for a building, do not ask for it in any style. ... To me, that is a sample of internationalism, not a sample of localism and limited effort.[169]

Following the symposium, Mumford continued to wrestle with what he viewed as the inadequacies of the International Style. He was dismayed that American architects, in abandoning the historical revivalism of the first half of the century, had merely substituted a machine aesthetic that was equally impervious to human needs. Moreover, much of modern architecture, in Mumford's opinion, had failed in its attempt to convey a monumental, symbolic expression, an opinion that Mumford evidently shared with the Swiss historian Sigfried Giedion.[170] Mumford addressed these issues in a series of lectures at Columbia University that were published in

1952 as *Art and Technics*. In his lecture on modern architecture, he urged his contemporaries to explore the possibilities of symbolic expression:

> Modern architecture crystallized at the moment that people realized that the
> older modes of symbolism no longer spoke to modern man; and that, on the
> contrary, the new functions brought in by the machine had something special to
> say to him. Unfortunately, in the act of realizing these new truths, mechanical
> function has tended to absorb expression, or in more fanatical minds, to do away
> with the need for it. As a result, the architectural imagination has, within the last
> twenty years, become impoverished.[171]

Yet, despite praise for the works of Frank Lloyd Wright and Matthew Nowicki,
Mumford did not explain how a more monumental modern architecture should
appear.

In no group of buildings was the need for a monumental, symbolic expression
more urgent in Mumford's opinion than the United Nations in New York City.
Completed in 1951, the United Nations was designed by the New York firm of
Harrison and Abramowitz with the consultation of an international team of architects that included Le Corbusier, Oscar Niemeyer, and Matthew Nowicki, among
others.[172] As with Rockefeller Center, Mumford devoted a number of "Sky Line"
columns to the United Nations as its planning and construction progressed.[173] He
was initially concerned by the cramped site chosen for the complex in Midtown
Manhattan overlooking the East River, and he argued instead for the wholesale
clearance of a large area of Lower Manhattan. As the complex took shape, however,
he became even more alarmed that the high-rise Secretariat Building had usurped
the symbolically more important General Assembly Building as the complex's visual
focal point:

> What we have ... is not a building expressive of the purposes of the United
> Nations but an extremely fragile aesthetic achievement, whose main lines con-
> form to the ideals of a boom period of shaky finance and large-scale speculation.
> This sort of modernism goes only skin deep. As a conscious symbol, the Secretar-
> iat adds up to zero; as an unconscious one, it is a negative quantity, since it symbol-
> izes the worst practices of New York, not the best hopes of the United Na-
> tions.[174]

In subsequent columns, Mumford attacked the design of the United Nations
from a variety of social, functional, and aesthetic angles. The Secretariat received
the bulk of his negative criticism for its sealed curtain walls on the east and west
sides, which required the use of artificial ventilation, and, because of the sun's inces-
sant glare, the use of blinds and artificial lighting as well. Although he admitted
that, when viewed from the north, the combination of the Secretariat and the
Assembly was "a vision of delight," he concluded that on almost all other counts,

the complex fell short of its universal goals: "If the United Nations matures into an organ of effective world government, capable of affectionately commanding men's loyalties throughout the planet, it will be in spite of, not because of, the architecture of its first headquarters."[175] Although Mumford has been criticized for his harsh assessment of the United Nations, in retrospect, it does not seem entirely unreasonable for him to have wanted the United Nations to maintain a specific architectural identity within the larger urban fabric of New York City.[176] As seen from the East River, the complex blends almost imperceptibly with the other skyscrapers of Midtown Manhattan. Yet, Mumford was once again maddeningly silent when it came to suggesting design alternatives.

Mumford did admire several buildings constructed in New York City during the postwar building boom, even though he continued to rail against the design of what he now termed "human filing cases."[177] Among his favorites were two moderately scaled designs by the firm of Skidmore, Owings and Merrill: Lever House (1950–1952) on Park Avenue and the Midtown branch of Manufacturers Trust Company (1954).[178] Mumford reserved his highest praise, however, for Ludwig Mies van der Rohe's coolly elegant Seagram's Building (1958), despite Mumford's earlier contention that Mies had become mired in an "Ice Queen's palace of sterile formalism."[179] In reviewing the building for the *New Yorker*, Mumford also proved that he had not lost his sense of humor, noting that the building "must give all the little micelike Mieses who have been coming forth from the architectural schools a touch of panic, for this is not the particular academic cliché they have so sedulously identified with modern architecture."[180] Mumford admired the building's high level of craftsmanship and its generous allotment of open space in one of the most crowded areas of Manhattan. "Sombre, unsmiling, yet not grim, 375 [Park Avenue] is a muted masterpiece – but a masterpiece," Mumford concluded.[181]

* * *

Although Mumford continued to write occasional book reviews for the *New Yorker*, his career as an architectural critic in effect ended in 1963 when his last "Sky Line" appeared. He was by this time disgruntled by what he perceived as a lack of direction among architects, and he was also weary of advocating a sociological basis for modern design, especially when no one seemed to be listening. In a 1962 article provocatively titled "The Case against 'Modern Architecture,'" Mumford once again upbraided the architectural profession for its subservience to the machine and its preoccupation with aesthetic concerns. In his view, the profession needed to rethink its values:

> If modern architecture is not to continue its disintegration into a multitude
> of sects and mannerisms – international stylists, empiricists, brutalists, neo-
> romantics, and what not – it must rest on some principle of order; and that order

must ally architecture to an equally coherent theory of human development. The notion of mechanical progress alone will not do, because it leaves out the one element that would give significance to this progress, man himself; or rather, because it makes the human personality a mere tool of the processes that should in fact serve it.[182]

"The Case against 'Modern Architecture'" proved to be Mumford's last major address to the profession. Although he must have sensed that great changes were about to occur in modern architecture, he chose to retire as an active critic just as his ideas might have had a renewed impact.

In retrospect, Mumford's criticism was always most effective when directed against a unified movement, whether it was the Beaux-Arts tradition of the early twentieth century or the International Style that supplanted it. When the International Style itself began to splinter at midcentury, Mumford was unwilling to provide a formal alternative, nor as a critic was he required to do so. Nevertheless, this frustrated many younger architects and critics, even those who were favorably disposed toward Mumford's views. Wolf Von Eckardt, for example, argued this point succinctly in the *New Republic,* referring to Mumford's aforementioned article:

> The case against modern architecture has never been more poignantly stated. But it cannot constructively rest where Mumford leaves it – with a vague exhortation to use an "organic approach" to building and city design. This is where the shining Mumfordian nebulae are still rather gaseous. The word "organic" has been bandied about by just about every architect and architectural writer who could spell it. But it has yet to result in a single blueprint that a building contractor, client or onlooker can understand.[183]

Nearly thirty years later, historian Leo Marx reached essentially the same conclusion: "A conspicuous shortcoming of Mumford's proposals for coping with contemporary problems is the organicist's preference for holistic solutions. . . . Mumford seems to be saying that nothing can be changed until everything can be changed."[184] Such was Mumford's moral commitment to improving the quality of human life, however, that he set goals for architecture that were nearly, but not quite, impossible to achieve.

Following the tenets of his organic humanism, Mumford defined the success of modern architecture primarily by how well it served society, and secondarily by formal and technical criteria. In his view, architecture itself could not reform society; only committed men and women working together could bring about the eutopia he envisioned. Toward the end of his career, Mumford downplayed his role as an architectural critic, preferring to be remembered as a social philosopher who had tackled the most complex and pressing issues confronting modern civilization. Chief among them was the crisis affecting the city in the twentieth century.

Lewis Mumford, 1931. Courtesy of Sophia Mumford.

Lewis and Elvina Mumford, Atlantic City, c. 1903. Courtesy of Sophia Mumford.

Charles Graessel. Courtesy of Sophia Mumford.

Patrick Geddes. Courtesy of National Library of Scotland, Edinburgh.

Ebenezer Howard. Courtesy of The First Garden City Heritage Museum, Letchworth.

Lewis and Geddes Mumford. Courtesy of Monmouth College.

Lewis Mumford, 1932. Photograph by George Platt Lynes. Courtesy Estate of George Platt Lynes.

Geddes, Alison, and Sophia Mumford, Palo Alto, 1943. Courtesy of Sophia Mumford.

Catherine K. Bauer Wurster. Photograph by Carol Baldwin. Courtesy of Sophia Mumford.

Frank Lloyd Wright addressing the American Institute of Architects' convention on receipt of the Gold Medal, Dallas, 1949. Courtesy of the American Institute of Architects' Library and Archives.

Henry-Russell Hitchcock Jr. Private Collection.

Clarence S. Stein, New York City, c. 1960. Courtesy of the Cornell University Library, Division of Rare and Manuscript Collections.

Frederic J. Osborn. Courtesy of the Osborn Archives, Welwyn Garden City Central Library.

The Mumfords' House, Leedsville, near Amenia, New York, c. 1955. Courtesy of Sophia Mumford.

Lewis and Sophia Mumford, Ledbury, England, July 1957. Courtesy of Sophia Mumford.

Lewis Mumford, Leedsville, New York. Photograph by David Gahr. Courtesy of Sophia Mumford.

4

BUILDING THE
REGIONAL CITY

> The culture of cities is ultimately the culture of life in its higher
> social manifestations.
>
> — *The Culture of Cities*

The city occupied a special place in Lewis Mumford's writings.[1] In his view, the city was the primary setting for human intercourse, and its siting, plan, architecture, and institutions were the very framework of civilization. When cities languished, either through political, economic, or social neglect, civilization itself languished. Mumford's criticism of urbanism was directed to remedying what he saw as life-threatening problems in the congested cities of the twentieth century. A disciple of both Patrick Geddes and Ebenezer Howard, Mumford synthesized the most salient and workable aspects of their ideas into a coherent program of renewal that would encompass not only the city, but also its surrounding region.[2]

As with his architectural criticism, Mumford looked to history to bolster his argument for the transformation of the modern city. Although the New England village and its forerunner, the medieval town, were always his long-lost eutopian ideals, he eventually reached back to the prehistoric origins of civilization for evidence of the positive and negative forces that shaped cities. In the present, New York City was the specific yardstick by which he measured the advance and retreat of modern civilization. Mumford was exhilarated by the cultural and intellectual climate of Manhattan, but he was simultaneously repulsed by its overcrowding. His gradual retreat from New York City in the 1960s coincided not only with his retirement from "The Sky Line," but with its transformation into the urban quagmire that he had been predicting since the 1920s.

From the very beginning, Mumford viewed the city as much more than a plan or group of buildings. An acute observer of the human condition, he was convinced that cities were best judged not by formal criteria, but by how well they served their public. Urban spaces functioned best when the proper scale, orientation, and planning combined to facilitate maximum human interaction. It is no coincidence that in Mumford's early attempts at playwriting, his elaborate stage directions focused on urban settings. Everyday people "performed" in analogous situations, and Mumford was interested in why some buildings, neighborhoods, or civic centers worked, while others did not. In viewing the city in this way, Mumford was greatly influenced by the historical masques Geddes had staged in Edinburgh and London in the 1910s.[3] According to Mumford's biographer, Donald L. Miller, "The city, for Geddes and Mumford, was above all a stage, or physical setting, for the complex drama of living. In the city, with its sprawling cast of characters and pulsating energy, the drama of human life reached its highest pitch. A city's physical setting – its architecture and urban plan – could either frustrate this drama or intensify it."[4]

While Geddes's regional survey provided Mumford with the method for studying the modern city, Howard provided it with a new form. Mumford found much to admire in Howard's garden city proposal, including its relatively low density and scale and its interdependence with the surrounding region. In a 1917 essay, Mumford heralded Howard's garden city as a new model for urban development: "Thereafter city planning meant more than the mere application of beauty patches and cosmetics to an ugly, diseased, and dilapidated town. It meant the rejuvenation and revitalization of cities by the surest of all means: bringing the men within them back to the bosom of the great rough mother that bore them."[5] Like Howard, Mumford maintained that in order for the garden city to succeed, the cultural and educational opportunities of large metropolitan centers must be introduced to the hinterlands. Thus, the inhabitants of the garden city would not suffer the boredom that prevailed in so many provincial centers.

Mumford recognized that in the early twentieth century, the lure of the great metropolis was still draining the population from smaller towns across America. In his 1922 essay "The City," he argued that the chief cause of this rural ennui was that the typical American town had lost touch with its regional roots in its vain attempt to become a commercial metropolis akin to New York. Mumford found the situation in small-town America both bleak and depressing: "Up and down these second-hand Broadways, from one in the afternoon until past ten at night, drifts a more or less aimless mass of human beings, bent upon extracting such joy as is possible from the sights in the windows, the contacts with other human beings, the occasional or systematic flirtations, and the risks and adventures of purchase."[6] Mumford's somewhat vague, short-term solution to this problem was to "remould our mechanical and financial régime," so that small towns would be more attractive to their inhabitants.[7] In the long run, however, he believed that the study of regionalism would provide the means for both the rejuvenation of existing cities and the planting of new garden cities. Fortunately, Mumford found several sympathetic

American colleagues with whom he could share and develop his ideas about region-alism further.

* * *

In the fall of 1922, Charles Harris Whitaker introduced Mumford to Clarence Stein, an architect deeply committed to the improvement of housing and the planning of new communities.[8] The following spring, Whitaker, Stein, Mumford, and several like-minded architects, planners, and writers formed the Regional Planning Associ-ation of America.[9] It was a loosely run organization whose membership hovered around twenty, and whose core consisted of Stein, the president of the group; Mumford, its secretary; Henry Wright, a planner and landscape architect who was also Stein's partner; Frederick Ackerman, an architect who worked closely with Stein and Wright as well; and Benton MacKaye, a conservationist. Others in the group included the architects Robert Kohn, John Bright, and Henry Klaber; city planner Frederick Bigger; philanthropist Alexander Bing; and writer Edith Elmer Wood. In 1931, Catherine Bauer joined the association's inner circle as its executive secretary. The association essentially operated as an informal planning think tank, and its members met frequently in New York City and at the Hudson Guild Farm in northern New Jersey to discuss their ideas.[10]

To the wide-ranging interests of the association Mumford contributed his grow-ing knowledge of American culture, his keen interest in architectural history, his contacts with Geddes and the Sociological Society, and his own observations on housing and other planning issues. As secretary of the association and as its ablest and most prominent writer, Mumford would eventually become the chief spokes-man for its policies. No one member, however, dominated the association's interac-tions. In fact, Mumford believed that the camaraderie among its members was per-haps the greatest contributing factor to its initial successes in the planning of actual communities: "Essentially this little group was a society of friends: people so close in aim, so freely co-operative in act, that the principle of unanimity, of laboring with each other till they had clearly focussed their agreements, spontaneously oper-ated. On such a basis neither factionalism nor desire for priority or publicity marred the work in hand."[11]

From its inception, the association presented an alternative to the largely cos-metic planning promoted by the earlier City Beautiful movement, which, except for the provision of new parks and recreation areas, was largely unconcerned with social issues. The postwar housing crisis in America, particularly the shortage of dwellings in New York City, initially dominated the group's agenda. This was a task for which its members were well prepared. Stein had actually studied at the Ecole des Beaux-Arts in Paris, and he later worked in the office of Bertram Gros-venor Goodhue. While in Goodhue's office, Stein helped to design the mining village of Tyrone, New Mexico, and this seems to have precipitated his lifelong interest in housing issues. Before their association with Stein, Wright and Ackerman both worked for Kohn on the war housing program, which was under the auspices of the United States Shipping Board.

Beyond the pressing issue of housing, the broader mission of the association was to promote the "regional city."[12] As conceived by Mumford in collaboration with the other members of the association over the course of the 1920s, the regional city was essentially a combination of Geddes's regionalism and Howard's garden city. The regional city was to be a new, almost entirely self-sufficient urban form, closely integrated with both the surrounding agricultural hinterlands and the outlying primeval wilderness. In this way, the regional city could take every possible advantage of its site, climate, and natural resources. The inhabitants of the regional city were its most important resource, and local languages, customs, folkways, literature, and other aspects of cultural identity would flourish there as well. Via efficient transportation links, the regional city would be connected to other new or revitalized cities, creating the evenly dispersed network of "social cities" that Howard had envisioned. Ambitious in concept and eutopian in vision, the regional city was the association's permanent, workable solution to the urban chaos that prevailed in the United States.

The association also embraced a strong conservationist policy that distinguished it from the British Garden City movement, and this was due primarily to Benton MacKaye, who is primarily known as the creator of the Appalachian Trail. MacKaye had spent his early childhood in New York City, but he subsequently moved to the rural village of Shirley Center, Massachusetts, where he developed a lifelong interest in the natural environment. Upon his graduation from Harvard University, he worked as a forester with the U.S. Department of Agriculture. Drawing upon his conservationist background, MacKaye worked to integrate the garden city more completely with the natural environment in which it was to be situated. He looked primarily to the New England village as his theoretical model, the form and layout of which were intimately known to him from his youth.

Although Mumford was probably closest in friendship with Stein, it was in MacKaye that the critic found perhaps the group's most versatile mind and kindred spirit.[13] Mumford and MacKaye shared a common intellectual background steeped in the American transcendentalist tradition, and they encouraged each other in their written work. In particular, they admired the writings of Henry David Thoreau, whom they considered to be one of America's first regionalists. Upon reading Mumford's analysis of Thoreau in *The Golden Day*, MacKaye felt compelled to write:

> Of course I drink in & relish what you say of Thoreau, and bulge my chest to have my name on the same page. But it is all so tantalizing, for it makes me want to sit

down with this author (as of yore) & have coffee & have it out. Under your hat I'm making out more attempts to mobilize my thoughts between two covers. And, as usual, I find these thoughts interwoven with your own. I intend to crib from you.[14]

True to his word, MacKaye quoted Mumford's work and ideas at length in his 1928 book, *The New Exploration*.

The two men shared not only a literary kinship but also an appreciation of regional folklife and folkways. Mumford later recalled that during a weekend of meetings at the Hudson Guild Farm, the association was "among the first urban groups to revive the square dances and the Appalachian folk-ballads, under the guidance of MacKaye."[15] The other members also benefited greatly from MacKaye's insight into the nature of community life, an insight that matched his knowledge of environmental issues. In a 1924 letter to MacKaye, Mumford wrote:

Both [Henry] Wright and Clarence [Stein], a couple of weeks ago, made the confession that they could plan the physical garden cities, but had nothing to put into them – couldn't visualize them on their social and civic side. This is where you come in Benton, and this is why I hark back again and again to the Appalachian and the New Colonial ideas. We want motive power and content for the program; and we must be audacious enough, it seems to me, to suggest a new way of life.[16]

Significantly, when Geddes visited the United States in 1923, he participated in a spirited meeting of the association at the Hudson Guild Farm, where, according to Mumford, a special bond developed between Geddes, the botanist, and MacKaye, the conservationist.[17]

From almost the very beginning, the association was affiliated with the British based International Garden Cities and Town Planning Federation.[18] Stein and Wright cemented this tie when, in 1924, they traveled to Great Britain to meet with Ebenezer Howard and Raymond Unwin and to study the new garden cities and garden suburbs there.[19] Unwin was a key figure in the Garden City and Arts and Crafts movements, and he proved to be a major influence on the association, especially in matters related to site planning.[20] Along with his brother-in-law and partner Barry Parker, Unwin had designed Letchworth Garden City (1903–1904) and Hampstead Garden Suburb (1905–1907). Mumford, it should be recalled, had met Unwin in 1920 over tea at Unwin's cottage in Hampstead.

At Letchworth Unwin had experimented with the design of working-class housing, and he was more broadly concerned with ideal population densities in community planning. His motto, "nothing gained by overcrowding" was carefully heeded by the association in their own work.[21] Like Unwin, the association advocated the elimination of costly streets from residential developments to allow for more green space. In matters of design, too, the association followed Unwin's conservative lead, but with a distinctly American twist. Unwin designed houses in the traditional Arts and Crafts style that were consistent with his Ruskinian nostalgia for the vernacular architecture of preindustrial English villages. For similar reasons, the architects in the association would choose the colonial revival style for their developments in order to link them to the American past.

The members of the association believed initially that the surest way to provide new housing was through private initiative on the model proposed by Howard. As built, their residential developments at Sunnyside Gardens, Queens, and Radburn, New Jersey, would not be ostentatious, since housing affordability remained one of their primary goals. Several of Mumford's colleagues shared his admiration for economist Thorstein Veblen, and they deliberately avoided adding the kinds of costly amenities to their houses that served only to satisfy bourgeois tastes.[22] The fledgling association thus had the practical experience and theoretical knowledge required to begin limited experiments in housing, but at the same time they needed to publicize their views effectively if these experiments were to succeed.

* * *

Although small in membership, the Regional Planning Association of America soon became an influential force in architecture and planning circles. Under Whitaker's direction and editorship, the *Journal of the American Institute of Architects* regularly featured the contributions of Mumford and other members of the association during the 1920s. The association also played a policy-making role within the American Institute of Architects itself, since several association members were on the institute's Committee on Community Planning. Mumford, in fact, drafted the committee's reports to the institute's 1924 and 1925 annual meetings.[23]

Mumford quickly became the association's most effective spokesman, publicizing the group's regionalist ideology in both the professional journals and the popular press. In several articles, Mumford established a clear dialectic among city planners: those who favored the technologically oriented, metropolitan approach that had largely supplanted the City Beautiful movement by the early 1920s versus those who favored the organically based regional approach. In a 1925 article for the *Journal of the American Institute of Architects,* for example, Mumford wrote:

> I think that a good many Americans would like to promote a genuine organic growth of communities; but they see that this involves a breach between their purposes and those for which the business groups will undertake any planning at all; and they are not yet prepared to admit that it may be more helpful and realistic to do nothing at all in city planning than it is to do the wrong thing on a grand scale.[24]

Two years later, Mumford argued that if garden cities were to be realized, they must be an integral part of broader regional planning measures: "If we aim only at a garden-city we shall probably not even achieve a garden-city. For a city is not, like an isolated work of art, the work of any one man or group: it is the result of a whole network of social, economic and regional relationships."[25]

The association's most influential forum for its ideas on regionalism was the May 1925 issue of the *Survey Graphic,* which coincided with the meeting in New York City of the International Town, City, and Regional Planning and Garden Cities Congress.[26] The congress attracted many important participants from abroad, including Ebenezer Howard, Raymond Unwin, Barry Parker, Charles B. Purdom, Walter Curt Behrendt, and Ernst May.[27] The congress facilitated the exchange of planning ideas among the participants, both in New York City and, in less formal circumstances, at the Hudson Guild Farm in New Jersey.

The special issue of the *Survey Graphic* must have ignited much discussion at the congress. Inspired by MacKaye and edited by Mumford, the issue was filled almost entirely with the association's propaganda. Stein, Wright, Ackerman, and MacKaye all wrote essays for the magazine, and other contributors included Stuart Chase, the economist; Alfred E. Smith, then governor of the state of New York; and Purdom, the financial director of Welwyn Garden City. It was Mumford's introductory essay, however, that set the tone for the entire issue. In it, he discussed the "fourth migration," the culminating stage in the settlement of America. According to Mumford, the first three migrations were the pioneers' initial trek across the North American continent, their eventual settlement in factory towns, and their subsequent removal to the nation's large financial centers.

Mumford argued that the fourth migration presented an attractive alternative to the metropolitan congestion of the third phase. New technology would lead the way in a great population dispersion stretching from coast to coast. The railroad, supplemented by the automobile and the airplane, would facilitate the movement of people and goods; the telephone and radio would bring information and culture to the countryside; and electrical power would improve the standard of living for all. At the conclusion of his essay, he urged his readers to seize this special opportunity: "Fortunately for us, the fourth migration is only beginning: we may either permit it to crystallize in a formation quite as bad as those of our earlier migrations, or we may turn it to better account by leading it into new channels."[28] Although the special issue of the *Survey Graphic* did not bring about the widespread changes envisioned by the various authors, it pleaded a strong and effective case for regionalism to those attending the congress.

The members of the association soon had another chance to promote their cause, this time in an official capacity. In 1923, Governor Smith had appointed Clarence Stein chairman of the New York State Commission of Housing and Regional Planning.[29] Stein's most important achievement in this capacity was the compilation in 1926 of the nation's first statewide regional planning report to which Mumford, MacKaye, and Wright made significant contributions. Not surprisingly, its conclusions regarding decentralization were strikingly similar to those in the *Survey Graphic,* although this time tailored specifically to the problems of New York State. The report's sweeping objectives were "to broaden out the valley belt, to develop logically the undersettled regions, to give aid to farming and lumbering, to prevent further overcentralization in cities while assisting economy for the manufacturers by proper use of hydroelectric power, to coordinate water supply and to furnish a proper basis for local action."[30] Charts and graphs by Wright underscored their arguments. Yet, as historian Carl Sussman has noted, the report was largely ignored because it demanded public planning initiatives at a time when the private sector opposed any action that would undermine urban land values.[31] In fact, all economic trends during the 1920s pointed toward increasing centralization, especially in New York City.

At the same time that the Regional Planning Association of America was attempting to influence public planning policy, the Russell Sage Foundation was funding the activities of a rival metropolitan New York planning group, the Regional Plan Committee, later known as the Regional Plan Association. The Regional Plan Association, which, significantly, did have the backing of the business community, was then in the process of assembling data for its highly influential *Regional Plan of New York and Its Environs,* published in multiple volumes between 1927 and 1931.[32] As the plan gradually took shape over the course of the decade, the two groups became locked in an ideological tug-of-war. The Regional Planning Association of America, of course, favored a regional approach that called for decentralization through the building of garden cities in the vicinity of New York. Conversely, the drafters of the plan wanted to rebuild the New York metropolitan area along its existing lines of development.

Mumford assumed the role of spokesman for the Regional Planning Association of America in its fight against the plan's metropolitan bias. As early as 1924, Mumford privately expressed his doubts to MacKaye about the direction that the plan, then in its infancy, was taking.[33] The Russell Sage Foundation presented some preliminary findings at the International Town, City, and Regional Planning and Garden Cities Congress the following year. The plan at this stage made no provision for garden cities, and this disappointed Mumford, his American colleagues, and many in the British contingent to the congress.[34] In another section of the congress's exhibition area, the members of the association had mounted their own display, which presented the preliminary findings of the New York State Commission of Housing and Regional Planning. Mumford highlighted the contrasting approaches of the two groups' exhibits in an article for the *Journal of the American Institute of Architects:*

> These plans stood symbolically at opposite poles: one assumes that technical ability can improve living conditions while our existing economic and social habits

continue; the other holds that technical ability can achieve little that is fundamentally worth the effort until we reshape our institutions in such a way as to subordinate financial and property values to those of human welfare.[35]

On more than one occasion, Mumford and Thomas Adams, the director of the Regional Plan of New York, exchanged letters in an attempt to work out their ideological differences, but ultimately, their views could not be reconciled.[36] Essentially, Mumford, the idealist, would not give in to Adams, the pragmatist. In January 1930, Adams wrote to Mumford: "I am sorry we cannot count on support from your able pen because, with all deference, your duty to the public is more important than your intellectual enjoyment as a critic."[37] In the face of such a personal affront, Mumford kept a level head. Soon afterward, he responded: "The garden city, from my private point of view, is not an auxiliary kind of planning: it is the main objective, and if we can contrive the machinery to produce garden cities, they may reduce the necessity for plans that are based upon a continuous upward curve of population growth within the limited area of the Regional Plan."[38]

Planning circles tended to overlap in a complicated fashion during this period, and the ideological split between the Regional Planning Association of America and the Regional Plan Association caused a great deal of consternation among those involved. Mumford's and Adams's differences were exacerbated by their shared personal connections to Patrick Geddes and Ebenezer Howard. Adams had previously been associated with the Garden City movement in Great Britain, as secretary of the Garden City Association, as general manager of Letchworth, and as president of the Town Planning Institute.

Clarence Perry, a peripheral member of the Regional Planning Association of America, was also a major contributor to the Regional Plan of New York.[39] Perry had pioneered the concept of the "neighborhood unit" in planning theory, and it was prominently featured in the published plan.[40] Perry's ideal neighborhood unit was to be relatively self-contained, having its own residences, shops, churches, and recreational facilities. An elementary school was to be located strategically at its center with no house more than a half-mile distant from the school. The association endorsed the neighborhood unit and, in fact, incorporated aspects of this concept into its design for the town of Radburn, New Jersey.[41] In other chapters of the published plan, the association's housing experiments at Radburn and Sunnyside Gardens, Queens, were highlighted as examples of progressive community planning. To complicate matters even further, Sunnyside Gardens had been financed in part by money from the Russell Sage Foundation, the chief backer of the Regional Plan of New York.[42]

Nevertheless, by the time the final volume of the plan appeared in 1931, the whole study was a profound disappointment to the Regional Planning Association of America's members, who had previously admired Adams's work. The association met in March 1932 to discuss its measured response to the plan as a whole, a response to be formulated by Mumford.[43] Following the meeting, Clarence Stein wrote to his wife, the actress Aline MacMahon:

> Did you get the telegram I sent to Pasadena? If so you know that Lewis Mumford knocked out Thom. Adams in the first round, to the delight of the Regional Planners. Around the ring were [Frederick] Ackerman, [Henry] Wright, Geddes Smith, [Robert] Bruere, … [Carol] Aronovici, the [Russell] Blacks, both of them, and Miss [Catherine] Bauer. Oh, yes, and Bruce Bliven of the New Republic for which Lewis is going to write the article on the Plan of N. Y. and Environs. It is going to be strong stuff.[44]

With the backing of the association, Mumford did indeed present his criticism of the plan in print. He gave a preliminary analysis of some of its positive and negative aspects in the *New Yorker* in May 1932, but he did not unleash his sweeping indictment of the plan as a whole until the following month in a two-part article for the *New Republic*.[45] In particular, Mumford was distraught by what he believed was the plan's lack of focus and its many ideological contradictions: "The report talks garden cities but drifts toward further metropolitan centralization; it talks neighborhood planning and better housing, but drifts toward our present chaotic methods of supplying both; it talks of objective standards of light and air for building but drifts toward overintensive uses of even suburban areas."[46]

In a point-by-point analysis, Mumford went on to criticize the framers of the plan for failing to provide an alternative to metropolitan growth. The plan continued to centralize business activity in Midtown Manhattan, and it tolerated the skyscraper as a building form. Furthermore, the plan underestimated the economic seriousness of the housing situation in the city's neighborhoods while advocating the untrammeled spread of the population into suburbia. Thus, despite its name, Mumford argued, the plan was anything but regional:

> The lack of a sociological concept of the city is at one with the planners' lack of an organic geographical concept of the region: it means a failure to approach the problem scientifically and to make use of such tentative results as already have been achieved. Maps, charts, tabulations, surveys, statistical analyses, are useful accessories of thought: they do not take the place of it.[47]

Mumford concluded that this type of megalopolitan planning was "even more shallow" than the cosmetic efforts promoted by the City Beautiful movement a generation earlier.[48]

Stung by Mumford's criticism, Adams lashed back in a rebuttal to the editors of the *New Republic*. Adams accused Mumford of a youthful idealism and naïveté about the specifics of city planning, noting that the planner must stick to a middle course if progress is to be made. In his own defense, Adams even invoked the name of

Patrick Geddes: "This is the main point on which Mr. Mumford and I, as well as Mr. Mumford and Geddes, differ – that is, whether we stand still and talk ideals or move forward and get as much realization of our ideals as possible in a necessarily imperfect society, capable of only imperfect solutions of its problems."[49] Of course, Mumford, the eutopian thinker, would have agreed in principle to Adams's statement to a certain degree. To Mumford, however, imperfect solutions could not be equated with what he believed were bad solutions in place of genuine regional planning. As Carl Sussman has observed, Mumford's article did not "tumble the enormous stature" of the Regional Plan of New York, but it did prepare Mumford for his sweeping criticism of the modern metropolis in *The Culture of Cities* (1938).[50]

* * *

Although the broad goal of the Regional Planning Association of America was the development of the regional city, its immediate focus in the decade following World War I was on housing, an area in which visible changes could be effected in a relatively short period of time. The diversion of the construction industries to wartime production had left the United States seriously deficient in new housing for its returning veterans, and Whitaker focused on this issue in the pages of the *Journal of the American Institute of Architects*. The magazine contained frequent reports on housing developments and legislation in Great Britain and Europe, in addition to lengthy analyses of the situation in America written by members of the association.

In a departure from the popular American ideal, Mumford and his colleagues believed that the freestanding, single-family house was nearly obsolete and that attached housing was the most practical and economical route to pursue. Henry Wright conducted extensive research into housing costs, concluding that since an increasingly larger share was being consumed by household appliances and municipal utilities, savings could be achieved only through effective community planning.[51] Construction and labor costs were not significant factors in Wright's view.

Mumford and the other members of the association thus remained skeptical of the mass-produced house, as proposed by Le Corbusier, Buckminster Fuller, and others in the architectural profession. Although Mumford recognized that limited savings might be achieved in the factory, he believed that without comprehensive planning and innovative financing, the end results would be as unsatisfactory as any speculative housing then on the market.

In a 1930 article for the *Architectural Record*, Mumford discussed the history and development of the mass-produced house, including such contemporary projects as Fuller's "Dymaxion House" and the Rasch brothers' unusual suspended apartment house. For all of its alleged economies, mass production was not cost-effective, according to Mumford: "To cut the cost of the shell in half is to lower the cost of the house a bare ten per cent."[52] Citing the findings of Stein's report for the New York State Commission of Housing and Regional Planning, Mumford argued that the real solution lay in the lowering of interest rates on new construction. This "would reduce the costs far more drastically than the most ingenious cheese-paring on the structure," he concluded.[53]

Still, mass production remained an appealing option to many in the architectural profession as the housing crisis deepened during the depression. In a 1931 article for the *New Republic,* the architectural critic Douglas Haskell proposed a complete rethinking of modern domestic design along the lines of mass production, a scheme that Mumford found naive given the complexity of the housing problem.[54] In a subsequent article, Mumford argued that Haskell ignored the real economic and planning issues behind low-cost housing:

> No decent "house of the future" can be designed in a factory alone. To forget this is to foster specious hopes; and if the mechanized house is placed upon the market before appropriate community and regional plans are made for it, the result will be the same drab, inefficient and nasty environment that the speculative builder creates today. A high total efficiency in the mechanized house, without modern community planning, is a myth.[55]

Fortunately, Mumford had tangible proof to back his assertions, for he was able to point to the association's own experiments in community planning. Sunnyside Gardens, Queens, and Radburn, New Jersey, were not true garden or regional cities, but they were among the most progressive and affordable residential communities yet attempted in America.

* * *

To help the country get out of the postwar housing morass, the Regional Planning Association of America not only wrote about the problem but also attacked it in concrete terms. Under the patronage of Alexander Bing, a member of the association and a wealthy businessman, the limited-dividend City Housing Corporation was founded in 1924 to finance the development of new communities based on garden city principles. Over the next four years, Clarence Stein and Henry Wright undertook the planning and construction of Sunnyside Gardens in the Long Island City section of Queens.[56]

The site chosen for Sunnyside Gardens, a seventy-seven acre plot next to the Long Island Railroad yards and across the East River from Midtown Manhattan, was hardly garden-like in its appearance. Nevertheless, Stein and Wright designed a well-landscaped, mixed-density development of apartment buildings, terrace houses, and a separate garage cluster. The use of the terrace block as the standard residential unit helped reduce the costs of construction and utilities. Frederick Ackerman, who was the principle architect for the project, further economized by designing the brick terrace houses with only minimal colonial revival detailing such as porches and railings.

Although the city had already imposed a relatively uniform street grid on the site, Stein and Wright were determined to provide open spaces in the new community. Following the lead of Raymond Unwin in England, they grouped their terrace houses around the perimeter of each block, opening the center for communal recreation areas. The houses themselves were oriented for maximum sunlight and cross-ventilation.

Without a protective greenbelt, Sunnyside Gardens was eventually surrounded by other developments, but the quality of its construction and the generosity of its open spaces set it distinctly apart from other residential neighborhoods in Queens and Brooklyn. The new community was among the most successful, affordably priced housing experiments in New York City during the 1920s, and it soon attracted a wide range of skilled workers, business professionals, artists, and writers, including Mumford and his family. In 1925, Mumford and his wife Sophia moved from Brooklyn Heights to an apartment in Sunnyside Gardens, and two years later, they bought a house in the development. They continued to live at Sunnyside Gardens for at least part of every year until the mid-1930s, when they made a farmhouse in the upstate village of Amenia their permanent home.

As one of the first residential communities to be carved out of this section of Queens, Sunnyside Gardens quickly achieved a high level of social cohesiveness as a neighborhood. In his autobiography, Mumford attributed the community's success to its "spirit":

> If Sunnyside was to teach me in the most direct way possible . . . how good a well-planned quarter of the city might be, it also taught me another lesson that bites deep into the story of all man's efforts to solidify his most vital impulses by translating them into brick and stone. Buildings are vehicles of the spirit only so long as the spirit that produced them remains alive and at intervals renews itself. After the spirit departs, there is something derisive and ironical in the structure left behind.[57]

The "spirit" of Sunnyside Gardens was certainly due in part to the many friends and relatives of the Mumfords who moved there, including Henry Wright.[58]

Mumford promoted Sunnyside Gardens in a variety of journals during this period. His most extensive review of the project appeared in the *Nation* under the humorous headline, "Houses – Sunnyside Up." In the piece, Mumford described the unusual site plan and residential amenities of Sunnyside Gardens in some detail, but he reserved his greatest praise for the sound economic base on which the community was built:

> Given the conditions under which the ordinary builder works, the City Housing Corporation, by limiting its profits to 6 per cent, has achieved immeasurably supe-

rior results. Sunlight, fresh air, open spaces, opportunity for play, good house design – these are not the idle dreams of Utopians; Mr. Alexander Bing, the initiator
of this development, has shown that they can be a sound business proposition.[59]

In a 1927 article for the *American Federationist,* Mumford pitched his vision of community planning based on the model of Sunnyside Gardens toward American labor:
"A good house can not exist in a city by itself; it can come only as part of a community plan, and until we learn to design our communities and our houses coopera-
tively, treating each separate unit as a part of the whole, we shall not succeed much
better than the jerry-builder does today."[60]

Mumford was even more forceful when addressing architects and planners on
Sunnyside Gardens. In a 1928 article, Mumford attacked most suburban architecture
for being "picturesque," and in its stead, he argued for more simply designed housing along the lines of Sunnyside Gardens.[61] Comprehensive community planning,
he argued, precluded such individual attention to style: "No one of [Stein, Wright
and Ackerman's] houses has any remarkable individuality; the 'style' is just the sim-
plest possible treatment of common brick, with windows of standard size; but every
section of a block, grouped around a common garden, has a distinct individuality
and the total result is something that has genuine style."[62]

* * *

The initial success of Sunnyside Gardens emboldened the Regional Planning Association of America to plan an even larger community during the second half of the
1920s. With the blessing of Ebenezer Howard, the association met at the Hudson
Guild Farm in October 1927 for a two-day conference to discuss the possibility of
creating a new regional city in the New York metropolitan area.[63] The following
year, the City Housing Corporation purchased a parcel of land approximately two
miles square in Bergen County, New Jersey. The association named the new community Radburn.[64] However, expediency soon dictated that Radburn be developed
as a garden suburb along the lines of Hampstead rather than a true garden city like
Letchworth or Welwyn.

The "Radburn idea," as worked out by Stein and Wright for this site, brought
together five basic design elements: residential superblocks, functional traffic separation, pedestrian overpasses and underpasses, the reorientation of houses with living
areas facing the garden and service areas facing the street, and continuous parkland
at the center of each superblock.[65] With its gently curving streets and service drive-
ways distinctly separated from parks and playgrounds, and its garages attached to
every house, Radburn was designed expressly to control the automobile's impact
on suburban life.

With great interest, Mumford scrutinized the new community under construction. He believed that the most innovative component of the Radburn idea was

the system of overpasses and underpasses that kept pedestrians away from automobile traffic. Around 1930, as Mumford was researching *The Brown Decades,* he realized that a similar system of traffic separation had been devised by Frederick Law Olmsted in Central Park.[66] Many years later, Stein himself admitted this: "I don't know whether I ever told you the joke on myself. Pop Stein and I used to walk downtown through the park during much of the period I was working on Radburn. It was a long time before I noted that what we considered was original in Radburn had been done with so much skill in the Park."[67]

Mumford was convinced of the superiority of the Radburn idea to anything that had yet been proposed by American planners, and he promoted the new development in print even more enthusiastically than Sunnyside Gardens. In a 1930 article, in which he asked the reader to take an imaginary airplane ride, Mumford cited Radburn as an alternative to aimless suburban sprawl:

> A certain compactness in planning which is necessitated by our effort to avoid extravagant underground utilities will provide a better view from the air than the loose scattered suburban type of planning which was once so popular in America: while the same economies will lead to a better massing of the smaller units than is now possible with individual houses. Enveloping the residential areas, and touching the business and industrial districts, runs a continuous belt of park, as in Radburn: here are the footpaths that provide for the safety and health of mothers and children. Radburn would in fact serve as a complete embryo of the modern type of city, were the architecture as rigorously conceived as the planning.[68]

Only on this last point did Mumford criticize Stein, Wright, and Ackerman's work. Whereas a limited construction budget required that the terrace houses at Sunnyside Gardens be designed as plainly as possible, the individual houses of Radburn were designed more explicitly in the popular colonial revival mode with gabled roofs and shutters. Still, this did not entirely dampen Mumford's enthusiasm. To Mumford, Radburn was the first concrete step in the creation of a regional city, and by implication, a whole new way of life in the twentieth century.

Related to the planning of Radburn was Benton MacKaye's proposal for "townless highways," a nationwide system of limited-access interurban parkways. Mac-Kaye believed that such a system would reduce traffic congestion, eliminate roadside commercial eyesores, and increase pedestrian safety. Instead of penetrating the heart of cities, the townless highways would be brought to the outskirts of communities like Radburn, where the separation of vehicular and pedestrian traffic was effected on an even more specialized scale. MacKaye and Mumford elaborated on this scheme in a joint article for *Harper's Magazine.* "Result: quiet homes and fast motor travel, not by ignoring the advantages of motor transportation but by boldly facing them and providing for them," they concluded.[69]

The influence of the Radburn idea was enormous, extending not only to such later federal projects as the Greenbelt towns but also to planning developments in

Great Britain.[70] Raymond Unwin, who had been such an important mentor to the association, incorporated many of its features into his planning reports for London in the late 1920s and early 1930s.[71] After World War II the Radburn idea was utilized in the design of the British new towns, as explained later in this chapter. Yet, beyond the overriding importance of this interchange with Great Britain, the association also kept abreast of housing developments on the European continent, developments that were radically different in appearance from the cozy, village atmosphere of Letchworth. Indeed, as historian Stanley Buder has noted, "the connection between the Garden City movement and [English] Arts and Crafts 'rusticity' by the mid-1920s appeared anachronistic."[72] This was particularly evident to Mumford.

* * *

The Regional Planning Association of America had long studied European housing as a possible economic model for the United States to emulate, but Mumford became increasingly interested in the architecture of the new European Siedlungen during the late 1920s. At Sunnyside Gardens and at Radburn, Stein, Wright, and Ackerman had designed the houses in a traditional colonial revival mode, stylistically somewhat akin to Unwin's Arts and Crafts vernacular. Conversely, the architects of the Siedlungen wholeheartedly embraced the new machine aesthetic, including flat roofs, concrete or stuccoed wall surfaces, and ribbon windows. To Mumford these modern forms seemed more expressive of modern life than the somewhat conservative work of his American and British colleagues.

Mumford kept informed about new housing developments in Europe through the pages of *Die Form* and the *Journal of the American Institute of Architects* and through personal contacts with such notable modern architects as Ernst May and Walter Gropius. In particular, Mumford praised May's work, perhaps because it most effectively synthesized garden city principles with a modern aesthetic. May and Unwin had, in fact, once worked together in England.[73] As *Stadtarchitekt* of Frankfurt, May supervised one of the largest new housing programs in Weimar Germany and, indeed, in all of Europe.

Mumford did not visit Frankfurt or any of the other new housing sites in person until 1932, but he received a foretaste of these new developments from his colleague Catherine Bauer, who, as already discussed in chapter 3, embarked on such a tour in 1930.[74] Armed with Mumford's introductions, Bauer met many of the leading modern architects, including May in Germany and J. J. P. Oud in the Netherlands. Oud left a particularly vivid impression on Bauer, as she indicated in a letter to Mumford from September of 1930: "I immediately liked him better than all the architects in Europe – whether because he was so unexpectedly direct & informal or because he is attractive in the American sense . . . , I can't say. In any case, he's probably the only exponent of the Neue Sachlichkeit whose words – however eloquent – you don't automatically start to discount."[75] As for Oud's Mathenesse housing development, Bauer added: "It's *very* good I'm sure – the plan is neat & exciting – & the colors really gay & satisfactory."[76]

Bauer was especially excited by what she found in Germany. She admired the Wiessenhof Siedlung in Stuttgart, and in particular the model dwelling by Le Corbusier.[77] In August 1930, she viewed Ernst May's new Siedlungen outside Frankfurt at Römerstadt and Praunheim.[78] The following month, when she stopped to visit the Bauhaus in Dessau, she also investigated nearby housing projects by Mart Stam and Walter Gropius. "The Gropius [Törten] Siedlung . . . is *excellent* . . . and I was amazed to hear that these really charming and well-planned little houses are the *cheapest existing dwellings* in Germany," she wrote to Mumford.[79] Expressed with the enthusiastic conviction of a fresh convert to modernism, Bauer's positive opinions of the new Siedlungen must have been very hard for Mumford to resist.

Mumford drew extensively on Bauer's firsthand knowledge of the European scene in his writings after 1930, most notably his housing essay for the Museum of Modern Art's "Modern Architecture: International Exhibition," which opened in the winter of 1932. As already discussed in chapter 3, Mumford focused primarily on the social and economic aspects of modern housing in his essay, arguing that effective community design must be freed from the strictures of speculative development. Moreover, he urged architects, planners, and politicians to adopt a unified approach to the contemporary housing situation, which was quickly reaching a state of crisis in the early years of the depression.

Mumford's essay covered many leading examples of American and European housing, including Clarence Stein and Henry Wright's Sunnyside Gardens and Radburn, May's Frankfurt-Römerstadt, and Otto Haesler's Rothenberg Siedlung at Kassel, Germany. Mumford deliberately sidestepped the question of architectural style, although he tended to emphasize the clean lines of the *neue Sachlichkeit*. In his ideal vision, architecture was only a contributing factor to a whole new way of living:

> These buildings are not complete by themselves, like a tomb that functions equally well with or without a corpse; they need the cooperation of the sky, the earth, the forms of men and women, the play of children, the moving routine of daily life itself. Then and then only does the whole live; the aesthetic arises out of the actual. The eye is gratified by the new architecture, not alone because its order and composure is the essence of all sound architecture; the eye is likewise happy because every other function of the mind and body is in effective rhythm.[80]

Mumford was not directly involved in organizing the material to be exhibited at the museum. As one of the exhibition's curators, Philip Johnson assumed this responsibility, and he was assisted by Stein, Wright, and Bauer.[81] As installed, the housing section included large photographs and text panels written by Bauer that underscored Mumford's message in the catalog.[82] On one wall, a photograph of a back alley of speculative housing in Long Island City, Queens was juxtaposed with a view into a verdant, inner courtyard of nearby Sunnyside Gardens. The superiority of the planned, limited-dividend development was a message not easily lost on the viewer.

Mumford still had not yet seen many of the European Siedlungen that he praised so highly in the exhibition. He remedied this situation when he received a Guggenheim fellowship later that spring, which enabled him to undertake research in Europe for his book *Technics and Civilization*. When the editors of *Fortune* asked him to write a series of articles on European housing, he agreed to expand his itinerary accordingly.[83] Mumford traveled to Great Britain, France, the Netherlands, Austria, and Germany in search of new housing developments. Catherine Bauer accompanied him on part of his journey, gathering much of the necessary research and leading him to many of the sites she had visited two years earlier.[84] Although generally disappointed by the modern architecture that had been so highly touted by Henry-Russell Hitchcock Jr. and Philip Johnson in the Museum of Modern Art's exhibition, Mumford was favorably impressed by the new housing. He especially liked May's Römerstadt, with its long rows of terrace houses and gardens oriented for maximum sunlight along the Nidda River valley. In May 1932, Mumford wrote to his wife Sophia:

> I have seen in Römerstadt, the most beautiful Siedlung I have yet laid eyes on. A good thing you are not with me: you'd never be content to live in Sunnyside or anywhere else if you walked through the houses & gardens & looked over the Nidda Valley.... It gave me a real notion of what our new cities might be like: a real fulfillment, & infinitely better than most of the other examples of modern architecture I have seen.[85]

While in Europe, Mumford also attended two major housing exhibitions: "Das Wachsende Haus" in Berlin and "Die Wiener Werkbundsiedlung" in Vienna, where almost all of the major European modernists were represented.[86] Yet, despite his favorable impressions of the new housing, it was the small-scaled city of Lübeck that impressed him the most. He found it "quiet, but full of life: crowded, but surrounded by parks & water and green space"; best of all, it was only a short walk from the city to the countryside.[87] Ironically, Mumford had discovered that the most completely livable regional city in Europe dated from the Middle Ages.

Mumford's first *Fortune* article written that fall discussed the housing situation in England. He reviewed the history of English housing reform, concluding that public subsidies were what accounted for most of the progress in improving the living conditions of the lower classes. Mumford stressed to his business readership, however, that government intervention in England did not stifle private initiative: "Municipal housing, public credit, state subsidies did not interfere with private enterprise: they merely extended new construction into a realm which private enterprise had not touched and could not touch."[88]

Housing on the Continent was the subject of his second *Fortune* article, in which he discussed the functionalist architecture of the new Siedlungen, using extensive illustrations of works by Ludwig Mies van der Rohe, Walter Gropius, Ernst May, and J. J. P. Oud, among others. Mumford's newly informed assessment of continental housing was even more positive than what he had written for the Museum of Modern Art's catalog the previous year:

> I have visited these new housing communities from one end of Europe to the other, with and without official guides; I have talked to the people who live in them; I have looked at the buildings in sunshine and rain; and I wonder that people even bother to circulate criticisms which are so easily refuted by inspection. An occasional stucco wall that has cracked or a roof that has not been sufficiently insulated does not take away from the character of the whole achievement: a high standard of technical excellence and a durable product.[89]

Mumford's third article summarized the various means by which the European governments provided housing assistance as well as their commitment to comprehensive community planning.[90] Up until this point, Mumford's series had been informative and optimistic. He only hinted at the adverse political situation then facing modern architects in Germany and the generally bleak economic climate that threatened progressive housing ventures all across Europe. Still, the editors of *Fortune* must have considered the series too radical, or perhaps even too socialistic, since they canceled Mumford's remaining two articles.[91]

The situation for progressive housing in the United States was even bleaker than in Europe. Gradually, the depression sapped the economic strength of the City Housing Corporation, the development arm of the Regional Planning Association of America. In 1934, the corporation was forced into bankruptcy, with the result that Radburn was never completed on its intended scale and was later engulfed by conventional suburban development.[92] The residents of Radburn struggled to meet their mortgage payments during this difficult period, but at Sunnyside Gardens, the mood was more rebellious. The residents there organized a debilitating mortgage strike in 1935, an action made possible by the strong social bonds that the design of Sunnyside Gardens had helped to foster.[93] The bankruptcy of the City Housing Corporation ultimately underscored the failure of such privately held, limited stock companies to effect large-scale changes in the urban environment. Mumford and his colleagues in the association realized that a radically different economic approach was necessary.

* * *

The depression intensified the need for new residential construction in the United

States, and Mumford and the other members of the Regional Planning Association of America began to agitate vigorously for an increased federal role in housing on the model already established in Europe. The association was especially critical of the Hoover administration's relative inactivity on this issue. In a 1930 article written for the *New Republic,* Mumford posed a number of penetrating questions:

> By what means can the rehousing of the unskilled worker be achieved, other than by moving up into vacated quarters? How can financial support be combined with intelligent community planning and architectural control? What is the relation of land increment, the cost of money, the cost of assembling separate parcels of land, the cost of labor, the cost of municipal utilities, to the final costs of housing? ... How far will group housing and community building be aided by industrial decentralization and regional planning? How far are they helped or hindered by the automatic growth of big cities?[94]

Furthermore, Mumford argued that the housing problem had existed well before the depression and that drastic steps were necessary to solve it, including the replacement of all substandard housing and the construction of new communities. To this sweeping program, the editors of the *New Republic* offered their wholehearted endorsement.[95]

Impatient with the lack of progress by the Hoover administration, Mumford lashed out again at the federal government the following year in an editorial for the *New Republic.* He decried the administration's bias toward home ownership at a time when even the upper classes were experiencing financial difficulties. "The situation is one that calls for a heroic declaration of war," Mumford wrote, "but the members of the President's Conference [on Home Building and Home Ownership] were not, alas, the stuff of which heroes are made."[96] Once again he called for the demolition of substandard housing and the building of "a thousand new communities on modern lines," and once again, his words fell on deaf ears.[97]

Mumford continued to hammer away at the federal government for its lack of action on the housing crisis even after Franklin Delano Roosevelt took office. Although several New Deal programs did provide for urban and rural housing, they were not comprehensive enough to satisfy Mumford and his colleagues.[98] In 1934, several members of the association, including Mumford and Henry Wright, organized the Housing Study Guild in order to focus their energies more effectively on this pressing issue.[99] That same year, Mumford and Wright collaborated with architect and guild member Albert Mayer on a series of articles for the *New Republic,* pointing out the inadequacy of the federal government's response.[100] The Roosevelt administration's initial focus on slum clearance was both wasteful and shortsighted, they maintained, and instead they proposed a national housing program whose key components included the establishment of a federal housing administration, the hiring of technical directors trained in advanced housing principles, systematic research in community development, the allotment of $5 billion in annual funds, and public ownership of the land.[101]

Although their proposed housing program was never implemented, the association's members subsequently advised the Roosevelt administration on various New Deal initiatives. Roosevelt had been relatively receptive to the association's ideas from the time when he was governor of New York State. In fact, during the summer of 1931, he had addressed a conference on regionalism at the University of Virginia organized by the association.[102] Unfortunately, the association's influence was reduced considerably because its individual members pursued advisory roles in separate federal agencies. Benton MacKaye was appointed to the Tennessee Valley Authority, Frederick Ackerman to the Public Works Administration, and Catherine Bauer to the Federal Housing Authority.[103] Clarence Stein and Henry Wright parted company personally and professionally in 1933, which contributed to the dissolution of the association that same year.[104] Subsequently, they played a diminished role on the Greenbelt towns, a New Deal program that in many ways represented the culmination of the association's efforts in community planning.

The Greenbelt towns were intended to be a series of experimental, moderate-income communities planted on the outskirts of major cities nationwide.[105] They were developed under the auspices of the federal government's Resettlement Administration, whose director, Rexford Tugwell, was sympathetic to the association's ideas.[106] Four towns were planned, but only three were actually built, and of this group, Greenbelt, Maryland (1935–1937) was the most fully realized. Although Stein, Wright, and Catherine Bauer advised on Greenbelt, Hale Walker was the chief site planner, and Douglas D. Ellington and R. J. Wadsworth were the architects.[107]

Greenbelt was located midway between Baltimore and Washington, D.C., and it was especially notable for its eponymous girdle of parkland, a characteristic feature of Ebenezer Howard's garden city that both Sunnyside Gardens and Radburn lacked. Its crescent-shaped plan included many components of the Radburn idea, such as residential superblocks and pedestrian underpasses. In comparison with the architecture of Radburn, Greenbelt's was strikingly modern in appearance. Some of the terrace houses had flat roofs, cantilevered door hoods, and casement windows, not unlike the European Siedlungen. Unfortunately, the Greenbelt towns proved to be among the most short-lived of the New Deal programs. In 1936 Congress abolished the Resettlement Administration in the aftermath of a court challenge, effectively halting the government's town planning efforts.[108] Mumford was not involved directly in the Greenbelt program, but its discontinuation left him profoundly disappointed nevertheless.

While his colleagues were accepting government appointments, Mumford characteristically maintained his independent status as a writer. By this time, his attention was focused on *The Renewal of Life* volumes. His research into modern housing provided essential background material for the second volume, *The Culture of Cities* (1938), to be discussed later in this chapter. He continued to investigate and write about new developments in the field, but by the mid-1930s he essentially relinquished his advocacy role to his colleagues. With Mumford's encouragement, Bauer wrote *Modern Housing* (1934), a survey of new developments in Europe and America based on her extensive travels and in-depth research.[109] Henry Wright's *Rehousing Urban America,* a "manual of good housing practice," appeared the following year.[110]

* * *

Mumford's eutopian vision of the regional city was initially shaped by his reading of Patrick Geddes and Ebenezer Howard, subsequently nurtured through his involvement with the Regional Planning Association of America, and further modified by his contact with the European Siedlungen. Thus by the mid-1930s Mumford's eutopian ideal had evolved from the picturesque, privately funded garden city to the modern, publicly supported regional city for which Römerstadt or Greenbelt provided the model. Still, as an urban critic, Mumford was open to other alternatives, and it is useful to examine his reaction to the radically different ideas promoted by Le Corbusier and Frank Lloyd Wright during this same period.[111]

Given Mumford's dislike of Le Corbusier's architecture, it at first seems surprising that Mumford found anything to admire in Le Corbusier's audacious vision of a modern skyscraper city. Yet in a 1930 review of Le Corbusier's *City of Tomorrow,* Mumford discussed the advantages as well as the shortcomings of the architect's vision. Of its shortcomings, Mumford wrote: "Le Corbusier is against antiquarianism, sentimentalism, handicraft, irregular contours in the landscape, organic planning and growth, historical and regional traditions: he is in favor of the machine, bareness, geometry, hanging gardens – which he quaintly prefers to those which are closer to the earth – flat surfaces and mathematical simplicity."[112] Conversely, Mumford liked the City of Tomorrow's functional plan, whose successes he somewhat ironically attributed to the architect's Beaux-Arts background: "Le Corbusier's method is excellent. Instead of starting with the tangle of compromises and vested interests and ancient habits that make up the modern city, he begins with the essential functions to be served, and creates a schematic city capable of meeting these requirements."[113] Nevertheless, Mumford's qualified appreciation of the City of Tomorrow – later to be rechristened by Le Corbusier as the Ville Radieuse or "Radiant City" – was subsequently replaced by harsh criticism when it became clear that the architect favored extraordinarily high densities for the modern metropolis: "Of the biological and social consequences of overcrowding, whether done in the present muddled pattern or in Le Corbusier's elegant geometrical equivalent, he is ostentatiously ignorant – or shall I say innocent?"[114]

Mumford's analysis of Wright's urbanism, or more accurately, Wright's antiur-

banism, was more complicated, given the often volatile personal relationship between critic and architect. In the design of new communities, the association had
adopted Raymond Unwin's concerns about achieving the right population densities. In their view, a community's density must be high enough to maintain a vital
cultural and social life for its inhabitants, but low enough to provide safer and more
salubrious surroundings.

Wright's ideas concerning community planning and population dispersal thus
caused Mumford considerable consternation. During the depression, Wright formulated an ideal community that he called Broadacre City. It was to be a sprawling
community, neither urban nor rural, zoned according to functional usage. Houses,
although varying in size, were to be allotted at least an acre of land. Transportation
over such a vast area was facilitated by the automobile and, for longer distances,
by the airplane and helicopter. When Wright exhibited his enormous model of
Broadacre City at Rockefeller Center in 1935, Mumford reviewed it for the *New
Yorker,* congratulating the architect for finally addressing "the conception of a whole
community."[115] Mumford admired the inclusion of generous parks and forests in
the plan, the Radburn-like separation of traffic, and the design of the individual
houses. Mumford's only real criticism of Broadacre City was Wright's design for
free-standing "minimal" houses: "Wright, who hates the very word 'housing,' has
created a design for single-family houses for the lower-income groups which com-
pares very unfavorably, I think, with the European and American [terrace] 'housing'
he detests."[116] This reaction perplexed Wright. In a letter to Mumford in April
1935, the architect wrote:

> I don't know what you can mean by preferring the German tenement and
> slum solution as preferable to the Broadacre's minimum house and maximum
> of space.
> There can be no possible comparison between the two as to privacy, light and
> air, living accommodations – or what have you – at $600.00....
> I must confess, you puzzle me Lewis.[117]

To this accusation, Mumford prepared a carefully worded response:

> The thing about which we fundamentally disagree is not what you put forward
> but what you reject. I think it is silly to lump all the good and bad things that have
> been done in European housing as a "slum solution." You can only do this by
> holding dogmatically that anything except a single family house on its own broad
> acre of land is a slum.
>
> For me, on the other hand, the type of city you have so admirably worked out in
> Broadacre City is one of a half a dozen potential urban types that we can develop
> in order to achieve the maximum possibilities of life. My own scheme of life has a

place in it for Römerstadt as well as for Broadacre City, because concentration, when not pushed to the point of congestion, offers certain possibilities of intercourse that dispersion doesn't.[118]

As Mumford had come to realize in the years following the dissolution of the Regional Planning Association of America, there was no single solution to the successful design of cities in the twentieth century, and he would reflect on this point at great length in writing *The Culture of Cities*.

* * *

Mumford wrote *The Culture of Cities* (1938) for essentially the same reason that he had written *Technics and Civilization* four years earlier: the study of history would reveal many of the sources of modern civilization's problems as well as some creative solutions. Like Patrick Geddes, Mumford believed that cities were among the most fragile of "organisms" and that before treatment could be prescribed for their various ills in the present, an informed diagnosis had to be made by reconstructing their development in the past. In writing *The Culture of Cities,* Mumford benefited greatly from the practical experience that he had gained from his involvement with the Regional Planning Association of America and from his careful observations of European and American cities. Applying this knowledge to his characteristic analysis of the past, he embarked on an ambitious examination of the historical antecedents of the regional city and the rationale for its future development.

In compiling information for his original "Form and Personality" manuscript around 1930, Mumford was struck by the great lack of historical literature on cities:

> The history of the city has still to be written. This fact becomes more than curious when one recalls that the greater part of what is called history has taken place in and was determined by the forces and social institutions which were collected in cities. But the reason for our paucity of knowledge in this department is not far to seek: history is the great discipline of the eighteenth and nineteenth centuries, and during this period the city ceased to exist as an object of thought.[119]

Mumford noted further that it was "only in the twentieth century that Patrick Geddes outlined a descriptive sociology of cities," thus providing the critic with the proper methodology for writing such a study.[120]

Once Mumford decided to split his growing manuscript into a series of books, he set out to remedy this historical deficiency himself. Mumford began work on *The Culture of Cities* soon after *Technics and Civilization* was published, and in many ways the later study paralleled and complemented the earlier work. As its title indicated, *The Culture of Cities,* was to be far more than a history of city planning. Borrowing heavily from Geddes, Mumford chronicled the rise, fall, and renewal of Western cities beginning with the idyllic unity of the Middle Ages, leading to the

industrial disintegration of the nineteenth century, and concluding with the potential reintegration of the twentieth century.

Mumford's survey began with the medieval town, which he believed to be an
exemplary model of regionalism based on his travels through Europe. He urged his
contemporaries to look more closely at medieval planning innovations: "In the
domain of cities, we have tardily begun to realize that our hard-earned discoveries
in the art of laying out towns, especially in the *hygienic* laying out of towns, merely
recapitulate, in terms of our own social needs, the commonplaces of sound medieval
practice."[121] Mumford argued that following the Middle Ages, a combination of
political, economic, sociological, and religious factors conspired to overthrow the
organic balance of the city, including the civilization of the countryside, the disintegration of the guild system, and the breakdown of the church's authority.

Mumford's subsequent analysis of the development of Renaissance and baroque
cities focused on their political consolidation, their swollen size, and their deterio-
rated housing stock. He discerned a shift from a "life economy to a money economy"; the former was concerned with day-to-day living, whereas the latter was
increasingly involved with financial gain.[122] He also examined the fundamental
transformation in the conceptual organization of space during this period: "It remained for the Italians of the fifteenth century to organize space on mathematical
lines, within two planes, the foreground-frame, and that of the horizon line. They
not merely correlated distance with intensity of color and quality of light, but with
movement of bodies through the projected third dimension."[123] According to
Mumford, Renaissance and baroque cities were defined by their straight avenues,
which facilitated the regulation of building facades, the movement of traffic, and
the parading of soldiers. Completing this transformation was the breakup of the
cultural, spiritual, and architectural unity of the church: the choir became the concert hall, the nave was transmogrified into the bourse, the chapter-house was replaced by the gentleman's club (in the nineteenth century), and religious festivals
were secularized into plays. Although this breakup was not without its benefits, as,
for example, the plays of William Shakespeare were to prove, Mumford argued that
"art and culture were dispersed with respect to the population as a whole: dispersed
and put out of their reach."[124]

Although Renaissance and baroque cities were not replaced in the nineteenth
century, they were challenged and transformed by the emerging industrial cities. In
Mumford's account, essentially an elaboration of that found in *The Story of Utopias*,
Coketown was based on the triple foundation of an unorganized labor force, the
open market, and colonial exploitation. Technology abetted this destructive process, primarily in the form of the coal mine and the steam engine. Mining stripped
the open countryside of its organic beauty, while the railroad ripped through the
heart of every major city. Mumford labeled this type of willful destruction "Abbau"
or un-building, a process that had profound environmental repercussions: "The

natural balance of organisms within their ecological regions was upset, and a lower and simpler biological order – sometimes marked by the complete extermination of the prevalent forms of life – followed the Western man's ruthless exploitation of nature for the sake of his temporary and petty profit-economy."[125] According to Mumford, the defining characteristic of the industrial city was that "it worked out a minimum of life," with human needs sacrificed to the speculative interests of the jerry-builder, who laid out new residential quarters on the gridiron plan.[126]

After 1890, Megalopolis largely replaced the industrial city, its overblown form resulting from the vast increases in population during the nineteenth century and improved transportation and communication networks. To Mumford, Megalopolis's wide boulevards and neoclassical architecture symbolized not only its economic power, but increasingly during the 1930s, the "growing war-bureaucracy" of the state.[127] As tangible proof that this growth could not go on indefinitely, he pointed toward Megalopolis's many slums, and the relocation of many of its residents to the relative safety of the suburbs. Those who remained in the city led a doomed existence:

> Living thus, year in and year out, at second hand, remote from the nature that is outside them and no less remote from the nature within, handicapped as lovers and as parents by the routine of the metropolis and by the constant specter of insecurity and death that hovers over its bold towers and shadowed streets – living thus the mass of inhabitants remain in a state bordering on the pathological.[128]

How could Megalopolis escape its downward spiral into "Necropolis," Geddes's term for the final stage in urban growth? In Mumford's view, no problems affecting the modern city were incurable if its inhabitants were receptive to change, a process that Geddes called "insurgency." More than one-third of *The Culture of Cities* was given over to Mumford's prescription for change in the form of a new, organically based, regional order. At its foundation lay the conversion of society to a regional outlook in which the conservation of the environment would become a top priority, as would the preservation of the region's identity. On an economic level, individual property rights would be surrendered to the communal ownership of the land, and the political system would be restructured as well to better serve the region's interests. Furthermore, the quality of life in the region would be enhanced by the neotechnic opportunities that Mumford first outlined in *Technics and Civilization,* primarily the widespread distribution of clean electric power.

In this new regional framework, Mumford advocated the planting of garden cities. Although he noted that previous attempts had been only partly successful, this only underscored the need for a fresh approach to planning: "The slowness of the garden city in taking root is due to the fact that it is, so to speak, the native form only for a co-operative and socially planned society. . . . The garden city can take form . . . only when our political and economic institutions are directed toward regional rehabilitation."[129] Both Sunnyside Gardens and Radburn were discussed in *The Culture of Cities,* but Mumford pointed to Greenbelt as a more advanced prototype for future developments. He praised the "straightforward design" of Greenbelt's terrace houses with their concrete walls and flat roofs, and he urged the federal government to resume its commitment to a national housing program.[130]

As in *Technics and Civilization,* Mumford carefully selected illustrations for *The Culture of Cities.* The medieval city was represented by Lübeck, the baroque by Paris, and Megalopolis by New York City, all places that Mumford knew well. To help the reader visualize the new regional order, he included views of the Tennessee Valley Authority's dams and buildings, the most visible symbols of New Deal planning accomplishments. Moreover, to suggest the variety of forms the regional city might take, he juxtaposed a photograph of Wright's Broadacre City model with a photograph of Le Corbusier's plan for Nemours, North Africa; the montage was completed by aerial photographs of Radburn and Welwyn. New developments in modern housing, discussed at great length in the text, were represented by multiple views of Römerstadt and Greenbelt.

Mumford concluded *The Culture of Cities* with a general discussion of the projected form of the regional city, a form that he had developed earlier with his colleagues in the Regional Planning Association of America. The regional city would be planned along the lines of Radburn, developed with modern terrace houses and other buildings like those at Greenbelt, and linked to other such cities by the townless highway. Together these new cities would facilitate population dispersal and improve the general quality of life. Mumford noted that aspects of his vision were already in place. The automobile and the airplane were providing efficient transportation, and power grids were supplying necessary energy. Near the end of the book he wrote: "Man is at last in a position to transcend the machine, and to create a new biological and social environment, in which the highest possibilities of human existence will be realized, not for the strong and the lucky alone, but for all co-operating and understanding groups, associations, and communities."[131]

The publication of *The Culture of Cities* in 1938 established Mumford as a leading authority on urban history and planning in the United States and abroad. Mumford's photograph appeared on the cover of *Time* magazine, and illustrations from the book were given a lavish spread in *Life.*[132] Most critics raved about *The Culture of Cities,* and many of them commented on Mumford's maturation as a writer. Noting that the book was not "altogether easy reading," R. L. Duffus of the *New York Times* praised it nevertheless: "This is far more than a discussion of cities and city cultures. It is an attempt to analyze, historically and contemporaneously, the nature and trend of man's organized life."[133] In a review of *The Culture of Cities* for the *Nation,* Douglas Haskell discussed the book's moral tone, something that had always been present in Mumford's writings but that had become more pronounced during the 1930s. Haskell compared Mumford to a "preacher" who always presents to his audience "the high vision complete, permitting no impairment in the *idea* ."[134] Haskell, moreover, emphasized just how persuasive such an approach could be:

> In this moral certainty as to values and aims lies a great source of Mumford's leadership and power. It permits him, for example, to cut through such obstacles as the financial restrictions that hamstring the technical workers in the field, with the simple reiterated declaration that the restrictions are just not *right;* hence no solution can be found till they are done away with.[135]

Yet, Mumford's moral certainty also provided more than ample ammunition for his detractors. In a review of *The Culture of Cities* written for the *Partisan Review,* the art historian Meyer Schapiro attacked Mumford on several counts. As an important theorist of style, Schapiro was especially appalled by what he viewed as Mumford's inappropriate use of this organizing rubric, especially of the term "baroque" to cover "practically the whole of post-mediaeval society from the 15th century to the 19th."[136] Schapiro was also critical of Mumford's ill-defined, "fuzzy organicism" in both *Technics and Civilization* and *The Culture of Cities:*

> In Mumford's writings, the polar twins, organic and inorganic, are often nothing but heavily weighted homiletic counters, like the metaphors, life and death, light and darkness, in older religious speech. In characterizing an object as organic, Mumford sanctifies it, endows it with an aura. And in spite of his strenuous es- pousal of the organic, his social analyses, in their reduction of issues to bare polar conflicts, are often mechanical and primitive, and congested with Newtonian cat- egories of mass, force, inertia and space.[137]

Schapiro reserved his harshest criticism for Mumford's political views, particu- larly those regarding class structure. A Marxist, Schapiro could not abide Mumford's social liberalism, which fell somewhat to the left of the New Deal but far short of Schapiro's political and intellectual radicalism: "Nothing is more characteristic of Mumford as a social thinker than his general aversion from politics and his unclarity about the nature of the state. The mythical aggregate to which he constantly ap- peals, the undifferentiated we's and ours' of his tumescent proclamations, are his alternative to class groupings."[138] Despite Mumford's espousal of a "basic commu- nism" in *Technics and Civilization,* it was communitarian rather than communistic principles that underlay Mumford's eutopian vision of the regional city.[139]

* * *

Following the publication of *The Culture of Cities,* Mumford's opinions were eagerly sought by a number of municipal agencies, regional authorities, and planning groups.[140] In the summer of 1938, he was invited to visit Hawaii by Lester McCoy, chairman of the City and County Park Board of Honolulu, in order to prepare a planning report on the city's parks.[141] Mumford spent several weeks in Honolulu with his family, essentially conducting a regional survey in the manner of Patrick Geddes.

Moving well beyond its defined parameters, Mumford's report called for the integration of Honolulu and its surrounding region, with the park system providing vital links between city and countryside. Mumford was charmed by the natural beauty of Honolulu, but he was also concerned that the "wrinkles" were becoming apparent.[142] He made a number of sweeping proposals, including the redesign of the city's waterfront, the preservation of the city's mountainous greenbelt, the building of arterial parkways, and the creation of new parks and forest preserves. Invoking Camillo Sitte, Mumford noted that parks were much more than "the lungs and the breathing spaces of the city."[143] He wrote: "Park planning . . . cannot possibly stop at the edges of the parks: its greatest need is to infuse its standards of space and beauty and order into every other aspect of the city's developments. The park system is thus the very spearhead of comprehensive urban planning."[144]

Evidently, Mumford's further recommendation that the Honolulu Park Board and other municipal agencies be more effectively reorganized was coolly received by its members. They rejected the report, and McCoy resigned from the board in protest.[145] Several years later, Mumford republished it in *City Development* (1945), a collection of his essays on city and regional planning. He chose the book's title deliberately to recall Geddes's eponymous and equally overlooked report for Dunfermline, Scotland, written more than forty years earlier.

That same summer, the Northwest Regional Council invited Mumford to prepare a regional planning report for the whole Pacific Northwest. For two weeks, he toured the area, observing and taking notes. Mumford discovered a region rich in natural resources, but, except for the Portland and Seattle metropolitan areas, a region that was sparsely populated. He concluded in his brief report that comprehensive regional planning along with population dispersal could make a real difference in this underdeveloped part of the country: "The critical problem all regional planning faces today is the problem of resettlement, that is, redistributing population in places of maximum advantage for life: in sites that are physically healthy and stimulating, with a sufficient underpinning of natural resources, with a sufficient supply of social facilities and cultural institutions."[146]

Such an approach to rural development was possible, he argued, because of the newly created electrical power grids in the less populated areas of the Northwest. In the particular case of the Columbia River gorge, he called for the establishment of an independent planning agency to manage this natural resource with environmental sensitivity. As with his Honolulu report, however, the recommendations in Mumford's Northwest report largely went unheeded, although the construction of locks and dams on the Columbia River did eventually open up that part of the region to further development and settlement. Still, by the late 1930s, the political backing was weakening in the United States for the kind of large-scale regional planning Mumford advocated. For the most part, the ambitious programs put into place by the New Deal were being trimmed rather than expanded.

* * *

At the end of the decade, Mumford and several other members of the Regional Planning Association of America reunited briefly to collaborate on *The City,* a documentary film produced for the 1939 New York World's Fair.[147] At first, they had hoped to interest the fair's organizers in building a housing exhibition, along the lines of the 1927 Wiessenhof Siedlung. Mumford and Henry Wright both served briefly on the planning committee of the "Fair of the Future," as it was initially called.[148] Another member of the association, Robert Kohn, was part of the team that selected the fair's theme, but in the end, the housing concept was scrapped in favor of "Building the World of Tomorrow."[149] Three commercial exhibits that showcased planning concepts – "Futurama," "Democracity," and the "Town of Tomorrow" – were ultimately included in the fair, but their technological biases were far removed from the association's regionalist vision.

Frustrated in their attempts to influence the fair's organizers, the members of the association instead concentrated their energies on creating a documentary film that would recount the story of housing in America. As completed, the scope of *The City* was even more expansive, chronicling the rural birth, the industrial decay, the megalopolitan death, and the anticipated regional rebirth of American cities. Of course, these were themes already familiar to readers of Mumford's articles and books.

An extraordinary array of creative talents worked on the film. Clarence Stein initiated the project, and along with fellow association members Kohn and Frederick Ackerman, he served on the board of Civic Films, the production arm of the sponsoring American Institute of Planners. Filmmaker Pare Lorentz conceived of *The City's* general outline. Ralph Steiner and Willard Van Dyke directed the film, and Henwar Rodakiewicz wrote the scenario. Mumford wrote the narrative, which was in turn read by the actor Morris Carnovsky. The musical score was composed by Aaron Copland.[150] At the core of the film's propagandistic message was the association's regionalist vision, as it had been expressed in Mumford's writings of the 1920s and 1930s. Although the scenario for the film was completed before Mumford was invited to contribute the narrative, it loosely paralleled *The Culture of Cities,* while at the same time it recalled themes from his earlier books *Sticks and Stones* and *The Story of Utopias.*

The City is divided into five parts filmed in various locations along the east coast of the United States: the New England village (Shirley Center, Massachusetts), the industrial city (Pittsburgh), Megalopolis (New York City), the highway (no specific location indicated), and the new regional city (a composite of Radburn; Greenbelt; Chatham Village, Pittsburgh; and Jones Beach, Long Island, among other places). Ironically, it is the Megalopolis sequence in the film, rather than the final and somewhat lengthy section on the regional city, that is the most entertaining, with its quick cutting and mechanical repetition. This sequence in the film is not narrated. In the other sections of the film, however, the somewhat folksy tone of Mumford's narrative intensifies the images as it ranges from overwhelming despair to sunny optimism. The text for the industrial sequence is particularly poignant: "It don't make us happier to know there's millions like us living here on top of it. There are prisons where a guy sent up for crime can get a better place to live than we can give our children. Smoke makes prosperity, they tell you here, smoke makes prosperity, no matter if you choke on it."[151] Neither Steiner nor Rodakiewicz particularly liked Mumford's narrative at the time, but as Mumford later noted, the filmmakers did not really grasp the association's message concerning the regional city.[152]

The film premiered at the Museum of Modern Art in May 1939, but unfortunately, Mumford was unable to attend. "It's a beautiful job and it tells our story clearly," Stein wrote to Mumford after the event.[153] Ackerman concurred:

> I think the film has character; it isn't Hollywood and it isn't Broadway. Your narrative was very good; and the meanings added by it were at no times a burden. . . .
> "The City" contains some impressive passages and some thrills; and there is plenty of grim humor running through it. It keeps saying: "Aren't we all?"[154]

The City was screened at the fair's Science and Education Auditorium twice a day, four times a week for nearly the duration of the fair.[155] It was quickly acclaimed by critics as a highlight among the fair's many attractions. "If there were nothing else worth seeing at the fair," wrote Archer Winsten of the *New York Post,* "this picture would justify the trip and all the exhaustion."[156] The *Architectural Review* called the film "more vivid and emotional" than either Futurama or Democracity, although the reviewer noted that the regional city sequence appeared "surprisingly flat and lifeless in comparison with the teeming energy of the [megalopolitan] city."[157]

As might be expected, Mumford's reaction to the "World of Tomorrow" was almost wholly negative. In his view, the fairgrounds sprawled unnecessarily and without any perceivable order across Flushing Meadows, and the pavilions were too overtly commercial. "As for the Fair as a whole, it has no architectural character whatever," Mumford wrote in the *New Yorker.* "It is just a cozy sector of chaos."[158] He was especially dismayed by the consumer-driven, technologically oriented future presented in exhibits such as Democracity, Futurama, and the Town of Tomorrow, and he pointed his finger at the fair's organizers for failing to include a more innovative exhibit on modern community design:

> Today [the community planners'] wreckage is strewed about the Fair, so thoroughly smashed and disfigured that their own fathers could scarcely identify the corpses. Democracity, in the Perisphere, is one of these wrecks; the Town of Tomorrow is another. As for the film "The City," ... it is a belated attempt at salvage. But although the city shown there is more human and more up-to-date and more close to actuality than the others, it necessarily leaves off, in the real town of Greenbelt, Maryland, at the point where a new demonstration should properly begin.[159]

Yet, the regionalist eutopia that Mumford and his colleagues presented to the public in 1939 was perhaps just as mythical as the various technological utopias displayed in the other pavilions at the fair. When viewed from a perspective of more than fifty years later, *The City*'s futuristic vision has proven to be just as elusive, although paradoxically, its cinematic impact has not diminished.

The City proved to be the Regional Planning Association of America's swansong. Death had already thinned the group's ranks by the end of the decade. Charles Harris Whitaker had died in 1938, although he was not very active in the group after its first few years. Henry Wright had died two years earlier, not long after his split with Clarence Stein. To Mumford, the dissolution of this partnership was perhaps the most grievous loss of all. In a 1949 letter, Mumford commended Stein on a piece about the association, a piece that prompted Mumford's own reflections about the group:

> Your tributes to Henry moved me deeply, too; all the more because I felt when your estrangement with him took place that it was more than a personal matter, that the country itself was the loser, too. And I still feel that way. If we could have somehow kept together between 1933 and 1936 and gotten Roosevelt's ear the whole history of housing and planning in this country would have been different – and far better.[160]

The demise of the association and the end of the New Deal effectively brought the most creative period in American regional planning to a close.[161] The association's considerable legacy included two planned communities, the Appalachian Trail, a documentary film, consultation on various New Deal programs, and numerous articles on housing and community planning, but it did not include a true regional city. Great Britain, and not the United States, proved to be the most fertile ground for the development of the regional city after World War II.

* * *

The Culture of Cities had been especially popular in Great Britain, where Mumford's opinions were highly regarded in planning circles still sympathetic to the ideas of Ebenezer Howard and Patrick Geddes. One such planner, Frederic J. Osborn, wrote to congratulate Mumford on the book, thus initiating a correspondence and friendship that lasted for more than three decades.[162] Osborn was a key figure in the Garden City movement.[163] Early in his career, he had worked closely with Howard, first as the housing manager of Letchworth and, subsequently, as estate manager of Welwyn. In later years, Osborn was the honorary secretary of the Garden Cities and Town Planning Association, the predecessor of the Town and Country Planning Association.

The friendship between Mumford and Osborn deepened during World War II over their mutual concern for the uncertain fate of Great Britain. At the height of the war, when the nation was under aerial attack by Nazi Germany, Osborn, with great optimism, asked Mumford to write a planning report that would address the social, economic, and architectural issues Great Britain would confront in the post-war period. Mumford complied, and his report, *The Social Foundations of Post-War Building* (1943), predicted a brighter future for Great Britain under comprehensive regional planning. Mumford introduced the concept of the "balanced personality" living in the "balanced environment," a concept that he developed further in *The Condition of Man* (1944) as the "organic person."[164] London in its prewar state was not such an environment, and Mumford called for drastic changes:

> There is a sense in which the demolition that is taking place through the war has not yet gone far enough. Though many of the past structures are still serviceable, and some of them truly venerable, the bulk of our building no longer corresponds to the needs and possibilities of human life. We must therefore continue to do, in a more deliberate and rational fashion, what the bombs have done by brutal hit-or-miss, if we are to have space enough to live in and produce the proper means of living.[165]

At about the same time, Mumford was asked by the *Architectural Review* to criticize the monumental *County of London Plan* (1943) being prepared by Sir Patrick Abercrombie and J. H. Forshaw for implementation after the war. Mumford was preoccupied with the writing of *The Condition of Man,* however, and two years elapsed before he wrote his lengthy and somewhat harsh review of the plan for the magazine. The plan recommended only limited decentralization, with the building of satellite cities to reduce the population of London.

Not surprisingly, Mumford's criticism was essentially the same as that he had leveled at Thomas Adams and the Regional Plan of New York the previous decade: the rebuilding of London must not occur within the old urban framework, but rather, it must be done afresh with the creation of true regional cities to alleviate metropolitan pressures. Any plan for London, according to Mumford, must be a long-range one:

> My capital criticism of the County of London Plan, is that in the very face of their own obvious sympathies and interests, the authors were not planning for a hundred years. Had they done so, they would have put men first. On the contrary,

they were planning in the hope that they could somehow hold the pre-war population of London a little while longer, without disturbing drastically the conven-
tions, economic, political, legal, social, that have been so steadily depleting the
man-power of the country as a whole.[166]

Mumford urged London's planners to take a number of bold, corrective steps, including the reorganization of residential neighborhoods to stimulate population
growth, the restructuring of urban land values, the removal of industry to new population centers outside of the city, and the creation of a regional authority more powerful than the London County Council. In fact, independent of Mumford's criticism,
Abercrombie strengthened his call for decentralization and the building of satellite
towns in his *Greater London Plan* (1944), which superseded the earlier study.[167]

When the air finally cleared over Great Britain at the end of World War II, the
garden city idea received renewed scrutiny from planners and government officials
eager to reduce overcrowding in the nation's cities. In his capacity as secretary of
the Town and Country Planning Association, Osborn continued to promote the
garden city to the general public and to lobby the government for its implementation in the postwar period. Largely through Osborn's efforts, Mumford was awarded
the Ebenezer Howard Memorial Medal in 1946, and the same year Osborn published a new edition of Howard's *Garden Cities of To-morrow* so that a new generation
of readers could be introduced to this seminal work.[168] Mumford himself prepared
a new introduction to the text in which he cautioned the reader to distinguish
between the garden city and its numerous suburban imitators: "*The Garden City, as
Howard defined it, is not a suburb but the antithesis of a suburb: not a more rural retreat, but
a more integrated foundation for an effective urban life.*"[169]

Osborn's efforts on behalf of the garden city soon yielded tangible results. As a
member of the Labour Party's Postwar Reconstruction Committee and an adviser
to the Greater London Plan, he emerged as a key player in the campaign leading
to the passage of the New Towns Act of 1946 and the Town and Country Planning
Act of 1947.[170] The new towns that resulted from this legislation were a series of
self-contained urban communities surrounded by greenbelts on the garden city
model. They were developed by the government on the outskirts of major British
cities, but far enough away to prevent their absorption into megalopolitan sprawl.
Eight of the first fifteen new towns were located in the greater London area in
order to relieve the city's massive overcrowding. Although Osborn advised only
informally on the actual design and planning of the new towns, he became their
chief international propagandist.

Construction on the new towns proceeded quickly, so that when Mumford visited Great Britain in 1953, Osborn was able to direct the critic to Crawley, Hemel
Hempstead, and Harlow, which were "neck and neck in the lead" in the group.[171]
These three communities were typical of the first new towns, with their terrace
housing and pedestrian shopping precincts. In contrast to Letchworth and Welwyn,

the architecture of the new towns was decidedly modern, although somewhat banal in execution. Significantly, the British planners incorporated several aspects of the Radburn idea into the new towns. Superblocks defined many residential neighborhoods, and pedestrian overpasses and underpasses crossed busy through roads.

In general, Mumford admired the new towns, but his one overriding criticism was that they were too spacious, with population densities too low to facilitate human interaction. He addressed this concern in a 1953 "Sky Line": "In its revolt against congestion and sordor, a space-hungry generation has, I fear, developed eyes that are bigger than its stomach. Such openness not merely reduces urbanity, but it also reduces social amenity and is economically wasteful."[172] Somewhat earlier, he elaborated on these same concerns to Osborn privately:

> There are many potential forms for a modern community besides the open (suburban) pattern you advocate and The High Paddingtons the *Architectural Review* people admire, and I find that issues that have caused the two sides to lock horns are unreal to me; unreal and stultifying to the imagination. The planners of the New Towns seem to me to have over-reacted against nineteenth-century congestion and to have produced a sprawl that is not only wasteful but — what is more important — obstructive to social life.[173]

Mumford's criticism of the new towns was, of course, similar to that he had leveled at Frank Lloyd Wright's Broadacre City almost two decades earlier. Such sprawl, in Mumford's view, not only adversely affected social intercourse, but it effectively prevented communities from achieving their true regional balance.

Although Mumford was ultimately disappointed by the new towns themselves during his 1953 trip to Great Britain, he was greatly encouraged by Lansbury Neighbourhood, an urban renewal project near the very heart of London. Lansbury's population density of 136 people per acre seemed almost ideal to Mumford, falling between the high densities of most London neighborhoods and the low densities of the outlying suburbs and new towns. He was also impressed by the variety in Lansbury's housing stock, ranging from single-family houses to six-story apartment buildings. In a review of Lansbury for the *New Yorker,* Mumford applauded its high design standards:

> Indeed, Lansbury is probably the freshest piece of design since Ernst May's Römerstadt.... And the reason Lansbury Neighbourhood has turned out to be so good is simple. Its design has been based not solely on abstract esthetic principles, or on the economics of commercial construction, or on the techniques of mass production, but on the social constitution of the community itself, with its diversity of human interests and human needs.[174]

Lansbury, however, was exceptional in its urban adaptation of the medium-density garden city model since most postwar housing near the center of London consisted of high-rise apartment blocks. These were essentially adaptations of Le Corbusier's Ville Radieuse, which was by then the most popular model for public housing in Great Britain and the United States.

* * *

In the attempt to broaden the parameters of "The Sky Line" in the postwar period, Mumford examined several of the most significant urban renewal projects undertaken in Europe and America. Rotterdam, like London, had been extensively bombed during World War II, and its center was extensively rebuilt during the 1950s. Mumford visited the city in 1957, finding much to admire in the new construction that had risen from the rubble. He applauded the rebuilding of the city's center at a lower density than before the war, and he especially liked the new pedestrian shopping precinct.

Mumford reserved his greatest praise, however, for two new public sculptures created for the heart of Rotterdam, sculptures that reaffirmed his belief in the key role of the visual arts in the renewal of civilization. The first was Ossip Zadkine's war memorial, which, according to Mumford, effectively represented the suffering that the citizens of Rotterdam had endured under the Nazi occupation. With great detail, Mumford described the expressionist sculpture of a human figure larger than life-size, its torso twisted in agony and its arms outstretched in defiance, mimicking the nearby cranes on the waterfront. "This is an image as terrible, in its immediacy, as Picasso's 'Guernica,' yet conceived with a power that promises the resurrection Rotterdam has experienced," Mumford wrote.[175]

The other public sculpture to elicit Mumford's praise was Naum Gabo's "Flower," an eighty-foot-high steel abstraction in front of Marcel Breuer's new Beehive Department Store. Mumford was not generally attuned to nonrepresentational modern art, but in Gabo's work he sensed an organic intent, one confirmed by the sculpture's popular nickname. Moreover, Mumford believed that Gabo was one of the few modern artists to have met effectively the challenge of the machine:

> In The Flower, what is positive, healthy, organically creative, confidently in command of our new energies and eager to plumb new potentialities, has come together in an original design. What we have achieved through mathematical calculation, the physical sciences, the skills and audacities of engineering has here become a visible structure, under the sway of a formative human purpose that transcends mere utilitarian ways and means.[176]

On that same European visit, Mumford journeyed south to Marseilles in order to inspect Le Corbusier's controversial Unité d'Habitation, a high-rise residence intended by the architect to be a universal prototype for collective housing in the late twentieth century. Despite Le Corbusier's embrace of a more organic design aesthetic in the postwar period, Mumford remained unconvinced that the architect's subservient attitude toward the machine had changed. Mumford reviewed the Unité d'Habitation for the *New Yorker,* and although he allowed that "up to a point, considered abstractly as a visual experience, the exterior of the building is a success," he attacked its overall design on functional grounds.[177] He was especially critical of the oblong dimensions of the interlocking apartment units, which required the use of artificial lighting and ventilation at their centers. The highly touted corridor of shops, he noted, was largely unoccupied since there were not enough residents to patronize it. On the whole, Mumford deemed the building an extravagant folly: "In designing Unity House, Le Corbusier betrayed the human contents to produce a monumental esthetic effect. The result is an egocentric extravagance, as imposing as an Egyptian pyramid, which was meant to give immortality to a corpse, and – humanly speaking – as desolate."[178]

Mumford also carefully scrutinized one of the most ambitious urban renewal projects ever attempted in an American city. In 1956–1957, he wrote a six-part series on Philadelphia, beginning with a historical survey of its architecture.[179] He essentially reconstructed a "Brown Decades" of Philadelphia's past that did much to revive the reputation of the nineteenth-century architect Frank Furness, who was then held in general contempt for his overscaled, idiosyncratic designs. Mumford devoted most of the series to the redevelopment of the city's historic core near Independence Hall, and this marked a striking departure in his urban criticism.[180] Although he had always believed in the conservation of worthy monuments, he had never before been an advocate of large-scale historic preservation. In creating a livable environment, Mumford had tended to favor Ebenezer Howard's approach of building afresh, but in later years Mumford came to a greater appreciation of Patrick Geddes's method of urban rehabilitation through "conservative surgery." Mumford lauded the restoration of Independence Hall, the centerpiece of the redevelopment effort, especially since changes to the structure over time were left intact. He was less satisfied, however, by the formal mall created to the north of the building, noting that "these three separate blocks are neither functionally nor visually one."[181] Mumford further criticized the re-creation of lost buildings, believing that new buildings in the vicinity could defer to their historic surroundings without being designed in the colonial or federal modes.

Yet, considering Mumford's appreciation of nineteenth-century architecture in *The Brown Decades,* it may initially seem surprising that he did not speak out more forcefully against the large-scale demolition of many important landmarks from this period in the vicinity of Independence Park. He did offer some support for preserving Furness's Provident Trust Company (1876–1879) located across the street from the park, a building in whose design the architect "pushed ugliness to the point where it almost turned into beauty, or at least a brutal creativity."[182] In the case of Thomas U. Walter and William Johnston's Jayne Building (1849–1851), which stood in the way of the park, however, Mumford shrank from the preservation challenge:

Much as I cherish the Jayne Building in memory, because of its possible effect on Louis Sullivan, when he worked in Furness' office across the street, I believe that its destruction would be a relatively small price to pay for turning its deep site into a handsome garden.... Those of us who have long labored to rescue the industrial and commercial buildings erected between 1850 and 1890 from undeserved neglect have a special duty to avoid misplaced piety and esthetically callous antiquarianism. Our job is to work for a more positive and healthy attitude toward the whole problem of urban renewal in this area.[183]

In retrospect, Mumford's dismissal of the Jayne Building seems unconscionable since its significance in the history of the American skyscraper had already been firmly established.[184] Nevertheless, his first allegiance was to the continued vitality of the city. To Mumford, the introduction of open space into the crowded urban fabric was paramount.

* * *

In Mumford's writings, no city received more scrutiny than his native New York. Mumford spent most of his life in and around New York City, and his perceptions on urban life were shaped positively by its many outstanding educational and cultural opportunities, and negatively by its exaggerated scale and overcrowding. At times he needed to withdraw from the city to reflect on its many problems, and to secure the kind of peaceful work environment that he needed for his writing. In 1926, Mumford and his wife began renting a cottage near Amenia in Dutchess County, New York; three years later, they bought a nearby farmhouse, where they lived for at least part of every year until his death in 1990.

Like Ralph Waldo Emerson and Henry David Thoreau, Mumford was revitalized by his contact with the land, but at the same time he realized that contact with New York City – particularly its libraries, its universities, its museums, and its inhabitants – was also important to his continued intellectual development. Ideally, Mumford hoped that many of the distinct advantages of city and country life could be integrated, as Howard had proposed in *Garden Cities of To-morrow.* He was unable to find such a happy median in the modern world, however, and so he continued to travel back and forth between his farmhouse and a series of urban residences.

New York City remained the primary subject of "The Sky Line," even after Mumford consciously stretched the boundaries of the column following World War II. His criticism of New York City could be applied to any other major city, only there, conditions were exaggerated to an extreme. What was wrong with Manhattan was emblematic of what was wrong with civilization, and Mumford constantly warned his readers that, left uncontrolled, the economic and technological forces that shaped the island increasingly threatened the quality of life for its inhabitants. By the mid-1950s, the postwar construction boom had intensified the physical congestion of the city to such an extent that Mumford wondered what place architecture would hold in its future:

> What happens in New York to the art of building is bound up with what happens to the city as a place to work and live in. If it ceases to be a milieu in which people can exist in reasonable contentment instead of as prisoners perpetually plotting to escape a concentration camp, it will be unprofitable to discuss its architectural achievements – buildings that occasionally cause people to hold their breath for a stabbing moment or that restore them to equilibrium by offering them a prospect of space and form joyfully mastered.[185]

In the face of such a bleak outlook, Mumford redoubled his efforts to encourage the rebuilding of the city on a more human scale.

Housing continued to be one of Mumford's chief concerns, but his vision of new, lower-density neighborhoods for New York City was effectively blocked by Robert Moses, the Commissioner of Parks and Coordinator of the Office of City Construction.[186] Mumford had initially been a supporter of Moses' plans for new parkways, parks, playgrounds, beaches, and recreation areas during the 1930s.[187] After World War II, however, Mumford became more and more concerned about the power that the administrator wielded over the planning process in New York, power that could be used to relieve or to further congestion in the city. Mumford expressed these concerns privately to Frederic J. Osborn in 1947:

> [Moses] is a gifted administrator, but it is hard for an honest man to tell whether he has done the city more harm or more good, on a balance of considerations, by his past performances. There is no doubt about the competence of his staff or the high quality of their technical ability: what is lacking in Moses is social insight. His influence has been mainly responsible for the fact that all our recent New York housing developments since 1938 have been in the form of thirteen-storey skyscrapers.[188]

Indeed, Moses advocated the Corbusian model of multiple high-rise apartment buildings in a park setting as the most expedient way to eliminate urban blight while easing the housing shortage. Consequently, Mumford was forced to take one of his strongest public stands against what he viewed as a dangerously misguided housing policy.

The arena for the Mumford–Moses battle was Stuyvesant Town, a new residential neighborhood erected on a sixty-one-acre urban renewal parcel on the Lower East Side of Manhattan.[189] In the late 1940s, the Metropolitan Life Insurance Company, with Moses' approval, built a phalanx of thirteen-story apartment buildings in one large superblock. The apartment buildings on the perimeter of the site created a visual barrier to the surrounding neighborhood, and, in fact, access to the complex was limited for security reasons. Although Stuyvesant Town was intended for middle-class residents, its design portended future public housing projects all across the country.

Mumford, of course, despised high-rise buildings of any sort, but he was especially concerned about residential towers, the antithesis of the low-density housing he had championed as a member of the Regional Planning Association of America. In the first of two "Sky Line" columns devoted to the project in 1948, he condemned Stuyvesant Town's density of 393 people to the acre, its unrelieved architectural monotony, and its private security force. According to Mumford, Stuyvesant Town exemplified the "architecture of the Police State."[190] Although he did admit that the tall buildings allowed in more light and air than the tenements they replaced and that the interior arrangements of the apartments were generous, he would not change his mind regarding the project's high population density.

Mumford's column provoked an angry response from Moses, who, in a letter to the *New Yorker,* countered the critic's every point. At the end of his diatribe, published in full within the context of a second "Sky Line" column, Moses accused Mumford of hating the city of his birth:

> It is a sad bird who fouls his own nest. People who don't like New York anyway, and others, who think big insurance companies should promptly be taken over by the government, will be happy to believe that there is a dreadful mess at Stuyvesant Town, hidden until Mr. Mumford courageously held it up to scorn in *The New Yorker.* On the other hand, I can testify that smarter visitors, not poisoned by jaundice and envy … have frankly expressed amazement and real admiration at the almost unbroken series of modern multiple houses for people of small and moderate means, built by a combination of public and quasi-public enterprise.[191]

Mumford responded to Moses' charges with lengthy annotations, printed along with the letter. Instead of backing down from his original assessment of Stuyvesant Town, Mumford intensified his original argument against high residential densities. On a broader level, he argued that planning in the postwar period must avoid the shortsightedness that had characterized earlier epochs: "The ability to get things done quickly is not as important as the ability to get the right things done in the right way in the right order. Many generations of New Yorkers will have to pay for the mistakes that have already been made."[192] This was, of course, essentially the same criticism that Mumford had leveled at the County of London Plan several years earlier and the Regional Plan of New York more than a decade before that.

One housing development in New York City did earn Mumford's almost unqualified approval, however. In Queens, far from the costly land that dictated high-rise apartments for Manhattan, the New York Life Insurance Company created an entire neighborhood of mostly low-rise housing called Fresh Meadows at about the same time that Stuyvesant Town was being built. The two projects demonstrated strikingly different approaches to community planning in Mumford's view:

> Both the design and the execution of this development deserve diligent scrutiny. The Metropolitan Life Insurance Company's Stuyvesant Town, in lower Manhattan, and the New York Housing Authority's projects are painful lessons in how not to rebuild New York. Fresh Meadows is a fine antidote. And it is a far too concrete and practical demonstration for the Authority's Mr. Robert Moses to dismiss it as the idle dream of long-haired theorists.[193]

Mumford praised Fresh Meadows's site plan, with its short curving streets and open spaces, and its reasonable density of seventeen families to the acre. His only major objections were to the high-rise buildings at the development's center and to the size of the individual rooms of the apartments, less generous than those at Stuyvesant Town. On the whole, he concluded, Fresh Meadows was "a beautiful community – complex and many-sided and serene."[194] It should be noted that Fresh Meadows was located near the site of a failed, turn-of-the-century development named Utopia, the irony of which was not lost on Mumford.

In his fight against Robert Moses' planning policies during the 1950s, Mumford shifted his focus from housing to highway construction. To Mumford, the automobile was perhaps the most destructive of all machines, especially where the city was concerned. Although he had collaborated with Benton MacKaye twenty years earlier on the townless highway concept, postwar highway engineers had subverted their basic premise. The new expressways and bridges did not bypass the city; on the contrary, highways were being driven through the very heart of the metropolis, squeezing the life out of its neighborhoods and introducing such a volume of traffic that transportation was reduced to a slow crawl. The parking lots required for the storage of cars were filling up as soon as they were built. Moreover, easy automobile access to Staten Island, Long Island, and Westchester County threatened the bucolic nature of these areas, paving the way for their complete suburbanization.[195] It is curious that in waging this second battle neither Moses nor Mumford ever learned to drive a car.[196]

Mumford devoted four "Sky Line" columns to this morass, describing in almost Spenglerian terms the increasing nightmare of traffic that was choking the city.[197] He advocated urban decentralization on a broader level and, on a more specific level, the return to a balanced system of public transportation. Recalling the 1926 planning report for New York State by Clarence Stein and Henry Wright, Mumford bitterly noted that their worst predictions had come true, mainly because of Moses' reckless policies:

> Mr. Moses uses the word "regional planning" as a swearword, to indicate his abiding hatred of such comprehensive and forward-looking policies, just as he invokes the term "long-haired planner" to designate anyone who turns up with a proposal that does not fit into his own set of assumptions, most of them by now manifestly inadequate and badly out of date.[198]

Mumford continued to lobby against highway development in New York City and elsewhere, opposing such projects as Moses' unsuccessful 1958 bid to extend Fifth Avenue through Washington Square in Manhattan.[199] When Congress passed the Interstate Highway Act in 1957, Mumford could only conclude that "they hadn't the faintest notion of what they were doing."[200]

By the end of the decade, Mumford came to the unsettling realization that the New York City of his youth and adolescence had either disappeared or changed beyond recognition. Emblematic of this transformation was McKim, Mead and White's Pennsylvania Station (1902–1910), whose neoclassical architecture he had never really admired, but whose spaciousness he appreciated nonetheless. Mumford was an inveterate train traveler, and the slow, physical decline of Pennsylvania Station caused him great concern. At this point in his life, moreover, he was nostalgic enough about the past and contemptuous enough of modern architecture to speak out about the situation.

In a "Sky Line" written in 1958, Mumford took stock of what he viewed as detrimental additions to the station's interior, including advertising kiosks, a suspended plastic canopy, and harsh fluorescent lighting. These additions compromised the original clarity of the passenger concourse, without relieving the tangled circulation patterns on the platforms below it. The best renovation, in Mumford's view, would be simply to clean the station. He concluded on a particularly somber note: "If it was sad that [Pennsylvania Railroad president] Alexander Cassatt should have died in 1906, without seeing his great station erected, it was a mercy that he did not live until 1958, to witness its bungling destruction. It would take even mightier powers than these old railroad titans wielded to undo this damage."[201] When the railroad threatened to raze Pennsylvania Station a few years later, Mumford's column was an important factor in garnering public and professional opinion against it. Although the station was demolished in 1963, this action subsequently led to the creation of the New York City Landmarks Preservation Commission. By this time, Mumford was enjoying the success of his 1961 book, *The City in History,* the culmination of decades of observation and study in New York City and elsewhere.

* * *

During the 1950s, Mumford began to give serious consideration to revising *The Culture of Cities,* his most influential book up until that point. He condensed the historical narrative of the book and its central thesis about the regional city in an article that appeared in Talbot Hamlin's *Forms and Functions of Twentieth-Century Architecture* (1952).[202] Soon, however, Mumford began to think in terms of an even larger historical study, realizing that *The Culture of Cities* had not gone far enough in identifying the forces that had shaped the city before the medieval period. Moreover, the chaotic state of the modern city was beginning to exceed his worst predictions, and he felt compelled to warn his readers once again of the consequences of uncontrolled growth.

In preparation for his new book, Mumford made an exhaustive study of recently available archaeological and anthropological literature and data, particularly the works of Henri Frankfort and V. Gordon Childe. To refresh his memory of European cities, he traveled abroad in 1957, stopping at major cities and towns in England, Belgium, the Netherlands, France, and Italy.[203] Finally, during the summer of 1960, Mumford traveled to Greece for the first time in preparation for his chapters on classical civilizations.[204] The following year he completed his new book, now retitled *The City in History*.[205]

Mumford's analysis of the prehistoric era began with the paleolithic cave and the transition to the neolithic village. He made the radical hypothesis that it was the container rather than the oft-cited tool that propelled man's progress at this early stage of his development. The container, with its capacity to hold things gathered by humans, became Mumford's enduring metaphor for the city through the ages. He identified the emergence of kingship and the cult of war as consolidating forces in early civilizations, and he drew many startling parallels with the present in his analysis: "The ancient city, in its very constitution, tended to transmit a collective personality structure whose more extreme manifestations are now recognized in individuals as pathological. That structure is still visible in our own day, though the outer walls have given way to iron curtains."[206]

In Mumford's view, classical civilization reached its apex in the medium-sized towns of ancient Greece, where city growth was controlled by colonization as the need arose. Such towns prefigured the garden city: "Cos, Cnidus, and Epidauros were no less symbols of the Greek concern for wholeness and balance than the Olympic games or the Delphic shrine; and the lessons they taught played a part in later town planning, though they have not yet been fully assimilated even today."[207] Conversely, the swollen imperial metropolis of Rome was characterized by poor sanitation and gruesome public spectacles. Mumford warned that the deteriorating state of the contemporary metropolis closely paralleled that of ancient Rome:

> Every overgrown megalopolitan center today, and every province outside that its life touches, exhibits the same symptoms of disorganization, accompanied by no less pathological symptoms of violence and demoralization. Those who close their eyes to these facts are repeating, with exquisite mimicry, the very words and acts, equally blind, of their Roman predecessors.[208]

Following the discussion of classical civilizations, *The City in History* rejoined the narrative of *The Culture of Cities* during the medieval period. Mumford continued to view the Middle Ages as a high point in Western civilization because of the organic synthesis that was achieved through Christianity's emphasis on individual, spiritual transformation. With power centralized in the church rather than the state, medieval town planning served human needs more effectively, as in the case of Venice. Mumford's analysis of the formal and economic disintegration of the city during the postmedieval period remained essentially unchanged, as did his use of the term "baroque" to encompass the fifteenth through the eighteenth centuries. Mumford singled out the radial, canal-linked plan of Amsterdam, however, as an example of intelligent expansion in the face of rampant commercialism during this period.

Mumford's analysis of Coketown, the next phase of urban development, was also taken largely from his previous book, but the sections on Megalopolis and regionalism were now replaced by an extensive analysis of the suburban sprawl that threatened the modern city. More than twenty years separated the publication of *The City in History* from *The Culture of Cities,* and Mumford had clearly lost much of the optimism that had characterized the earlier work. In the intervening period, he had seen his worst fears about society's blind pursuit of technology realized in the development of the atomic bomb and the proliferation of the automobile. In Mumford's view, urban centers had become increasingly congested, polluted, and inhospitable places in which to live and work, and thus they earned the appellation, "The Bursting Container."[209] He noted bitterly that the section "A Brief Outline of Hell" found in *The Culture of Cities* could not be republished "because all its anticipations were abundantly verified."[210] Moreover, architects and planners had not effectively risen to the challenge of urban renewal, and he found much of their work to be banal, and in some cases, inhumane.

Mumford ultimately believed in the city's ability to endure, but he argued in the conclusion to *The City in History* that the nuclear arms race must be stopped and that society's values must be reoriented toward more peaceful ends. To Mumford, the city *was* civilization, and a meaningful human existence was inconceivable without it:

> Through its own complex and enduring structure, the city vastly augments man's ability to interpret these processes and take an active, formative part in them, so that every phase of the drama it stages shall have, to the highest degree possible, the illumination of consciousness, the stamp of purpose, the color of love. That magnification of all the dimensions of life, through emotional communion, rational communication, technological mastery, and above all, dramatic representation, has been the supreme office of the city in history. And it remains the chief reason for the city's continued existence.[211]

Mumford supported the text of *The City in History* with extensive illustrations and lengthy captions that together form an important, and somewhat optimistic, subtext to the main narrative. Photographs of Delphi, Athens, Rome, and Pompeii were used to illustrate the classical city. Aerial views of Venice and various plans of

Amsterdam demonstrated the soundness of organic planning principles from the medieval and baroque periods, respectively. Mumford's composite vision of the regional city, almost entirely absent in the text, reemerged in photographs of Radburn, Fresh Meadows, Harlow New Town, and the Tennessee Valley Authority. New developments in urban renewal and historic preservation were represented by Rotterdam and Philadelphia.

The City in History has remained the best known of Mumford's many books on architecture and planning, not least because it was given the National Book Award for nonfiction in 1962.[212] A six-part television series based on the book and produced for the National Film Board of Canada brought Mumford's dire warnings about the modern city to an even broader audience.[213] The book was enthusiastically received by Mumford's colleagues, many of whom believed it to be the summation of his life's work. Frederic J. Osborn found that "this book makes a stronger impact on my understanding than *The Culture of Cities* did, greatly as I admired it. I cannot doubt that [*The City in History*] will be a success and add greatly to your influence on the people interested in urban affairs."[214] It also made a deep impression on Clarence Stein:

> I have read "The City in History" from cover to cover. It has taken time, because ... I had to read the beginning and the end – first – and then visit Venice and Amsterdam – before I really read the whole story. Lewis, it is one of the great books of our times – perhaps of all times – I will have to read it again before I can tell you.[215]

On the whole, reviewers in the popular press and professional circles agreed with Stein's and Osborn's positive assessments. Writing for the *New York Times,* Allan Temko called it the "crowning achievement" of Mumford's career.[216] "The book is more than urban history," Temko continued, "it is moral philosophy of a high order and tragic poetry."[217] Christopher Tunnard also reviewed the book favorably in the *Journal of the American Institute of Planners:* "This is certainly not history for its own sake – it is history for *our* sake, and the reminders are on every page."[218]

Still, some reviewers criticized Mumford's pessimistic thesis and moralizing tone. Although Henry S. Churchill noted that the book was "full of insights and penetrating observations," he faulted Mumford for delivering a negative indictment of the city without providing a workable blueprint for its rehabilitation:

> Moral reform is not a function of the planner, although moral – i.e. Mumfordian sociological – understanding might be. Yet nowhere in *The City in History* is there any relation shown between the *form* of the city and moral values, no guide to the planner who wishes to act thoughtfully, but who must act anyhow, because that is his job. And, if The City is of and in itself the product of an ineradicable trauma, if there is no escape, why struggle?[219]

Not surprisingly, Robert Moses despised the book, voicing his disapproval in an article for the *Atlantic Monthly*. Moses compared Mumford to the Old Testament prophet Jeremiah, accusing him of attempting to "poison" the younger generation: "There is, indeed, much wrong with cities – big and little – but the answer is not to abandon or completely to rebuild them on abstract principles. Only on paper can you disperse concentrations of population and create small urban stars with planned satellites around them."[220]

From the opposite end of the political and social spectrum came an indirect attack on Mumford from Jane Jacobs, an urban critic residing in New York. Jacobs's book *The Death and Life of Great American Cities* appeared the same year as Mumford's, and it was a sweeping indictment of the whole principle of decentralized planning. Jacobs argued that the various planning movements of the twentieth century had all sapped the vitality out of large cities, and she lumped these movements together under the single scornful heading, "Radiant Garden City Beautiful."[221]

Curiously, both Mumford and Jacobs believed in a sociological approach to understanding urban centers with all of their human variety. In practice, however, they differed over the form that the modern city should take. Mumford, of course, looked to the regional city as the ideal solution, whereas Jacobs maintained that the best neighborhoods were not planned at all. Her ideal was the high-density city block, like that of her adopted Greenwich Village, in which people of many diverse groups and ages mixed at all hours without fear of crime. A variety of periods and styles in buildings helped to foster this diversity, as did a wide range of residential types and commercial establishments placed cheek by jowl. In her view, children were safer playing on the sidewalks of the urban street under the supervision of either parents or shopkeepers than in city parks or playgrounds.

Mumford, with his inbred sense of order, could not tolerate such a slapdash approach to city planning, nor could he personally resist responding to Jacobs's charges. In a searing review of *The Death and Life of Great American Cities*, Mumford attacked her thesis point by point, accusing her of marshaling faulty data and of neglecting the real underlying causes of social pathology in the modern city: the megalopolitanism that she praised. Mumford noted that he was a born and bred New Yorker – and incidentally a one-time resident of Greenwich Village – whereas Jacobs was not. He faulted her for overlooking other vibrant residential areas of the city and for dismissing the positive values of its larger parks: "Certainly it was not any mistake of Frederick Law Olmsted's in laying out Riverside Drive, Morningside Park, and St. Nicholas Park that has made these large parks unusable shambles today."[222] Mumford instead prescribed an organic decongestant for what ailed American cities:

> One cannot control destructive automatisms at the top unless one begins with
> the smallest units and restores life and initiative to them – to the person as a
> responsible human being, to the neighborhood as the primary organ not merely

of social life but of moral behavior, and finally to the city, as an organic embodiment of the common life, in ecological balance with other cities, big and little, within the larger region in which they lie.[223]

The Mumford–Jacobs debate overflowed from the pages of the *New Yorker* into the national press, and it is one that still concerns planners today.[224] Mumford's preferred medium-density regional city could never match the excitement and creativity of a high-density metropolitan city such as New York. Conversely, it is difficult to ignore the attraction of more spacious surroundings, especially for families with small children. In the meantime, the American middle class continues to flee the city for the safety and anonymity of the suburbs and exurbs, an outward flow that neither Mumford nor Jacobs could effectively stanch, their moral pronouncements notwithstanding.

To those critics who faulted *The City in History* for not providing enough practical direction for change in the present, Mumford responded with *The Highway and the City* (1963), a collection of essays from the *New Yorker* and other periodicals. Although he acknowledged that this was no substitute for a companion volume to the larger work, he claimed that "at least these chapters will indicate by concrete example some of the fashionable blind alleys we must avoid, and some of the desirable goals toward which we may profitably direct our efforts."[225]

In 1968, Mumford published *The Urban Prospect*, yet another collection of his essays and speeches, this time in response to the racial strife and social upheaval that had rocked many American inner-city neighborhoods. *The Urban Prospect* included Mumford's testimony in April 1967 before the Ribicoff Committee of the U.S. Senate, a committee charged with disbursing housing and urban renewal funds. Mumford made an impassioned plea to the committee to refrain from pouring billions of dollars into failed programs like public housing and slum clearance. Although he had lost much of his faith in planners, he had not yet renounced his belief in regional planning. Careful, coordinated efforts, he argued, were the key:

> Go slow! Experiment with small measures and small units, until you have time to prepare better plans and to organize new public agencies to carry out those plans.... Remember that you cannot overcome the metropolitan congestion of the last century, or the cataclysmic disintegration of urban life during the last thirty years, by instituting a crash program.[226]

* * *

By the early 1960s, Mumford realized that his vision of the regional city would not come to pass in his lifetime, despite the best efforts of his colleagues in the Regional Planning Association of America and in the Town and Country Planning Association of Great Britain. Nevertheless, in his introduction to Frederic J. Osborn's *New*

Towns (1963), Mumford emphasized the progress that had been made toward achieving this eutopian goal in Great Britain:

> With the institution of the new towns policy on a large scale the way has been opened to carry Howard's bold vision to a fuller, if not its final, consummation, by a systematic application of his principles to all the components of the city, and by the deliberate union of many related cities into a new kind of urban unit ... [which] will have all the dynamism of a great metropolis.[227]

When *Garden Cities of To-morrow* appeared in a new paperback edition in 1965, Mumford cited this as further proof of the book's continuing validity, bringing "to an almost hilarious climax this book's astonishing career. At least it produces hilarity ... in a few people like Osborn, Clarence Stein, and myself, who staked our reputations on persistently advocating the ideas first put forth by Ebenezer Howard some sixty-seven years ago."[228]

Mumford's continued optimism about the city was an extraordinary testament to his faith in society's ability to renew itself. The city would always have the potential to regenerate itself since it was essentially a social container made up of individuals free to choose their own destinies. Mumford's optimism owed much to his study of urban history. If the medieval city was able to rise from the ruins of Roman civilization, certainly the same process could be repeated in the twentieth century. Cities such as Venice and Amsterdam were positive reminders of what had been accomplished in the past, while experimental models such as Radburn and Greenbelt were but a foretaste of the regional city to come. As the conscience of the planning profession, Mumford himself could not design a concrete example of a regional city. It remained for architects and planners to bring his eutopian vision down to earth.

CONCLUSION: LEWIS MUMFORD, 1895–1990

Form in modern architecture cannot come at once; for its complete expression would involve a creative transformation of modern civilization. Indeed, no smaller end is worth working for.

— "Form in Modern Architecture"

After several years of poor health that forced his retirement from active writing, Lewis Mumford died on January 26, 1990, at the age of ninety-four. Perhaps not surprisingly, posthumous tributes to Mumford have tended to emphasize his contributions to architecture and urban planning over his work in literary criticism, sociology, or philosophy.[1] Although it may still be too soon to gain a clear perspective on his manifold accomplishments in other areas, the extraordinary breadth of his architectural and urban criticism has secured for him a firm place in the American pantheon that he largely created. His ideas have continued to generate discussion among architects and planners, even as they have distanced themselves from the social issues that he valued so greatly.

Mumford remains a complex figure vis-à-vis the introduction and criticism of European modernism in the United States. As a young man, he was eager for his architectural colleagues in America to throw off the yoke of revivalism, only to be disappointed when the International Style proved to be as heavily burdened by formal clichés. Mumford did not believe modern architecture should be defined by new materials or their arrangement into novel forms, but rather by how well it served and enriched the lives of its users. He saw glimmers of such an architecture in the best work of Frank Lloyd Wright, Matthew Nowicki, and a handful of others but for the most part found technological interests blindly placed ahead of human needs.

In Mumford's eyes, the worship of the machine was having a particularly devastating effect on the American landscape. Cities, which had been overbuilt since the early twentieth century, had sprawled well beyond their livable boundaries, isolating their inhabitants from nature, which was so essential to their well-being. Echoing his mentor Patrick Geddes, Mumford warned that once the basic ecological balance between urban and rural areas was disturbed, Megalopolis would surely degenerate into Necropolis. On the surface, Mumford's solution was simple. It consisted of a "fourth migration" of citizens from the older overcrowded metropolitan centers to regionally balanced communities, similar in plan and appearance to Radburn, Greenbelt, or Fresh Meadows. Unfortunately, with the demise of the Resettlement Administration of the New Deal, the United States lost the political and financial apparatus to implement such a change in Mumford's lifetime.

* * *

As a philosopher, historian, and critic, Mumford channeled his intellectual energies into the pursuit of a single lifelong goal: eutopia, the good place, to be located in the imperfect here and now. Although admittedly a lofty goal, eutopia was in Mumford's view not only desirable but also attainable, and even necessary. Yet, whereas eutopia seemed just within reach in the closing chapters of *The Culture of Cities* (1938), by the time he wrote *The City in History* (1961), it was an all but abandoned hope. Ironically, the root cause of Mumford's later pessimism was "utopia."

Toward the end of his career, Mumford regarded utopia – the "perfect place" – as nearly the polar opposite of eutopia. This had not always been the case, for initially he believed that as a construct utopia could have a positive influence in directing the course of human activity:

> Utopia, as the expression of rational possibilities, is an integral feature of purposive living; for no human life is fully rational unless it anticipates its own life-course and controls its present actions and present needs in the light of some more general plan, some larger system of values, into which all the parts of its existence tend to fit.[2]

To Mumford, of course, eutopia – "the possibility of renovating society, through the application of reason and social invention to political and economic institutions" – was the more practical and desirable goal.[3]

World War II was a turning point for Mumford, both personally and professionally. He was profoundly disturbed by the invention and detonation of the atomic bomb, and he devoted the rest of his career to averting what he strongly believed was impending nuclear catastrophe. As a result, he began to rethink many of his basic assumptions about civilization, including the role of utopias. In researching the prehistoric origins of civilization for *The City in History*, Mumford discerned the existence of an authoritarian power structure that had the ability to destroy the very populace it governed. The city was utopia, he concluded a few years later, whose inexorable progress was made possible through the power of the machine.[4]

Mumford explored this idea further in the two-volume *Myth of the Machine* (1967 and 1970), the last of his large works.[5] In volume 1, *Technics and Human Development,* he introduced the concept of the human-powered "megamachine" in ancient civilizations, best exemplified by the army of slaves that built the pyramids.[6] Volume 2, *The Pentagon of Power,* traced the modern reemergence of the megamachine, as it was vastly enhanced by new technologies. Mumford argued that this latest incarnation of the megamachine was the result of a collusion between science and government, and its destructive capabilities had already been revealed in the atomic bomb. The link between utopia and the megamachine was all too clear. The forces of absolutism and conformity had always been negative elements in utopian thought, but in the drive toward technological perfection in the twentieth century, these forces had grown nearly uncontrollable: "The pervasive character of all utopias is their totalitarian absolutism, the reduction of variety and choice, and the effort to escape from such natural conditions or historical traditions as would support variety and make choice possible. These uniformities and compulsions constitute utopia's inner tie to the megamachine."[7] Only a complete reorientation of human values away from technological perfection and toward organic equilibrium could save civilization from ruin.

As a writer and speaker, Mumford continually warned his audiences about the dangers of modern technology. When he addressed a gathering in honor of the fiftieth anniversary of the "International Style" exhibition in 1982, for example, he surprised many with the tenor of his remarks: "We are in the deepest crisis mankind has known and what's left to us may not be worth salvaging. I wrote about the atom bomb three weeks after it was dropped and it has hung over us like a cloud ever since. Maybe it's too late; maybe it isn't. Let us pray."[8] This pessimistic assessment of the future of civilization was not the spontaneous outburst of an octogenarian, but rather a careful conclusion drawn from his own writings on the destructive proclivities of modern technology, writings that he felt were increasingly ignored in his own time.

One suspects that Mumford would have been gratified by the fall of the Iron Curtain just before his death in 1990, since it demonstrated the kind of organic renewal he had been advocating since World War II. The transformation of Eastern Europe from totalitarian to democratic rule happened mainly because it was the will of the people, and it was accomplished largely through grass-roots politics rather than technological warfare. One suspects, too, that Mumford would have felt vindicated by the signing of nuclear reduction and nonproliferation treaties by the United States, the former Soviet Union, and other world powers in the years following his death, and hopeful about the United Nations' more active role in mediating world affairs. Nevertheless, civil and international wars continue to be fought and the technological utopia that he railed against remains in place. Were Mumford alive today, he almost certainly would be urging his readers to seize even greater control of the machine and to work toward a more peaceful transformation of society.

* * *

"Utopian" was a label that Mumford disdained, since it cast him in the role of an unchanging ideologue preoccupied with society's perfection. He did not outline a utopian framework in his writings on architecture and urban planning, arguing instead that the reconstruction of the physical environment coupled with personal renewal could lead to an improved but free society. Although Mumford ultimately connected utopianism with totalitarianism, he equated eutopianism with communitarianism, regionalism, and an organic way of life. "Damn utopias!" Mumford once wrote to his colleague Catherine Bauer. "Life is better than utopia."[9]

NOTES

CHAPTER 1

1. The chief sources for Lewis Mumford's life are his autobiography, *Sketches from Life: The Autobiography of Lewis Mumford, The Early Years* (New York: Dial Press, 1982), and two other autobiographical collections of his selected writings, *Findings and Keepings: Analects for an Autobiography* (New York and London: Harcourt Brace Jovanovich, 1975); and *My Works and Days: A Personal Chronicle* (New York and London: Harcourt Brace Jovanovich, 1979). In addition, Mumford wrote two semiautobiographical pieces for the *New Yorker* during the 1930s: "A New York Childhood: Ta-Ra-Ra-Boom-De-Ay," *New Yorker,* 22 December 1934, 18–23; and "A New York Adolescence: Tennis, Quadratic Equations, and Love," *New Yorker,* 4 December 1937, 75–89. Both pieces were used as source material for *Sketches from Life,* and the latter was reprinted in part in *Works* (44–52). Mumford also wrote a semiautobiographical novella in verse, "The Little Testament of Bernard Martin Aet. 30," in *The Second American Caravan: A Yearbook of American Literature,* ed. Alfred Kreymborg, Mumford, and Paul Rosenfeld (New York: Macaulay, 1928) 123–169. This novella was reprinted in *Findings* (107–149). Mumford's papers are deposited in the Special Collections of Van Pelt Library, University of Pennsylvania, Philadelphia (hereafter referred to as Mumford Papers). The only full-length biography of Mumford is Donald L. Miller's *Lewis Mumford: A Life* (New York: Weidenfeld and Nicolson, 1989). See also Frank G. Novak Jr.'s short but perceptive study, *The Autobiographical Writings of Lewis Mumford: A Study in Literary Audacity* ([Honolulu]: University of Hawaii Press, 1988).
2. Miller, *Lewis Mumford,* 4.
3. Mumford, *Sketches,* 43.
4. Ibid., 12.
5. Frank Lloyd Wright, *An Autobiography* (New York: Duell, Sloan and Pearce, 1943), 11.
6. Mumford, *Sketches,* 44.
7. Ibid., 50.
8. Ibid., 53.
9. Mumford, "New York Childhood," 21.
10. Mumford, *Sketches,* 18
11. Ibid., 26, 109.
12. Ibid., 75.
13. Mumford Papers, folder 8142; Mumford, *Sketches,* 82–84.

14. On the lasting importance of the Stuyvesant curriculum in Mumford's intellectual development, see Arthur P. Molella, "Mumford in Historiographical Context," in *Lewis Mumford: Public Intellectual,* ed. Thomas P. Hughes and Agatha C. Hughes (New York and Oxford: Oxford University Press, 1990), 21–42.
15. Mumford, *Sketches,* 101.
16. Mumford Papers, folder 8143.
17. Mumford, *Sketches,* 101.
18. Mumford Papers, folder 8146.
19. See, for example, Mumford, "An Improved Electrolytic Detector," *Modern Electrics,* April 1912, 40. Mumford contributed several other short articles to this magazine. For further discussion see Molella, "Mumford in Historiographical Context."
20. Mumford, *Sketches,* 95–98, 103.
21. Mumford Papers, folder 8146.
22. Mumford, Louis Morinsky, William Bender, and Joseph Hindin, "Dr. Bilby's Aeroplane," TS, c. 1910, Mumford Papers, folder 8148.
23. Mumford, "New York Adolescence," 75.
24. Program for "Dr. Bilby's Aeroplane," 11 January 1911, Mumford Papers, folder 8144.
25. Stuyvesant High School Commencement Program, 27 June 1912, Mumford Papers, folder 8146.
26. Mumford, *Sketches,* 159, 161.
27. Ibid., 137.
28. Ibid., 140.
29. Ibid., 141.
30. Mumford eventually accepted two honorary degrees: LL.D., University of Edinburgh, 1965; and Dr. Arch., University of Rome, 1967. On Mumford's relations with the academic establishment, see Thomas S. W. Lewis, "Mumford and the Academy," *Salmagundi* 49 (Summer 1980): 99–111.
31. Mumford, *Sketches,* 123–125.
32. Ibid., 144.
33. Mumford, "The Golden Day Revisited," introduction to *The Golden Day: A Study in American Literature and Culture,* 2d rev. ed. (Boston: Beacon Press, 1957), xiii – xiv.
34. Most of Mumford's drawings and watercolors are deposited at Monmouth University, West Long Branch, New Jersey. For a brief history of this collection, see Kenneth R. Stunkel and Vincent DiMattio, "Lewis Mumford's Life in Art Comes to Light," *Horns of Plenty: Malcolm Cowley and His Generation* 2 (Fall 1989): 29–30; and Kenneth R. Stunkel, "Lewis Mumford: Guardian and Critic of Civilization," *Horns of Plenty: Malcolm Cowley and His Generation* 2 (Fall 1989): 30–44. A catalog of the Monmouth collection by Stunkel and DiMattio is forthcoming. See also Molly Sullivan, *Lewis Mumford's New York: A Personal View* (New York: City College of New York, 1992). I do not share Sullivan's view that Mumford was influenced by the "Ashcan School" of American painting, since Mumford's urban sketches rarely emphasize the human figure.
35. Mumford, *Sketches,* 98.
36. The Monmouth collection contains more than fifteen self-portraits executed by Mumford between 1917 and 1930. Stunkel, "Lewis Mumford: Guardian and Critic," 40.
37. Stunkel and DiMattio, "Lewis Mumford's Life in Art," 29.
38. Mumford, random note, 1918, published in *Works,* 31. In his autobiographical writings, Mumford used the abbreviation R. N. along with the date when referring to such random notes, begun "partly in imitation of Samuel Butler" (R. N. 1914, published in *Works,* 26).

39. Several biographies of Geddes have been written, of which the best and most recent are Helen Meller, *Patrick Geddes: Social Evolutionist and City Planner* (London and New York: Routledge, 1990); and Philip Boardman, *The Worlds of Patrick Geddes: Biologist, Town Planner, Re-Educator, Peace-Warrior* (London, Henley, and Boston: Routledge and Kegan Paul, 1978).

40. Mumford, *Sketches*, 144.

41. Patrick Geddes and J. Arthur Thomson, introduction to *Evolution* (London: Williams and Norgate, 1911), viii – ix.

42. Ibid., xiv.

43. Mumford, *Sketches*, 144–145.

44. Charles Zeublin, "The World's First Sociological Laboratory," *American Journal of Sociology* 4 (March 1899): 577–592.

45. Meller, *Patrick Geddes*, 40. For a discussion of Geddes's valley section, see Rosalind Williams, "Lewis Mumford as a Historian of Technology in *Technics and Civilization*," in *Lewis Mumford: Public Intellectual*, 51–56.

46. Mumford, *Sketches*, 144.

47. Ibid., 150.

48. Patrick Geddes, *Cities in Evolution: An Introduction to the Town Planning Movement and to the Study of Civics* (London: Williams and Norgate, 1915), 3–4.

49. Mumford, *Sketches*, 330.

50. On the life and work of Sir Ebenezer Howard, see Robert Beevers, *The Garden City Utopia: A Critical Biography of Ebenezer Howard* (New York: St. Martin's Press, 1988); Dugald MacFadyen, *Sir Ebenezer Howard and the Town Planning Movement* (1933; reprint, Cambridge: Massachusetts Institute of Technology Press, 1970); Stanley Buder, *Visionaries and Planners: The Garden City Movement and the Modern Community* (New York and Oxford: Oxford University Press, 1990); and Robert Fishman, *Urban Utopias in the Twentieth Century: Ebenezer Howard, Frank Lloyd Wright, and Le Corbusier* (New York: Basic Books, 1977), 21–88. On the history and diaspora of Howard's garden city, see Stephen V. Ward, ed., *The Garden City: Past, Present and Future* (London, Glasgow, New York, Tokyo, Melbourne, and Madras: E. & F. N. Spon, 1992).

51. Geddes, *Cities in Evolution*, 154; Mumford, *Sketches*, 335.

52. Ebenezer Howard, *Garden Cities of To-morrow*, 4th rev. ed., ed. Frederic J. Osborn, with an introduction by Mumford (Cambridge, Mass., and London: Massachusetts Institute of Technology Press, 1965), 48.

53. Mumford, "Nineteen Hundred Sixteen," TS, 1916, Mumford Papers, folder 8226. In his use of simplified spellings in this and other typescripts, Mumford was evidently practicing the shorthand of phonetician Henry Sweet.

54. Unpublished essay, 7 May 1916, Mumford Papers, folder 6940.

55. A selection from the approximately 160 letters in the Mumford–Geddes correspondence has been edited and annotated by Frank G. Novak Jr. in "Master and Disciple: Selections from the Patrick Geddes–Lewis Mumford Letters," *Horns of Plenty: Malcolm Cowley and His Generation* 2 (Fall 1989): 45–62. A definitive edition of the Mumford–Geddes correspondence is planned by Novak. Mumford excerpted some of his letters to Geddes in *Findings, Works*, and *Sketches*.

56. Mumford, *Sketches*, 155.

57. Mumford, R. N., 1916, published in *Findings*, 25.

58. Mumford, unpublished R. N., c. 1916, Mumford Papers, folder 8028.

59. Mumford, R. N., 1916, published in *Findings*, 25.

60. Mumford, unpublished R. N., 21 August 1916, Mumford Papers, folder 8027.

61. Ibid.
62. Ibid.
63. Mumford, unpublished R. N., Mumford Papers, unlocated.
64. Ibid.
65. Ibid.
66. Mumford to Patrick Geddes, 2 February 1920, published in Novak, "Master and Disciple," 52.
67. Mumford, *Sketches,* 171–172.
68. Mumford, "The Pittsburgh District," unpublished essay, August 1917, Mumford Papers, folder 8225.
69. Mumford, "The Year 1917," unpublished essay, Mumford Papers, folder 8224.
70. Mumford, "Washington Reconoissance [*sic*]," unpublished essay, 24 October 1919, Mumford Papers, folder 8225.
71. Ibid.
72. Ibid.
73. Mumford, "Nineteen Hundred Sixteen."
74. Mumford, *Sketches,* 176. See Mumford, introduction to unpublished essay, 1917, Mumford Papers, folder 8033.
75. Mumford, "Counter-Tendencies: An Outline of Regional Policy," unpublished outline, Mumford Papers, unlocated.
76. Mumford, *Sketches,* 111.
77. Mumford published his play *The Builders of the Bridge* in full and excerpts from other dramatic works in *Findings.* His play "The Invalids" was accepted by the Baltimore Players in 1918, but it was never staged (ibid., 21).
78. Mumford, "Survival of the Fittest," dramatic script, c. 1914–1915, published in *Findings,* 16.
79. Mumford, "The Invalids," dramatic script, 1916, published in *Findings,* 21.
80. Mumford, "Who Is Regius Storm?" unpublished postscript to "The Invalids," 1917, Mumford Papers, folder 7824. In 1961, Mumford wrote across the first page of a draft of "The Invalids": "Written by Regius himself in 1916–1917!" Mumford Papers, folder 7823.
81. Mumford, "The Year: 1918," 19 January 1919, unpublished essay, Mumford Papers, folder 8225.
82. Thorstein Veblen, *The Theory of the Leisure Class* (1899; reprint, with an introduction by John Kenneth Galbraith, Boston: Houghton Mifflin Company, 1973), 110–111.
83. Mumford, "The Brownstone Front," unpublished dramatic script, c. 1917–1919, Mumford Papers, folders 7825–7826.
84. Ibid.
85. Ibid.
86. Ibid.
87. Mumford, "Nineteen Hundred Sixteen."
88. Mumford, *Sketches,* 130.
89. Ibid., 195.
90. Ibid., 198.
91. Ibid., 202.
92. Ibid., 203. On the partnership of McKim, Mead, and Bigelow, see Richard Guy Wilson, "The Early Work of Charles F. McKim: Country House Commissions," *Winterthur Portfolio* 14 (Autumn 1979): 235–267.
93. Mumford, *Sketches,* 203.
94. Mumford, unpublished bibliography, Mumford Papers, folder 8030.

95. Mumford, *Sketches*, 203.
96. Mumford, "The Year: 1918."
97. Ibid.
98. Mumford to Patrick Geddes, 2 February 1920, published in Novak, "Master and Disciple," 52.
99. Mumford, unpublished housing essay for *Journal of the American Institute of Architects,* 1918, Mumford Papers, folder 6969.
100. Mumford, *Sketches*, 204.
101. Mumford, unpublished drawings for housing competition, 1918, Mumford Papers, folder 8031.
102. See, for example, the designs for utilitarian workers' cottages in Frederick L. Ackerman, "What Is a House? IV," *Journal of the American Institute of Architects* 5 (December 1917): 591–639.
103. Mumford, *Sketches*, 204.
104. Ibid., 333.
105. Mumford, "The Year: 1918."
106. Mumford, *Sketches*, 184.
107. Mumford, unpublished notes for "The Marriage of Museums," 31 August 1916, Mumford Papers, folder 6968.
108. See Patrick Geddes, *City Development: A Study of Parks, Gardens, and Culture-Institutes, A Report to the Carnegie Dunfermline Trust* (1904; reprint, New Brunswick: Rutgers University Press, 1973), chaps. 14 and 25.
109. A physical link across Central Park to connect the two museums had been proposed in February 1916 by Henry Fairfield Osborn, president of the American Museum of Natural History. See the *Forty-Seventh Annual Report of the Trustees of the American Museum of Natural History for the Year 1915* (New York: American Museum of Natural History, 1916), 18–19.
110. Mumford, "The Marriage of Museums," *Scientific Monthly* 7 (September 1918): 252.
111. Ibid.
112. Ibid., 253.
113. Ibid.
114. Mumford, "The Heritage of the Cities Movement in America: An Historical Survey," *Journal of the American Institute of Architects* 7 (August 1919): 349.
115. Ibid., 354.
116. Ibid.
117. For a short biographical sketch of Whitaker, see Mumford, ed., *Roots of Contemporary American Architecture: A Series of Thirty-Seven Essays Dating from the Mid-Nineteenth Century to the Present* (New York: Reinhold, 1952), 434–435.
118. Mumford to Charles Harris Whitaker, 3 March 1920, Mumford Papers, folder 5914.
119. Charles Harris Whitaker to Mumford, 5 March 1920, Mumford Papers, folder 5313.
120. On the lack of criticism in American architectural journals, see Mary Woods, "The First American Architectural Journals: The Profession's Voice," *Journal of the Society of Architectural Historians* 48 (June 1989): 117–138.
121. Charles Harris Whitaker to Mumford, 6 November 1919, Mumford Papers, folder 5313.
122. G.B.P.(?) [acting for Charles Harris Whitaker] to Mumford, 20 March 1919, Mumford Papers, folder 5313.
123. Charles Harris Whitaker to Mumford, 24 December 1919, Mumford Papers, folder 5313.
124. Mumford, *Sketches*, 184.
125. Ibid., 217.

126. Ibid., 218.

127. Boardman, *Worlds of Patrick Geddes,* 176.

128. Mumford, *Sketches,* 212.

129. Mumford, reviews of *Town Improvement,* by Frederick Noble Evans, and *New Towns after the War,* by the New Townsmen, *Dial* 67 (20 September 1919): 274.

130. Claude Bragdon, *Architecture and Democracy* (New York: Alfred A. Knopf, 1918), 52.

131. Mumford, review of *Architecture and Democracy,* by Claude Bragdon, *Dial* 67 (4 October 1919): 318.

132. On the history of this tradition, see Donald Drew Egbert, "The Idea of Organic Expression and American Architecture," in *On Arts in Society: Selections from the Periodical Writings of Donald Drew Egbert* (Watkins Glen, N.Y.: American Life Foundation for the University of Victoria, 1970), 63–73.

133. Mumford, *Sketches,* 245–246.

134. Ibid., 252.

135. Ibid., 252–253.

136. Victor Branford to Mumford, 20 September 1919, Mumford Papers, folder 531.

137. Mumford to Victor Branford, October 1919, Mumford Papers, folder 5675.

138. Mumford to Victor Branford, 11 January 1920, Mumford Papers, folder 5676.

139. Mumford, "Current Criticism of 'The State,'" *Sociological Review* 11 (Autumn 1919): 136–140.

140. Mumford, *Sketches,* 254.

141. Ibid., 269.

142. Ibid., 273.

143. Ibid., 277.

144. Ibid., 293–294.

145. Miller, *Lewis Mumford: A Life,* 136.

146. Mumford, *Sketches,* 353.

147. Ibid., 185.

148. Mumford, "Miscellany," *Freeman* 1 (31 March 1920): 67.

149. Mumford, "Painting: Standards Old and New," *Freeman* 1 (7 April 1920): 90.

150. Mumford, "Miscellany," *Freeman* 1 (23 June 1920): 356; "Miscellany," *Freeman* 1 (4 August 1920): 497.

151. Mumford, "The Tate Gallery Reopens," *Freeman* 2 (22 September 1920): 38.

152. Mumford, "Ex Libris," review of *Daniel H. Burnham: Architect, Planner of Cities,* by Charles Moore, *Freeman* 4 (22 February 1922): 575.

153. Ibid.

154. Charles Harris Whitaker to Mumford, 20 February 1922, Mumford Papers, folder 5314.

155. Mumford, *Sketches,* 305.

156. Ibid., 304.

157. Mumford, "What's Wrong with Utopia?" unpublished essay, Mumford Papers, folder 8149.

158. Mumford, *The Story of Utopias* (1922; reprint, Gloucester, Mass.: Peter Smith, 1959), 267.

159. Patrick Geddes and Victor Branford, introduction to *The Coming Polity* (London: Le Play House Press, 1919), 14.

160. Mumford, *Sketches,* 303.

161. Casey Nelson Blake, *Beloved Community: The Cultural Criticism of Randolph Bourne, Van Wyck Brooks, Waldo Frank, and Lewis Mumford* (Chapel Hill and London: University of North Carolina Press, 1990), 206–207.

162. Mumford, *Utopias*, 15.

163. Ibid., 33.

164. Ibid., 99.

165. Ibid., 94–96.

166. Ibid., 193.

167. Ibid., 203.

168. Ibid.

169. Ibid., 229.

170. Ibid., 241–243.

171. Ibid., 281.

172. Ibid., 128.

173. Ibid., 297–298.

174. Mumford, "Herzl's Utopia," *Menorah Journal* 9 (August 1923): 167.

175. Alfred Zimmern, "Post-War Utopianism," review of *The Story of Utopias*, *Literary Review* 4 (20 January 1923): 397.

176. A. Emerson Palmer, "Utopias That Make the World Tolerable," review of *The Story of Utopias*, *New York Times Book Review*, 24 December 1922, 11.

177. Robert Morss Lovett, review of *The Story of Utopias*, *New Republic*, 13 December 1922, 74.

178. Victor Branford to Mumford, 28 November 1922, Mumford Papers, folder 532.

179. Patrick Geddes to Mumford, 25 December 1919, published in Novak, "Master and Disciple," 48–49.

180. Mumford, *Sketches*, 318.

181. Ibid., 321.

182. Mumford to Patrick Geddes, 6 July 1923, published in Mumford, *Findings*, 79.

183. Ibid, 80–81.

184. Patrick Geddes to Mumford, 6 November 1923, Mumford Papers, folder 1807.

185. Mumford, *Sketches*, 332.

186. Mumford, "Patrick Geddes, Insurgent," *New Republic*, 30 October 1929, 296.

187. Mumford to Patrick Geddes, 5 May 1925, Mumford Papers, folder 5832 [original in the National Library of Scotland, Edinburgh].

CHAPTER 2

1. This chapter is based on my earlier study of Lewis Mumford's contributions to American architectural history. See Robert Wojtowicz, "Lewis Mumford: The Architectural Critic as Historian," in *The Architectural Historian in America: A Symposium in Celebration of the Fiftieth Anniversary of the Founding of the Society of Architectural Historians*, Studies in the History of Art, vol. 35, ed. Elisabeth Blair MacDougall (Hanover and London: University Press of New England, 1990), 237–249.

2. On Mumford's general approach to the study of history, see Frank G. Novak Jr., "Lewis Mumford and the Reclamation of Human History," *Clio* 16 (February 1987): 159–181; and Charles Molesworth, "Inner and Outer: The Axiology of Lewis Mumford," in *Lewis Mumford: Public Intellectual*, ed. Thomas P. Hughes and Agatha C. Hughes (New York and Oxford: Oxford University Press, 1990), 241–255. On Mumford's investigation into American culture during the 1920s, see Alan Trachtenberg, "Mumford in the Twenties: The Historian as Artist," *Salmagundi* 49 (Summer 1980): 29–42; Joseph Duffey, "Mumford's Quest: The First Decade," *Salmagundi* 49 (Summer 1980): 43–68; Eddy Dow, "Van Wyck Brooks and Lewis

Mumford: A Confluence in the 'Twenties," *American Literature* 45 (November 1973): 407–422; and Eddy Dow, "Lewis Mumford's Passage to India: From the First to the Later Phase," *South Atlantic Quarterly* 76 (Winter 1977): 31–43.

3. Van Wyck Brooks to Mumford, 12 July 1922, published in *The Van Wyck Brooks–Lewis Mumford Letters: The Record of a Literary Friendship, 1921–1963,* ed. Robert E. Spiller (New York: E. P. Dutton and Company, 1970), 17.

4. Donald L. Miller, *Lewis Mumford: A Life* (New York: Weidenfeld and Nicolson, 1989), 149.

5. Van Wyck Brooks, "On Creating a Usable Past," *Dial* 64 (11 April 1918): 338.

6. Mumford, "The City," in *Civilization in the United States: An Inquiry by Thirty Americans,* ed. Harold E. Stearns (New York: Harcourt, Brace and Company, 1922), 11.

7. Robert Littell to Mumford, 28 August 1923, Lewis Mumford Papers, Special Collections, Van Pelt Library, University of Pennsylvania, Philadelphia (hereafter referred to as Mumford Papers), folder 3550.

8. Mumford, review of *The Enjoyment of Architecture,* by Talbot Faulkner Hamlin, *Freeman* 4 (8 March 1922): 622.

9. On Kimball's life and work, see Lauren Weiss Bricker, "The Writings of Fiske Kimball: A Synthesis of Architectural History and Practice," in *The Architectural Historian in America,* 215–235.

10. Mumford, "Early American Architecture," review of *Domestic Architecture of the American Colonies and of the Early Republic,* by Fiske Kimball, *New Republic,* 7 March 1923, 50.

11. Mumford, "Architectural Piety," *Journal of the American Institute of Architects* 11 (August 1923): 306.

12. Ibid., 304.

13. Mumford, "Architecture and History," *Journal of the American Institute of Architects* 12 (April 1924): 192.

14. Mumford, "The Autobiography of an Idea," review of *The Autobiography of an Idea,* by Louis H. Sullivan, *New Republic,* 25 June 1924, 133.

15. Ibid. Mumford was undoubtedly referring to the work of the Dutch expressionist Michael de Klerk in this passage, known to him through the pages of the architectural journals. See, for example, Clarence S. Stein, "Amsterdam – Old and New," *Journal of the American Institute of Architects* 9 (October 1922): 310–327.

16. Claude Bragdon to Mumford, 30 July 1924, Mumford Papers, folder 522.

17. Mumford, *Sketches from Life: The Autobiography of Lewis Mumford, The Early Years* (New York: Dial Press 1982), 424.

18. Ibid.

19. Ibid., 424–425. On his lecture notes and in his autobiography, Mumford incorrectly stated that the course was to be given initially in the fall of 1924. A course guide for the New School's 1923–1924 academic year lists Mumford's course for the fall term. Mumford Papers, folder 8067.

20. Mumford, *Sketches,* 425.

21. Mumford Papers, folder 6521.

22. Ibid.

23. Mumford Papers, folder 6519.

24. Mumford Papers, folder 6518.

25. Ibid.

26. Mumford Papers, folder 6519; Mumford, *Sketches,* 289.

27. Mumford, "American Architecture: The Medieval Tradition," *Freeman* 8 (19 December 1923): 344–346; "American Architecture: The Heritage of the Renaissance," *Freeman* 8 (2 January 1924): 394–396; "American Architecture: The Classical Myth," *Freeman* 8 (9 January

1924): 418–420; "American Architecture: The Diaspora of the Pioneer," *Freeman* 8 (13 February 1924): 538–540; "American Architecture: The Realization of Industrialization," *Freeman* 8 (27 February 1924): 584–586; and "The Imperial Age," *Journal of the American Institute of Architects* 12 (August 1924): 366–371.

28. Mumford, unpublished introduction to *Sticks and Stones,* Mumford Papers, folder 6512.

29. Ibid.

30. Van Wyck Brooks to Mumford, [April 1924], published in *The Van Wyck Brooks–Lewis Mumford Letters,* 26; notation on manuscript for *Sticks and Stones,* Mumford Papers, folder 6512; Horace B. Liveright to Mumford, 25 June 1924, Mumford Papers, folder 487.

31. Mumford to Horace B. Liveright, 24 February 1924, Mumford Papers, folder 5672.

32. Mumford, acknowledgments for *Sticks and Stones: A Study of American Architecture and Civilization* (New York: Boni and Liveright, 1924), 9.

33. Mumford, unpublished draft of *Sticks and Stones,* Mumford Papers, folder 6512.

34. Mumford, *Sticks and Stones,* 30–31.

35. Ibid., 41.

36. Ibid., 65.

37. Ibid., 66.

38. Ibid., 101.

39. Ibid., 106–107.

40. Ibid., 116.

41. Ibid., 179.

42. Ibid., 182.

43. Ibid., 238.

44. Ibid., 246.

45. Percy A. Hutchison, "American Architecture the Expression of Our Culture," review of *Sticks and Stones, New York Times Book Review,* 24 September 1924, 4.

46. Aymar Embury II, "Architecture and Life," review of *Sticks and Stones, Saturday Review of Literature,* 27 December 1924, 414.

47. Fiske Kimball, "A Machine Age," review of *Sticks and Stones, New York Herald Tribune Books,* 26 October 1924, 3.

48. Mumford, letter to the editor of the *New York Herald Tribune Books,* 27 October 1924, published 2 November 1924, 12.

49. Talbot Faulkner Hamlin, "Engineering or Architecture?" review of *Sticks and Stones, Nation,* 3 December 1924, 604.

50. Ibid.

51. Mumford, *The Golden Day: A Study in American Experience and Culture* (New York: Boni and Liveright, 1926), 92.

52. In the first edition of *The Golden Day,* Mumford grouped Hawthorne and Melville together under the heading of "Twilight." Not until the second revised edition did Mumford expand his categories to include "Night," under which he placed Melville separately. See *The Golden Day: A Study in American Literature and Culture,* 2d rev. ed. (Boston: Beacon Press, 1957), 71.

53. Mumford, *Golden Day* [1926], 205.

54. Mumford, "The Pageant of American Architecture," review of *The American Spirit in Architecture,* by Talbot Faulkner Hamlin, *Journal of the American Institute of Architects* 14 (September 1926): 410.

55. Mumford, "Art in America," review of *Art in America,* by Suzanne La Follette, *New Republic,* 5 March 1930, 77.

56. Ibid.

57. Mumford, *Sketches*, 429. Mumford writes that he and Mendelsohn first met in 1927, but surviving correspondence indicates that the two men had their initial encounter in 1925.

58. Mumford, *Sketches*, 428.

59. Ibid., 430.

60. Ibid., 429. On the strength of Mumford's praise, Byrne landed a commission to design a church in Cork, Ireland. Francis Barry Byrne to Mumford, c. 1927, Mumford Papers, folder 692. For a discussion of Byrne's life and work, see Sally Kitt Chappell and Ann Van Zanten, *Barry Byrne, John Lloyd Wright: Architecture and Design* (Chicago: University of Chicago Press, 1982).

61. Mary-Jane Grunsfeld to Mumford [January 1927], Mumford Papers, folder 1986.

62. Mumford, "New York *vs.* Chicago in Architecture," *Architecture* 56 (November 1927): 241.

63. Ibid., 243.

64. Ibid., 244.

65. On Wright's life and work, see Robert C. Twombly, *Frank Lloyd Wright: An Interpretive Biography* (New York, Evanston, San Francisco, and London: Harper and Row, 1973); and Robert C. Twombly, *Frank Lloyd Wright: His Life and His Architecture* (New York, Chichester, Brisbane, and Toronto: John Wiley and Sons, 1979).

66. Mumford, *Sketches*, 432.

67. Mumford, "The Social Back Ground [*sic*] of Frank Lloyd Wright," *Wendingen* 7 (1925): 74.

68. On Hitchcock's career as an architectural historian, see Helen Searing, "Henry-Russell Hitchcock: The Architectural Historian as Critic and Connoisseur," in *The Architectural Historian in America*, 251–263.

69. Inscribed issue of *The Hound and the Horn*, Mumford Papers, folder 8049.

70. Henry-Russell Hitchcock Jr. to Mumford, 8 November 1927, Mumford Papers, folder 2215. See Henry-Russell Hitchcock Jr., "The Decline of Architecture," *The Hound and the Horn* 1 (September 1927): 28–35.

71. Henry-Russell Hitchcock Jr. to Mumford, 8 November 1927. See Mumford, "American Taste," *Harper's*, October 1927, 569–577.

72. Henry-Russell Hitchcock Jr. to Mumford, 8 November 1927.

73. Mumford, *Sketches*, 423.

74. Henry-Russell Hitchcock Jr., review of *American Architecture*, by Fiske Kimball, *Creative Art* 3 (August 1928): xiii. The other book, which Hitchcock did not identify, was probably Geoffrey Scott's *Architecture of Humanism* (1914). See Hitchcock's appreciative comments on Scott in Hitchcock, "Humanism and the Fine Arts," in *The Critique of Humanism: A Symposium*, ed. C. Hartley Grattan (1930; reprint, Freeport, N.Y.: Books for Libraries Press, 1968), 233.

75. Henry-Russell Hitchcock Jr. to Mumford, 11 August 1928, Mumford Papers, folder 2215.

76. Mumford, "Frank Lloyd Wright and the New Pioneers," review of *Frank Lloyd Wright*, by Henry-Russell Hitchcock Jr., *Architectural Record* 65 (April 1929): 415.

77. Henry-Russell Hitchcock Jr. to Mumford, 21 June 1929, Mumford Papers, folder 2215.

78. Mumford, "Modern Architecture," review of *Modern Architecture: Romanticism and Reintegration*, by Henry-Russell Hitchcock Jr., *New Republic*, 19 March 1930, 131.

79. Henry-Russell Hitchcock Jr. to Mumford, [c. March] 1930, Mumford Papers, folder 2215.

80. Henry-Russell Hitchcock Jr. to Mumford, 11 August 1928.

81. Francis Barry Byrne to Mumford, 18 May 1928, Mumford Papers, folder 693.

82. Ibid.

83. Mumford, preface to *The Brown Decades: A Study of the Arts in America, 1865–1895*, 3d rev. ed. (New York: Dover, 1971): v.

84. Mumford, unpublished lecture notes, Mumford Papers, folder 6574.

85. Mumford, "American Taste," 572.

86. Mumford, "The Brown Decades," *Scribner's*, February 1931, 135–144; "The Brown Decades: Architecture," *Scribner's*, April 1931, 385–395; "The Brooklyn Bridge," *American Mercury*, August 1931, 447–450; and "The Brown Decades: Art," *Scribner's*, October 1931, 361–372.

87. George Grant Elmslie to Mumford, 20 April 1931, Mumford Papers, folder 1419.

88. Mumford to Frank Lloyd Wright, 1 July 1930, fiche M015D08. Copyright (c) The Frank Lloyd Wright Foundation.

89. Frank Lloyd Wright to Mumford, 7 July 1930, Mumford Papers, folder 5477. Copyright (c) The Frank Lloyd Wright Foundation.

90. Ibid.

91. Mumford, *The Brown Decades: A Study of the Arts in America, 1865–1895* (New York: Harcourt, Brace and Company, 1931), 55.

92. On the history and use of the term "Chicago school," see Robert Bruegmann, "The Marquette Building and the Myth of the Chicago School," *Threshold* 10 (Fall 1991): 6–23. Mumford used the term "Chicago school" only in passing. See Mumford, *Brown Decades* [1931], 165.

93. Mumford, *Brown Decades* [1931], 114.

94. Ibid., 131.

95. Ibid., 134.

96. Ibid., 163.

97. Ibid., 154.

98. Ibid., 165.

99. Ibid., 168–169.

100. Ibid., 88.

101. Ibid., 104.

102. See Mumford, "The Builders of the Bridge," published in *Findings and Keepings: Analects for an Autobiography* (New York and London: Harcourt Brace Jovanovich, 1975), 213–312. The play was never produced.

103. Mumford, *Brown Decades* [1931], 248.

104. Albert Guerard, "Mr. Mumford on the Arts," review of *The Brown Decades*, *New York Herald Tribune Books* (11 October 1931): 3.

105. Henry Hazlitt, "The Buried Renaissance," review of *The Brown Decades*, *Nation*, 11 November 1931, 520.

106. Matthew Josephson, "The Days of Brooklyn Bridge," review of *The Brown Decades*, *New Republic*, 11 November 1931, 357.

107. Unsigned review of *The Brown Decades*, *Architectural Forum* 56 (February 1932): 17.

108. Frank Lloyd Wright to Mumford, 9 December 1931, Mumford Papers, folder 5478. Copyright (c) The Frank Lloyd Wright Foundation.

109. Henry-Russell Hitchcock Jr. to Mumford, 5 November [1931], Mumford Papers, folder 2215.

110. Ibid.

111. Ibid.

112. Mumford, "Giants of Modern Architecture," reviews of *The Architecture of H. H. Richardson and His Times: 1838–1886,* by Henry-Russell Hitchcock Jr.; and *Louis Sullivan: Prophet of Modern Architecture,* by Hugh Morrison, *New Republic* 26 February 1936, 87.

113. Carl W. Condit, *The Rise of the Skyscraper* (Chicago: University of Chicago Press, 1952), 9.

114. See, for example, Alan Trachtenberg, *Brooklyn Bridge: Fact and Symbol*, 2d ed. (Chicago and

London: University of Chicago Press, 1979), 139; and Albert Fein, *Frederick Law Olmsted and the American Environmental Tradition* (New York: George Braziller, 1972), 162 n.

115. Robert L. Anderson, "The Brown Decades Revisited," *Journal of the [American] Society of Architectural Historians* 2 (July 1942): 23.

116. See, for example, Daniel Bluestone, *Constructing Chicago* (New Haven and London: Yale University Press, 1991).

117. Mumford, "On Judging Art," review of *Ananias, or the False Artist,* by Walter Pach, *New Republic,* 20 March 1929, 130.

118. Mumford, *The Condition of Man* (New York: Harcourt, Brace and Company, 1944), 390.

119. A. W. Vaughan, foreword to *The South in Architecture* (1941; reprint, New York: Da Capo Press, 1967), n.p.

120. Mumford, *The South in Architecture,* 17–18.

121. Ibid., 44.

122. Ibid., 80.

123. Ibid., 97.

124. Ibid., 96.

125. Ibid., 128.

126. Ibid., 116.

127. Ibid., 117.

128. Ibid., 121.

129. Frank Lloyd Wright, "Mumford Lectures," review of *The South in Architecture, Saturday Review of Literature,* 23 August 1941, 16.

130. Mumford to Frank Lloyd Wright, 30 May 1941, fiche M118A04. Copyright (c) The Frank Lloyd Wright Foundation.

131. Frank Lloyd Wright to Mumford, 3 June 1941, Mumford Papers, folder 5479. Copyright (c) The Frank Lloyd Wright Foundation.

132. Mumford, "A Backward Glance," in *Roots of Contemporary American Architecture: A Series of Thirty-Seven Essays Dating from the Mid-Nineteenth Century to the Present,* ed. Mumford (New York: Reinhold, 1952), 30.

133. Mumford, preface to *Sticks and Stones: A Study of American Architecture and Civilization,* 2d rev. ed. (New York: Dover, 1955), n.p.

134. Ibid.

135. Mumford, preface to *The Brown Decades: A Study of the Arts in America, 1865–1895,* 2d rev. ed. (New York: Dover, 1955), n.p.

136. Mumford to Alison Mumford, 4 August 1954, Mumford Papers, folder 6047.

137. Mumford to Thomas Hoving, 12 November 1975, Mumford Papers, folder 6012.

CHAPTER 3

1. Part of this chapter first appeared in Robert Wojtowicz, "Lewis Mumford: The Architectural Critic as Historian," *The Architectural Historian in America: A Symposium in Celebration of the Fiftieth Anniversary of the Founding of the Society of Architectural Historians,* Studies in the History of Art, vol. 35, ed. Elisabeth Blair MacDougall (Hanover and London: University Press of New England, 1990), 237–249. On Lewis Mumford's career as an architectural critic, see Elizabeth Borden Carlson, "Lewis Mumford: Twentieth-Century Architectural Critic" (Ph.D. diss., University of California at Santa Barbara, 1988); Paul Goldberger, "Organic Remedies: Building and the City," *Salmagundi* 49 (Summer 1980): 87–98; and David R.

Weimer, "Lewis Mumford and the Design of Criticism," *Arts and Architecture* 79 (September 1962): 14–15, 30–31.

2. For a discussion of criticism in nineteenth-century architectural journals, see Mary Woods, "The First American Architectural Journals: The Profession's Voice," *Journal of the Society of Architectural Historians* 48 (June 1989): 117–138.

3. Mumford, introduction to TS, "Houses, Machines, Cities," Lewis Mumford Papers, Special Collections, Van Pelt Library, University of Pennsylvania, Philadelphia (hereafter referred to as Mumford Papers), folder 7885.

4. On the writings of Van Rensselaer, see Lisa Koenigsberg, "'Lifewriting': First American Biographers of Architects and Their Works," in *The Architectural Historian in America*, 41–58.

5. Schuyler's life and work are discussed at length in William H. Jordy and Ralph Coe, "Montgomery Schuyler," editors' introduction to *American Architecture and Other Writings*, vol. 1, by Montgomery Schuyler (Cambridge, Mass.: Belknap Press, 1961), 1–89.

6. On Croly's career as an architectural critic, see Suzanne Stephens, "Architecture Criticism in a Historical Context: The Case of Herbert Croly," in *The Architectural Historian in America*, 275–287.

7. Claude Bragdon, *Architecture and Democracy* (New York: Alfred A. Knopf, 1918), 176.

8. Ibid., 26.

9. For a discussion of Douglas Haskell as an architectural critic, see Robert Benson, "Douglas Haskell and the Criticism of International Modernism," in *Modern Architecture in America: Visions and Revisions,* ed. Richard Guy Wilson and Sidney K. Robinson (Ames: Iowa State University Press, 1991), 164–183; and Robert Benson, "Douglas Haskell and the Modern Movement in American Architecture," *Journal of Architectural Education* 36 (Summer 1983): 2–9.

10. Mumford, ed., *Roots of Contemporary American Architecture: A Series of Thirty-Seven Essays Dating from the Mid-Nineteenth Century to the Present* (New York: Reinhold, 1952), 422–423, 427–428, 429, 430, 434–435.

11. Mumford, foreword to *Architecture as a Home for Man: Essays for Architectural Record,* ed. Jeanne M. Davern (New York: Architectural Record Books, 1975), ix.

12. Helen Meller, *Patrick Geddes: Social Evolutionist and City Planner* (London and New York: Routledge, 1990), 67–68.

13. Mumford, *Architecture* (Chicago: American Library Association, 1926), 10–11.

14. W. R. Lethaby, *Form in Civilization: Collected Papers on Art and Labour* (London: Oxford University Press, 1922), 119. Mumford wrote: "Architecture, properly understood, is civilization itself." See Mumford, *Sticks and Stones: A Study of American Architecture and Civilization* (New York: Boni and Liveright, 1924), n.p.

15. William Richard Lethaby to the book editor of the *Dial,* 26 October 1924, Mumford Papers, folder 2837.

16. Mumford, "Form in Modern Architecture: I. The Breakup of Form," *Architecture* 60 (September 1929): 127.

17. Patrick Geddes to Mumford, 2 April 1932, Mumford Papers, folder 1811.

18. Mumford, "Machinery and the Modern Style," *New Republic,* 3 August 1921, 265.

19. Mumford, "The City," in *Civilization in the United States: An Inquiry by Thirty Americans,* ed. Harold E. Stearns (New York: Harcourt, Brace and Company, 1922), 11–12.

20. For a detailed discussion of the Machine Age, see Richard Guy Wilson, Dianne H. Pilgrim, and Dickran Tashjian, *The Machine Age in America, 1918–1941* (New York: Harry N. Abrams, 1986).

21. Mumford, "Beauty and the Industrial Beast," *New Republic*, 6 June 1923, 38.
22. Ibid.
23. Mumford, "Decoration and Structure," *Commonweal* 2 (7 October 1925): 533.
24. Ibid.
25. Mumford, "The Economics of Contemporary Decoration," *Creative Art* 4 (January 1929): xxi.
26. Mumford, "That Monster – The Machine: Lewis Mumford vs. Genevieve Taggard: The Bourgeois Girls Like Their Ham Sliced Thin," *New Masses* 3 (September 1927): 23.
27. Genevieve Taggard, "That Monster – The Machine: Lewis Mumford vs. Genevieve Taggard: Do You Kill Your Own Hogs Too?" *New Masses* 3 (September 1927): 23.
28. Mumford, "That Monster – The Machine," 23.
29. Mumford, *Sticks and Stones*, 187.
30. Mumford, "Notes on Modern Architecture," *New Republic*, 18 March 1931, 120.
31. Ibid., 121.
32. Mumford, untitled cartoon, *Survey* 55 (15 December 1925): 336. In drawing this cartoon, Mumford may have been inspired by the German expressionist architect Eric Mendelsohn, whose fantastic sketches of industrial architecture had been published earlier in the *Dial*. See Herman George Scheffauer, "Dynamic Architecture: New Forms of the Future," *Dial* 70 (March 1921): 323–328.
33. Mumford, "Magnified Impotence," *New Republic*, 22 December 1926, 138–139.
34. Mumford, "The City of Tomorrow," reviews of *The Metropolis of Tomorrow*, by Hugh Ferriss; *Our Cities Today and Tomorrow: A Survey of Planning and Zoning Progress in the United States*, by Theodora Kimball Hubbard and Henry Vincent Hubbard; and *The City of Tomorrow and Its Planning*, by Le Corbusier, *New Republic*, 12 February 1930, 332.
35. Ibid.
36. Mumford, "The Destruction of the Shelton," *Commonweal* 3 (28 April 1926): 689.
37. Mumford, "Is the Skyscraper Tolerable?," *Architecture* 55 (February 1927): 68.
38. Mumford, "The Barclay-Vesey Building," *New Republic*, 6 July 1927, 176.
39. Ibid.
40. Ibid., 177.
41. Mumford, "Notes," 122.
42. W. Davenant Cavendish, "And Who Is Keats?" letter to the editor, *New Republic*, 6 May 1931, 331.
43. Mumford, response to letter written by W. Davenant Cavendish, *New Republic*, 6 May 1931, 331.
44. Mumford to Frank Lloyd Wright, 27 June 1931, fiche M023D03. Copyright (c) The Frank Lloyd Wright Foundation.
45. On Mumford's relationship with the German avant-garde, see Heinz Tschachler, *Lewis Mumford's Reception in German Translation and Criticism* (Lanham, Md., New York, and London: University Press of America, 1994), 15–23; and Miles David Samson, "German-American Dialogues and the Modern Movement Before the 'Design Migration,' 1910–1933" (Ph.D. diss., Harvard University, 1988), 337–436.
46. Barry Parker to Mumford, 4 June 1925, Mumford Papers, folder 3789.
47. Charles B. Purdom to Clarence S. Stein, 29 December 1924, Mumford Papers, folder 4664.
48. Ebenezer Howard to Clarence S. Stein, 26 April 1925, Mumford Papers, folder 4664.
49. Ibid.

50. Walter Curt Behrendt to Mumford, 22 May 1925, Mumford Papers, folder 362.

51. Walter Curt Behrendt to Mumford, 13 July 1925, Mumford Papers, folder 362.

52. Ibid.

53. Mumford, foreword to *Vom Blockhaus zum Wolkenkratzer: Eine Studie über Amerikanische Archi-tektur und Zivilisation,* trans. M. Mauthner (Berlin: Bruno Cassirer Verlag [1925]), 10. "Für die vorliegende Ausgabe aber habe ich mich entschlossen, einige der besten oder der chara-kteristischsten Beispiele jeder Periode in Abbildungen zu bringen, nicht um damit ein erschöpfendes Studienmaterial zu liefern, sondern um die Phantasie des Lesers in die rechten Kanäle zu leiten; leider zwingt diese Methode dazu, die große Masse roher und entarteter Architektur zu übergehen, die die ersten Industriestädte anfüllten, und der Leser muβ sich diesen Mangel an innerem Gleichgewicht immer vor Augen halten."

54. Mumford, "The Poison of Good Taste," *American Mercury,* September 1925, 94; "Amerikan-ische Baukunst," *Die Form* 1 (February 1926): 104.

55. Mumford, *Sketches from Life: The Autobiography of Lewis Mumford, The Early Years* (New York: Dial Press, 1982), 429; Wolf Von Eckardt, *Eric Mendelsohn* (New York: George Braziller, 1960), 19.

56. Eric Mendelsohn to Mumford, 8 January 1925, published in Oskar Beyer, ed., *Eric Mendel-sohn: Letters of an Architect,* trans. Geoffrey Strachan (London, New York, and Toronto: Abelard-Schuman, 1967), 75.

57. Eric Mendelsohn to Hendricus Wijdeveld, 18 February 1925, Nederlandse Documentatie Centrum voor de Boukunst, Amsterdam.

58. Eric Mendelsohn to Mumford, 24 December 1925, published in Beyer, ed., *Eric Mendelsohn: Letters,* 88.

59. Mumford, "The Poison of Good Taste," 94.

60. For his book *Russland, Europa, Amerika: Ein Architektonischer Querschnitt* (Berlin: Rudolf Mosse Buchverlag, 1929), Mendelsohn borrowed photographs of the John Ward House and Mount Vernon (9, 11) from Mumford's *Vom Blockhaus zum Wolkenkratzer* (plate opp. 18, plate opp. 76). However, a comparison of the respective photographs of Mount Vernon reveals that they are not identical. Several years later when writing *Technics and Civilization* (New York: Harcourt, Brace and Company, 1934), Mumford borrowed an image of a grain elevator from Mendelsohn's *Amerika: Bilderbuch eines Architekten* (Berlin: Rudolf Mosse Buchverlag, 1926). Cf. Mendelsohn, *Amerika,* 43, with Mumford, *Technics,* pl. XIV. On Mumford's relationship with Mendelsohn, see Stanislaus von Moos, "The Visualized Ma-chine Age: Or: Mumford and the European Avant-Garde," in *Lewis Mumford: Public Intellec-tual,* ed. Thomas P. Hughes and Agatha C. Hughes (New York and Oxford: Oxford Univer-sity Press, 1990), 189–198. I do not agree with von Moos that Mumford's writings reveal a "bias for architectural expressionism" (ibid., 189).

61. Ernst May to Mumford, 10 May 1925, Mumford Papers, folder 3194.

62. Ernst May to Mumford, 24 June 1925, Mumford Papers, folder 3194.

63. Letter of introduction for Walter Gropius to Mumford from Eric Mendelsohn [March(?)] 1928, published in Beyer, ed., *Eric Mendelsohn: Letters,* 99.

64. Mumford, "The American Dwelling-House," *American Mercury,* April 1930, 477.

65. Mumford, "Decoration and Structure," 533.

66. Mumford, "Architecture and the Machine," *American Mercury,* September 1924, 77.

67. Mumford, "Frank Lloyd Wright and the New Pioneers," review of *Frank Lloyd Wright,* by Henry-Russell Hitchcock Jr., *Architectural Record* 65 (April 1929): 415.

68. Mumford, "The Economics of Contemporary Decoration," xxi.

69. Mumford, *Sketches,* 459. On Bauer's early career, see Mary Susan Cole, "Catherine Bauer and the Public Housing Movement, 1926–1937" (Ph.D. diss., George Washington University, 1975).

70. Catherine K. Bauer [Wurster] to Mumford, 29 July [1930], Mumford Papers, folder 6338.

71. Mumford, "Bourgeois Culture and Machine Art/Bürgerliche Kultur und Maschine," trans. Ethel Talbot Scheffauer, *Die Form* 5 (7 June 1930): 324.

72. Harvey M. Watts to Howell Lewis Shay, 4 February 1931, published in Howell Lewis Shay, "Modern Architecture and Tradition," *T-Square Club Journal* 1 (February 1931): 14.

73. Leo Marx, "Lewis Mumford: Prophet of Organicism," in *Lewis Mumford: Public Intellectual,* 168.

74. Mumford, "Towards an Organic Humanism," in *The Critique of Humanism: A Symposium,* ed. C. Hartley Grattan (1930; reprint, Freeport, N.Y.: Books for Libraries Press, 1968), 358–359.

75. Mumford, "Form in Modern Architecture: I," 125–128; "Form in Modern Architecture: II. The Beginnings of Modern Form," *Architecture* 60 (December 1929): 313–316; "Form in Modern Architecture: III. The Social Contribution," *Architecture* 61 (March 1930): 151–153; "Form in Modern Architecture: IV. The Community as a Source of Form," *Architecture* 62 (July 1930): 1–4; and "Form in Modern Architecture: V. The Wavy Line versus the Cube," *Architecture* 62 (December 1930): 315–318.

76. Mumford, "Form in Modern Architecture: I," 128.

77. Mumford, "Form in Modern Architecture: V," 318.

78. Mumford to Catherine K. Bauer [Wurster], 2 July 1933, published in Mumford, *My Works and Days: A Personal Chronicle* (New York and London: Harcourt Brace Jovanovich, 1979), 309–310.

79. Mumford to Frank Lloyd Wright, 6 February 1932, fiche M028D02. Copyright (c) The Frank Lloyd Wright Foundation.

80. Mumford, *Sketches,* 433.

81. On the history of the "International Style" exhibition, see Terence Riley, *The International Style: Exhibition 15 and the Museum of Modern Art* (New York: Rizzoli, 1992).

82. Philip Johnson to Mumford, 3 January 1931, Mumford Papers, folder 2483.

83. Mumford to Catherine K. Bauer [Wurster], 9 February 1931, Mumford Papers, folder 6345.

84. Mumford to Catherine K. Bauer [Wurster], 3 September 1931, Mumford Papers, folder 6354.

85. Mumford, "Housing," in *Modern Architecture: International Exhibition* (New York: Museum of Modern Art, 1932), 184.

86. Wright was angered by his exclusion from the design commission for the 1933 Century of Progress Exposition in Chicago, of which Hood was a prominent member. See Frank Lloyd Wright to Raymond M. Hood, 3 February 1931. Copyright (c) The Frank Lloyd Wright Foundation. See also Mumford, "Two Chicago Fairs," *New Republic,* 21 January 1931, 271–272.

87. Frank Lloyd Wright to Mumford, 19 January 1932, Mumford Papers, folder 5478. Copyright (c) The Frank Lloyd Wright Foundation.

88. Telegram from Mumford to Frank Lloyd Wright, 21 January 1932, fiche M027D10. Copyright (c) The Frank Lloyd Wright Foundation.

89. Telegram from Frank Lloyd Wright to Mumford, 21 January 1932, Mumford Papers, folder 5478. Copyright (c) The Frank Lloyd Wright Foundation.

90. Mumford to Frank Lloyd Wright, 23 January 1932, fiche M027E03. Copyright (c) The Frank Lloyd Wright Foundation.

91. Mumford to Frank Lloyd Wright, 6 February 1932, fiche M028D02. Copyright (c) The Frank Lloyd Wright Foundation.

92. Catherine K. Bauer [Wurster] to Mumford, [29 January 1932], Mumford Papers, folder 6368; Riley, *International Style*, 82.

93. Henry-Russell Hitchcock Jr., "Architectural Criticism," *Shelter* 2 (April 1932): 2.

94. "Symposium: The International Architectural Exhibition," *Shelter* 2 (April 1932): 4.

95. Mumford, "The Sky Line: Organic Architecture," *New Yorker*, 27 February 1932, 45.

96. Ibid., 46.

97. Douglas Haskell, "Architecture: What the Man about Town Will Build," *Nation*, 13 April 1932, 442.

98. Catherine K. Bauer [Wurster], "Exhibition of Modern Architecture: Museum of Modern Art," *Creative Art* 10 (March 1932): 201.

99. Letter from Mumford to Sophia Mumford, 26 April 1932, Mumford Papers, folder 6302; letter from Mumford to Sophia Mumford, 9 May 1932, Mumford Papers, folder 6303. Donald L. Miller has claimed that Mumford also met with Ernst May, Le Corbusier, and Siegfried Giedion on this trip, but I have been unable to substantiate these encounters. See Donald L. Miller, *Lewis Mumford: A Life* (New York: Weidenfeld and Nicolson, 1989), 322–323.

100. Philip Johnson to Mumford, 18 April 1932, Mumford Papers, folder 2483.

101. Mumford to Sophia Mumford, 13 June 1932, Mumford Papers, folder 6304.

102. Miller, *Lewis Mumford: A Life*, 324.

103. Mumford, "Notes on Germany," *New Republic*, 26 October 1932, 280, 281.

104. Mumford to Douglas Haskell, 4 July 1932, published in Benson, "Douglas Haskell and the Criticism of International Modernism," 180.

105. The four volumes of *The Renewal of Life* are, in order, Mumford, *Technics and Civilization* (New York: Harcourt, Brace and Company, 1934); *The Culture of Cities* (New York: Harcourt, Brace and Company, 1938); *The Condition of Man* (New York: Harcourt, Brace and Company, 1944); and *The Conduct of Life* (New York: Harcourt, Brace and Company, 1951). For a discussion of *The Renewal of Life*, see Gale H. Carrithers Jr., *Mumford, Tate, Eiseley: Watchers in the Night* (Baton Rouge and London: Louisiana State University Press, 1991), 1–77.

106. On the evolution of Mumford's "Form and Personality" typescript into *Technics and Civilization*, see Rosalind Williams, "Lewis Mumford as a Historian of Technology in *Technics and Civilization*," in *Lewis Mumford: Public Intellectual*, 43–65.

107. Mumford, "Form and Personality," TS, c. 1930, Mumford Papers, folder 6591.

108. Ibid., folder 6592; J. J. P. Oud, *Hollaendische Architektur* (Munich: Albert Langen, 1926), 76.

109. Ibid.

110. Ibid., folder 6597.

111. Notes from Catherine K. Bauer [Wurster] to Mumford concerning "Form and Personality" TS, c. 1930, Mumford Papers, folder 6599.

112. Mumford to Van Wyck Brooks, 21 June 1933, published in *The Van Wyck Brooks–Lewis Mumford Letters: The Record of a Literary Friendship, 1921–1963*, ed. Robert E. Spiller (New York: E. P. Dutton and Company, 1970), 94.

113. Ibid., 95.

114. Mumford, *Sketches*, 464.

115. Ibid., 467.

116. Mumford, "Downfall or Renewal?" review of *The Decline of the West: I. Form and Actuality*, by Oswald Spengler, *New Republic*, 12 May 1926, 369. See also Mumford, "A Philosopher of History," review of *The Decline of the West: II. Perspectives of World History*, by Oswald Spengler, *New Republic*, 20 March 1929, 140–141.

117. Mumford, "The Decline of Spengler," review of *Man and Technics: A Contribution to a Philosophy of Life*, by Oswald Spengler, *New Republic*, 9 March 1932, 104.

118. Mumford, *Technics*, 214–215.

119. Ibid., plate XIV.

120. Ibid., plate XV. See Mumford, "The Art Galleries: Portrait of the Mechanic as a Young Man – Newcomers in Retrospect," *New Yorker*, 31 March 1934, 32–36.

121. Von Moos, "Visualized Machine Age," 212.

122. Mumford, *Technics*, 403.

123. Ibid., 363.

124. For a brief history of "The Sky Line," see Brendan Gill, "The Sky Line: Prospectus," *New Yorker*, 23 February 1987, 106–109.

125. See George Sheppard Chappell, "The Sky Line: Cheap Architecture – The Aeolian Building – Athletic Club Plans – New York Noises," *New Yorker*, 16 October 1926, 61; and George Sheppard Chappell, "The Sky Line: A Pat for the Tiger – Nautical – A Classical Touch," *New Yorker*, 11 February 1928, 65–66.

126. Robert A. M. Stern, Gregory Gilmartin, and Thomas Mellins, *New York 1930: Architecture and Urbanism between the Two World Wars* (New York: Rizzoli, 1987), 7.

127. Mumford, "Frozen Music or Solidified Static? Reflections on Radio City," *New Yorker*, 20 June 1931, 28–36. On the history and design of Rockefeller Center, see Alan Balfour, *Rockefeller Center: Architecture as Theater* (New York: McGraw-Hill, 1978); Carol Herselle Krinsky, *Rockefeller Center* (New York: Oxford University Press, 1978); and Victoria Newhouse, *Wallace K. Harrison, Architect* (New York: Rizzoli, 1989), 34–55.

128. Mumford, "Notes on Modern Architecture," 121.

129. Mumford, "Frozen Music or Solidified Static?" 36.

130. Wolcott Gibbs to Mumford, 10 June 1931, Mumford Papers, folder 3580.

131. Mumford, *Sketches*, 442.

132. Harold Ross to Mumford, 20 April 1933, Mumford Papers, folder 3580.

133. Harold Ross to Mumford, 11 April 1935, Mumford Papers, folder 3580; St. Clair McKelway to Mumford, 23 June 1937, Mumford Papers, folder 3581.

134. Mumford, "A New York Childhood: Ta-Ra-Ra-Boom-De-Ay," *New Yorker*, 22 December 1934, 18–23; and "A New York Adolescence: Tennis, Quadratic Equations, and Love," *New Yorker*, 4 December 1937, 75–89.

135. Mumford, *Sketches*, 442–443.

136. Mumford, "The Sky Line: The New York Lunchroom," *New Yorker*, 19 May 1934, 46.

137. Mumford, "The Sky Line: Two Theatres," *New Yorker*, 14 January 1933, 55.

138. Ibid., 55, 56.

139. On the controversy surrounding Rivera's mural, see Balfour, *Rockefeller Center*, 181–191.

140. Mumford, "The Art Galleries: Early Americans – Ben Shahn and Tom Mooney – Mr. Rivera's Mural," *New Yorker*, 20 May 1933, 66.

141. Mumford, "The Sky Line: Rockefeller Center Revisited," *New Yorker*, 4 May 1940, 73.

142. Ibid., 74.

143. On the history and design of the Cloisters Museum, see Stern et al., *New York 1930*, 126–131.

144. Mumford, "The Sky Line: Pax in Urbe," *New Yorker*, 21 May 1938, 60.

145. Ibid., 62.

146. Ibid., 63.

147. Ibid.

148. Ibid.

149. Mumford, "The Sky Line: Growing Pains – The New Museum," *New Yorker*, 3 June 1939, 54.

150. Alfred H. Barr Jr. to Mumford, 8 January 1939, Mumford Papers, folder 3461; see Mumford, "The Sky Line: Bauhaus – Two Restaurants and a Theatre," *New Yorker*, 31 December 1938, 40–42.

151. "Form of Forms," *Time*, 18 April 1938, 41.

152. Miller, *Lewis Mumford: A Life*, 424–425.

153. Mumford, *Condition*, 415.

154. Ibid., 419.

155. Mumford, "Civilized History," review of *A Study of History*, vols. 1–3, by Arnold J. Toynbee, *New Republic*, 27 November 1935, 64.

156. Mumford, "The Napoleon of Notting Hill," review of *A Study of History*, vols. 7–10, by Arnold J. Toynbee, *New Republic*, 8 November 1954, 16. On the intermediate volumes of the series, see Mumford, "Transcendental Dissolution," review of *A Study of History*, vols. 4–6, by Arnold J. Toynbee, *New Republic*, 1 April 1940, 445–446.

157. Harold Ross to Mumford, 13 January 1947, Mumford Papers, folder 3581.

158. Peter Blake, *No Place like Utopia: Modern Architecture and the Company We Kept* (New York: Alfred A. Knopf, 1993), 146.

159. Mumford assisted Walter Curt Behrendt and his wife Lydia in securing faculty appointments at Dartmouth College. See Miller, *Lewis Mumford: A Life*, 428–429.

160. See Mumford, "The Sky Line: The Marseilles 'Folly,'" *New Yorker*, 5 October 1957, 76–95.

161. Mumford, *Sketches*, 436.

162. Ibid., 437. On Wright's later career, see Mumford, "The Sky Line: A Phoenix Too Infrequent – I," *New Yorker*, 28 November 1953, 133–139; "The Sky Line: A Phoenix Too Infrequent – II," *New Yorker*, 12 December 1953, 116–127; and "The Sky Line: What Wright Hath Wrought," *New Yorker*, 5 December 1959, 105–129.

163. Mumford, *Sketches*, 439.

164. Mumford, *The Highway and the City* (New York: Harcourt, Brace and World, 1963), 139.

165. Mumford, "The Life, the Teaching and the Architecture of Matthew Nowicki [Part I]," *Architectural Record* 115 (June 1954): 139–149; "The Life, the Teaching and the Architecture of Matthew Nowicki, Part II: Matthew Nowicki as an Educator," *Architectural Record* 116 (July 1954): 128–135; "The Life, the Teaching and the Architecture of Matthew Nowicki, Part III: His Architectural Achievement," *Architectural Record* 116 (August 1954): 169–175; and "The Life, the Teaching and the Architecture of Matthew Nowicki, Part IV: Nowicki's Work in India," *Architectural Record* 116 (September 1954): 153–159. This series was subsequently republished in *Architecture as a Home for Man*, 63–101.

166. Mumford, *Architecture as a Home for Man*, 100.

167. Hugh Morrison, "After the International Style – What?" *Architectural Forum* 72 (May 1940): 345–347; Mumford, "The Sky Line: Status Quo," *New Yorker*, 11 October 1947, 104–110.

168. Mumford, "The Sky Line: Status Quo," 110.

169. Mumford, quoted in "What Is Happening to Modern Architecture?" *Museum of Modern Art Bulletin* 15 (Spring 1948): 18.

170. See Mumford, "Monumentalism, Symbolism and Style, Part One," *Magazine of Art*, October 1949, 202–207, 227–228; and "Monumentalism, Symbolism and Style, Part Two," *Magazine of Art*, November 1949, 258–263. On Mumford's relationship with Giedion, see von Moos, "The Visualized Machine Age," 216–227.

171. Mumford, *Art and Technics* (New York: Columbia University Press, 1952), 114.

172. On the history and design of the United Nations, see George A. Dudley, *A Workshop for Peace: Designing the United Nations Headquarters* (New York: Architectural History Foundation; Cambridge, Mass., and London: Massachusetts Institute of Technology Press, 1994); and Victoria Newhouse, *Wallace K. Harrison*, 104–43.

173. Mumford, "The Sky Line: United Nations Headquarters: The Ground Plan," *New Yorker*, 25 October 1947, 56–62; "The Sky Line: United Nations Headquarters: Buildings as Symbols," *New Yorker*, 15 November 1947, 102–109; "The Sky Line: Magic with Mirrors – I," *New Yorker*, 15 September 1951, 84–93; "The Sky Line: Magic with Mirrors – II," *New Yorker*, 22 September 1951, 99–106; "The Sky Line: Workshop Invisible," *New Yorker*, 17 January 1953, 83–88; and "The Sky Line: United Nations Assembly," *New Yorker*, 14 March 1953, 72–81. These columns were republished in *From the Ground Up: Observations on Contemporary Architecture, Housing, Highway Building, and Civic Design* (New York: Harcourt, Brace and Company, 1956), 20–70. On Mumford's analysis of the United Nations, see Lawrence J. Vale, "Designing Global Harmony: Lewis Mumford and the United Nations Headquarters," in *Lewis Mumford: Public Intellectual*, 256–282.

174. Mumford, *From the Ground Up*, 43–44.

175. Ibid., 56, 61.

176. See Vale, "Designing Global Harmony," 278–282.

177. Mumford, *From the Ground Up*, 95.

178. See Mumford, "The Sky Line: House of Glass," *New Yorker*, 9 August 1952, 48–54; and Mumford, "The Sky Line: Crystal Lantern," *New Yorker*, 13 November 1954, 197–204.

179. Mumford, *Architecture as a Home for Man*, 87.

180. Mumford, "The Sky Line: The Lesson of the Master," *New Yorker*, 13 September 1958, 126–129.

181. Ibid., 135.

182. Mumford, "The Case against 'Modern Architecture,'" *Architectural Record* 131 (April 1962): 161.

183. Wolf Von Eckardt, "Changing Our Unnatural Habitat," review of *The Highway and the City*, *New Republic*, 1 June 1963, 22.

184. Marx, "Lewis Mumford: Prophet of Organicism," 179.

CHAPTER 4

1. Part of this chapter first appeared in Robert Wojtowicz, "The Critic as Propagandist: Lewis Mumford and the 'Radburn Idea,'" in *Proceedings of the Fourth National Conference on American Planning History* (Richmond, Va.: Society for American City and Regional Planning History, 7–10 November 1991): 167–187. On Mumford's writings on urbanism, see Lewis F. Fried, *Makers of the City: Jacob Riis, Lewis Mumford, James T. Farrell, and Paul Goodman* (Amherst: University of Massachusetts Press, 1990), 64–118; and Paul Goldberger, "Organic Remedies: Building and the City," *Salmagundi* 49 (Summer 1980): 87–98.

2. For a discussion of Mumford's regionalism, see John L. Thomas, "In Retrospect: Lewis Mumford: Regionalist Historian," *Reviews in American History* 16 (March 1988): 158–172.

3. See Patrick Geddes, *Dramatisations of History* (Bombay: Modern Publishing Company; Edinburgh: P. G. and Colleagues, 1923).

4. Donald L. Miller, *Lewis Mumford: A Life* (New York: Weidenfeld and Nicolson, 1989), 197.

5. Mumford, "Garden Civilizations: Preparing for a New Epoch," *Town and Country Planning* 23 (March 1955): 139–140. Mumford originally penned this essay in 1917.

6. Mumford, "The City," in *Civilization in the United States: An Inquiry by Thirty Americans,* ed. Harold E. Stearns (New York: Harcourt, Brace and Company, 1922), 8.

7. Ibid., 20.

8. Mumford, *Sketches from Life: The Autobiography of Lewis Mumford, The Early Years* (New York: Dial Press, 1982), 336.

9. Minutes of the Regional Planning Association of America, 20 April 1923, Lewis Mumford Papers, Special Collections, Van Pelt Library, University of Pennsylvania, Philadelphia (hereafter referred to as Mumford Papers), folder 8033. For Mumford's account of the association, see Mumford, introduction to *The New Exploration: A Philosophy of Regional Planning,* by Benton MacKaye (1928; reprint, with a foreword by David N. Startzell, Harpers Ferry, West Virginia: Appalachian Trail Conference; Urbana-Champaign, Illinois: University of Illinois Press, 1990), vii–xxii; and Mumford, introduction to *Toward New Towns for America,* by Clarence S. Stein, 3d rev. ed. (Cambridge, Mass., and London: Massachusetts Institute of Technology Press, 1966), 11–17. See also Roy Lubove, *Community Planning in the 1920's: The Contribution of the Regional Planning Association of America* (Pittsburgh: University of Pittsburgh Press, 1963); Carl Sussman, ed., *Planning the Fourth Migration: The Neglected Vision of the Regional Planning Association of America* (Cambridge, Mass., and London: Massachusetts Institute of Technology Press, 1976); Daniel Schaffer, *Garden Cities for America: The Radburn Experience* (Philadelphia: Temple University Press, 1982); and Kermit C. Parsons, "Collaborative Genius: The Regional Planning Association of America," *Journal of the American Planning Association* 60 (Autumn 1994): 462–482. Short biographies of many of the association's members appear in Mumford, ed., *Roots of Contemporary American Architecture: A Series of Thirty-Seven Essays Dating from the Mid-Nineteenth Century to the Present* (New York: Reinhold, 1952), 419–437.

10. Mumford, *Sketches,* 338–339, 341.

11. Mumford, introduction to Stein, *Toward New Towns for America,* 15.

12. The term "regional city" first appears in the minutes of the Regional Planning Association of America for 8–9 October 1927. Mumford Papers, folder 8034.

13. On the friendship between Mumford and MacKaye, see John L. Thomas, "Lewis Mumford, Benton MacKaye, and the Regional Vision," in *Lewis Mumford: Public Intellectual,* ed. Thomas P. Hughes and Agatha C. Hughes (New York and Oxford: Oxford University Press, 1990), 66–99.

14. Benton MacKaye to Mumford, 6 March 1927, Mumford Papers, folder 3032.

15. Mumford, introduction to Stein, *Toward New Towns for America,* 15.

16. Mumford to Benton MacKaye, 18 December 1924, Mumford Papers, folder 5989 [original in Dartmouth College Library].

17. Mumford, *Sketches,* 342.

18. Minutes of the Regional Planning Association of America, 7 June 1923, Mumford Papers, folder 8033.

19. Lubove, *Community Planning,* 49.

20. On Unwin's life and work, see Frank Jackson, *Sir Raymond Unwin: Architect, Planner and Visionary* (London: A. Zwemmer, 1985).

21. Lubove, *Community Planning,* 49. See also Raymond Unwin, *Nothing Gained by Overcrowding! How the Garden City Type of Development May Benefit Both Owner and Occupier* (London: P. S. King, 1912).

22. Sussman, introduction to *Planning the Fourth Migration*, 7–8.

23. Mumford, "Report of Committee on Community Planning," *American Institute of Architects: Proceedings of the Fifty-Seventh Annual Convention* (1924), app. 6, 120–126; and "Report of Committee on Community Planning," *American Institute of Architects: Proceedings of the Fifty-Eighth Annual Convention* (1925), app. 10, 119–126.

24. Mumford, "Architecture and Broad Planning: II. Realities vs. Dreams," *Journal of the American Institute of Architects* 13 (June 1925): 199.

25. Mumford, "The Fate of Garden Cities," *Journal of the American Institute of Architects* 15 (February 1927): 38.

26. Mumford, *Sketches*, 344.

27. Mumford, "Architecture and Broad Planning," 198; Schaffer, *Garden Cities for America*, 71–72; Heinz Tschachler, *Lewis Mumford's Reception in German Translation and Criticism* (Lanham, Md., New York, and London: University Press of America, 1994), 20; Mumford to Patrick Geddes, 5 May 1925, Mumford Papers, folder 5832 [original in the National Library of Scotland, Edinburgh]. Geddes did not attend the congress as Schaffer has claimed.

28. Mumford, "The Fourth Migration," *Survey Graphic* 54 (1 May 1925): 133.

29. Mumford, *Roots*, 431.

30. *Report of the Commission of Housing and Regional Planning to Governor Alfred E. Smith* (Albany: New York [State] Commission of Housing and Regional Planning, 7 May 1926), republished in Sussman, ed., *Planning the Fourth Migration*, 194.

31. Sussman, *Planning the Fourth Migration*, 144.

32. On the history and development of the plan and the association's response to it, see David A. Johnson, "Regional Planning for the Great American Metropolis: New York between the World Wars," in *Two Centuries of American Planning*, ed. Daniel Schaffer (Baltimore: Johns Hopkins University Press, 1988): 167–196.

33. Mumford to Benton MacKaye, 18 December 1924, Mumford Papers, folder 5989 [original in Dartmouth College Library].

34. Johnson, "Regional Planning for the Great American Metropolis," 178.

35. Mumford, "Architecture and Broad Planning," 198.

36. On the life and work of Thomas Adams, see Michael Simpson, *Thomas Adams and the Modern Planning Movement: Britain, Canada and the United States, 1900–1940* (London and New York: Alexandrine Press, 1985).

37. Thomas Adams to Mumford, 9 January 1930, Mumford Papers, folder 4054.

38. Mumford to Thomas Adams, c. 31 January 1930, Mumford Papers, folder 6108.

39. Sussman, introduction to *Planning the Fourth Migration*, 20.

40. Clarence Arthur Perry, "The Neighborhood Unit: A Scheme of Arrangement for the Family-Life Community," in *Neighborhood and Community Planning*, vol. 7 of *Regional Plan of New York and Its Environs* (New York: Committee on Regional Plan of New York and Its Environs, 1929), 21–140.

41. Sussman, introduction to *Planning the Fourth Migration*, 20.

42. Schaffer, *Garden Cities for America*, 198.

43. Communication from Mumford to the Regional Planning Association of America, 12 March 1932, published in Sussman, *Planning the Fourth Migration*, 222.

44. Clarence S. Stein to Aline MacMahon, 24 March 1932, Mumford Papers, folder 4664.

45. Mumford, "The Sky Line: The Regional Plan," *New Yorker*, 21 May 1932, 64–66; "The Plan of New York [I]," *New Republic*, 15 June 1932, 121–126; and "The Plan of New York: II," *New Republic*, 22 June 1932, 146–154.

46. Mumford, "The Plan of New York [I]," 122.

47. Mumford, "The Plan of New York: II," 153.

48. Ibid., 154.

49. Thomas Adams, "A Communication: In Defense of the Regional Plan," *New Republic*, 6 July 1932, 208.

50. Sussman, *Planning the Fourth Migration*, 221.

51. Mumford, "Community Planning and Housing," *Journal of the American Institute of Architects* 11 (December 1923): 492.

52. Mumford, "Mass-Production and the Modern House [Part One]," *Architectural Record* 67 (January 1930): 17.

53. Ibid., 18.

54. See Douglas Haskell, "The House of the Future," *New Republic*, 13 May 1931, 344–345.

55. Mumford, "The Flaw in the Mechanical House," *New Republic*, 3 June 1931, 66.

56. On the history and planning of Sunnyside Gardens, see Stein, *Toward New Towns for America*, 21–35; Henry Wright, *Rehousing Urban America* (New York: Columbia University Press, 1935), 36–42; and Schaffer, *Garden Cities for America*, 119–133.

57. Mumford, *Sketches*, 413–414.

58. Miller, *Lewis Mumford: A Life*, 203, 241.

59. Mumford, "Houses – Sunnyside Up," *Nation*, 4 February 1925, 115–116.

60. Mumford, "American Architecture," *American Federationist* 34 (December 1927): 1484.

61. Mumford, "American Architecture To-day: II," *Architecture* 57 (June 1928): 301.

62. Ibid., 307.

63. Ebenezer Howard to Alexander M. Bing, 23 March 1927, published in Dugald MacFadyen, *Sir Ebenezer Howard and the Town Planning Movement* (1933; reprint, Cambridge: Massachusetts Institute of Technology Press, 1970), 164–165; minutes of the Regional Planning Association of America, 8–9 October 1927, Mumford Papers, folder 8034.

64. On the history and planning of Radburn, see Stein, *Toward New Towns for America*, 36–73; Wright, *Rehousing Urban America*, 42–46; and Schaffer, *Garden Cities for America*, 135–215.

65. Stein, *Toward New Towns for America*, 41–44.

66. Mumford, *The Brown Decades: A Study of the Arts in America, 1865–1895* (New York: Harcourt, Brace and Company, 1931), 93.

67. Clarence S. Stein to Mumford, 25 August 1947, Mumford Papers, folder 4664.

68. Mumford, "Form in Modern Architecture: IV. The Community as a Source of Form," *Architecture* 62 (July 1930): 4.

69. Mumford and Benton MacKaye, "Townless Highways for the Motorist: A Proposal for the Automobile Age," *Harper's*, August 1931, 353.

70. On the influence of Radburn on American planning, see Eugenie Ladner Birch, "Radburn and the American Planning Movement: The Persistence of an Idea," *Journal of the American Planning Association* 46 (October 1980): 424–439.

71. Jackson, *Sir Raymond Unwin*, 151–152.

72. Stanley Buder, *Visionaries and Planners: The Garden City Movement and the Modern Community* (New York and Oxford: Oxford University Press), 149.

73. Ibid., 151.

74. For Bauer's reflections on her first impressions of the new Siedlungen, see Catherine K. Bauer Wurster, "The Social Front of Modern Architecture in the 1930s," *Journal of the Society of Architectural Historians* 24 (March 1965): 48–52.

75. Catherine K. Bauer [Wurster] to Mumford, 3 October 1930, Mumford Papers, folder 6342.

76. Ibid.

77. Catherine K. Bauer [Wurster] to Mumford, 29 July [1930], Mumford Papers, folder 6338.

78. Catherine K. Bauer [Wurster] to Mumford, 9 August 1930, Mumford Papers, folder 6339.

79. Catherine K. Bauer [Wurster] to Mumford, 9 September 1930, Mumford Papers, folder 6341.

80. Mumford, "Housing," in *Modern Architecture: International Exhibition* (New York: Museum of Modern Art, 1932), 189.

81. Terence Riley, *The International Style: Exhibition 15 and the Museum of Modern Art* (New York: Rizzoli, 1992), 60.

82. Mumford to Frank Lloyd Wright, 6 February 1932, fiche M028D02. Copyright (c) The Frank Lloyd Wright Foundation. Riley, *International Style*, 60, 192–193.

83. Mumford, *Sketches*, 465.

84. Ibid.

85. Mumford to Sophia Wittenberg Mumford, 24 May 1932, Mumford Papers, folder 6303.

86. Mumford to Sophia Wittenberg Mumford, 6 June 1932, Mumford Papers, folder 6304; Mumford, "Machines for Living," *Fortune*, February 1933, 88.

87. Mumford to Sophia Wittenberg Mumford, 2 May 1932, Mumford Papers, folder 6303.

88. Mumford, "England's Two Million Houses, New," *Fortune*, November 1932, 82.

89. Mumford, "Machines for Living," 88.

90. Mumford, "Taxes into Houses," *Fortune*, May 1933, 48–49, 86–89.

91. Mary Susan Cole (Ph.D. diss., George Washington University, 1975), "Catherine Bauer and the Public Housing Movement, 1926–1937," 122–123.

92. Schaffer, *Garden Cities for America*, 193–194.

93. Ibid., 199.

94. Mumford, "The Chance for Civilized Housing," *New Republic*, 17 September 1930, 116–117.

95. "Housing – One Way to Prosperity," *New Republic*, 17 September 1930, 111–112.

96. [Mumford], "Housing versus Ownership," *New Republic*, 16 December 1931, 123.

97. Ibid.

98. On the history of New Deal housing and planning initiatives, see John Hancock, "The New Deal and American Planning: The 1930s," in *Two Centuries of American Planning*, ed. Daniel Schaffer (Baltimore: Johns Hopkins University Press, 1988), 197–230.

99. Schaffer, *Garden Cities for America*, 227.

100. Albert Mayer, "New Homes for a New Deal – I: Slum Clearance – But How?" *New Republic*, 14 February 1934, 7–9; Henry Wright, "New Homes for a New Deal – II: Abolishing Slums Forever," *New Republic*, 21 February 1934, 41–44; Mumford, "New Homes for a New Deal – III: The Shortage of Dwellings and Direction," *New Republic*, 28 February 1934, 69–72; Mumford, Albert Mayer, and Henry Wright, "New Homes for a New Deal – IV: A Concrete Program," *New Republic*, 7 March 1934, 91–94.

101. Mumford, Mayer, and Wright, "New Homes for a New Deal – IV," 93–94.

102. Mumford, *Sketches*, 478. For a discussion of the "Round Table on Regionalism" held at the University of Virginia, see Walter L. Creese, *T.V.A.'s Public Planning: The Vision, the Reality* (Knoxville: University of Tennessee Press, 1990), 42–52.

103. Mumford, "The Regional Planning Association of America: Past and Future," TS, 21 September 1948, Mumford Papers, folder 8035; Mumford, *Roots*, 421.

104. Kermit C. Parsons, "Clarence Stein and the Greenbelt Towns: Settling for Less," *Journal of the American Planning Association* 56 (Spring 1990): 169.

105. On the history and development of Greenbelt, Maryland; Greenhills, Ohio; Greendale, Wisconsin; and the aborted town of Greenbrook, New Jersey; see Stein, *Toward New Towns for America*, 118–187.

106. Parsons, "Clarence Stein and the Greenbelt Towns," 165.

107. Ibid., 174.

108. Hancock, "The New Deal and American Planning," 215–217.

109. Cole, "Catherine Bauer," 130. See Catherine K. Bauer [Wurster], *Modern Housing* (Boston and New York: Houghton Mifflin, 1934).

110. Wright, preface to *Rehousing Urban America,* xi.

111. On Wright's and Le Corbusier's contrasting theories of urbanism, see Robert Fishman, *Urban Utopias in the Twentieth Century: Ebenezer Howard, Frank Lloyd Wright, and Le Corbusier* (New York: Basic Books, 1977), 89–263.

112. Mumford, "The City of Tomorrow," reviews of *The Metropolis of Tomorrow,* by Hugh Ferriss; *Our Cities Today and Tomorrow: A Survey of Planning and Zoning Progress in the United States,* by Theodora Kimball Hubbard and Henry Vincent Hubbard; and *The City of Tomorrow and Its Planning,* by Le Corbusier, *New Republic,* 12 February 1930, 333.

113. Ibid.

114. Mumford, "Communitas," reviews of *When the Cathedrals Were White: A Journey to the Country of Timid People,* by Le Corbusier; and *Communitas: Ways of Livelihood and Ways of Life,* by Percival Goodman and Paul Goodman, *Virginia Quarterly Review* 23 (Summer 1947): 440.

115. Mumford, "The Sky Line: Mr. Wright's City – Downtown Dignity," *New Yorker,* 27 April 1935, 63.

116. Ibid., 64.

117. Frank Lloyd Wright to Mumford, 27 April 1935, Mumford Papers, folder 5478. Copyright (c) The Frank Lloyd Wright Foundation.

118. Mumford to Frank Lloyd Wright, 25 June 1935, fiche M053E02. Copyright (c) The Frank Lloyd Wright Foundation.

119. Mumford, "Form and Personality," TS, c. 1930, Mumford Papers, folder 6595.

120. Ibid.

121. Mumford, *The Culture of Cities* (New York: Harcourt, Brace and Company, 1938), 14.

122. Ibid., 90.

123. Ibid., 91.

124. Ibid., 106.

125. Ibid., 151.

126. Ibid., 179.

127. Ibid., 273.

128. Ibid., 258.

129. Ibid., 401.

130. Ibid., caption to plate IX (31). Since not all of Greenbelt's terrace blocks have flat roofs, Mumford was careful to include illustrations only of the most modern-looking units.

131. Ibid., 492.

132. "Art: Form of Forms," *Time,* 18 April 1938, cover and 40–43; "Metropolis: Lewis Mumford's Book Scraps Today's City, Plans a New and Saner U.S.," *Life* 23 May 1938, 52–59.

133. R. L. Duffus, "A History of the Urban Life: Mr. Mumford's 'The Culture of Cities' Links Past, Present and Future," review of *The Culture of Cities, New York Times Book Review,* 17 April 1938, 1.

134. Douglas Haskell, "The City, Past and Future," review of *The Culture of Cities, Nation,* 23 April 1938, 478.

135. Ibid.

136. Meyer Schapiro, "Looking Forward to Looking Backward," review of *The Culture of Cities*, *Partisan Review* 8 (July 1938): 13.

137. Ibid., 18.

138. Ibid., 19.

139. Here, I am using Stanley Buder's definition of communitarianism as the application of "intelligence to the experimental design of a community's institutions and environment" (*Visionaries and Planners*, 4).

140. Prior to this time, the closest Mumford had come to preparing a planning report was in 1925–1926 when he was asked by the *Evening Sun* to write a series of columns on the city of Baltimore. See Mumford, "The Bricks of Baltimore," *[Baltimore] Evening Sun*, 1 December 1925, sec. 2, 23; "Deserts versus Gardens," *[Baltimore] Evening Sun*, 4 December 1925, sec. 2, 25; "Modern Public Buildings," *[Baltimore] Evening Sun*, 8 December 1925, sec. 2, 27; "How to Ruin Baltimore," *[Baltimore] Evening Sun*, 10 December 1925, sec. 2, 27; and "The New Municipal Building," *[Baltimore] Evening Sun*, 11 February 1926, sec. 2, 23.

141. Mumford, *City Development: Studies in Disintegration and Renewal* (New York: Harcourt, Brace and Company, 1945), 84.

142. Mumford, *Whither Honolulu? A Memorandum Report on Park and City Planning* (Honolulu: City and County of Honolulu Park Board, [1938]), 3.

143. Ibid., 46.

144. Ibid., 45.

145. Mumford, *City Development*, 85.

146. Mumford, *Regional Planning in the Pacific Northwest: A Memorandum* (Portland, Oreg.: Northwest Regional Council, 1939), 18.

147. *The City*, a film produced by the American Institute of Planners and directed by Ralph Steiner and Willard Van Dyke with commentary written by Mumford, 1939. On the making of *The City*, see William Alexander, *Film on the Left: American Documentary Film from 1931 to 1942* (Princeton, N.J.: Princeton University Press, 1981), 247–257; and Howard Gillette Jr., "Film as Artifact: *The City* (1939)," *American Studies* 18 (Fall 1977): 71–85. On the design and planning of the fair itself, see Victoria Newhouse, *Wallace K. Harrison, Architect* (New York: Rizzoli, 1989), 80–93.

148. *The Fair of the Future, 1939: Social Theme, Physical Concept, Design Organization, Summary* ([New York]: Office of the Secretary, 11 December 1935, amended 10 February 1936).

149. Newhouse, *Wallace K. Harrison*, 81.

150. Gillette, "Film as Artifact," 73; Alexander, *Film on the Left*, 248–250.

151. Mumford, narrative for *The City*, quoted in Alexander, *Film on the Left*, 251.

152. Gillette, "Film as Artifact," 75–78.

153. Clarence S. Stein to Mumford, 12 May 1939, Mumford Papers, folder 890.

154. Frederick L. Ackerman to Mumford, 11 May 1939, Mumford Papers, folder 21.

155. Alexander, *Film on the Left*, 255.

156. Archer Winsten, "Movie Talk: 'The City' Opens Saturday at the World's Fair: Documentary of Unqualified Excellence Shows the Way to New Achievements," review of *The City*, *New York Post*, 23 May 1939.

157. "A World's Fair Film," review of *The City*, *Architectural Review* 86 (August 1939): 93, 94.

158. Mumford, "The Sky Line in Flushing: West Is East," *New Yorker*, 17 June 1939, 38.

159. Mumford, "The Sky Line in Flushing: Genuine Bootleg," *New Yorker*, 29 July 1939, 38.

160. Mumford to Clarence S. Stein, 5 July 1949, Mumford Papers, folder 6177 [original in Cornell University Library, Division of Rare and Manuscript Collections].

161. In 1948, Mumford, Stein, and Bauer reorganized the association as the Regional Develop-

ment Council of America, but with only limited success. See Mumford, "The Regional Planning Association of America"; and Parsons, "Clarence Stein and the Greenbelt Towns," 177.

162. Frederic J. Osborn to Mumford, 12 December 1938, published in *The Letters of Lewis Mumford and Frederic J. Osborn: A Transatlantic Dialogue, 1938–1970*, ed. Michael Hughes (New York and Washington: Praeger Publishers, 1972), 5–6.

163. On Osborn's life and work, see Arnold Whittick, *F. J.O. – Practical Idealist: A Biography of Sir Frederic J. Osborn* (London: Town and Country Planning Association, 1987).

164. Mumford, *The Social Foundations of Postwar Building,* Rebuilding Britain Series, no. 9 (London: Faber and Faber Ltd., 1943), republished in *City Development,* 185.

165. Ibid., 157.

166. Mumford, "Lewis Mumford on the Future of London," *Architectural Review* 97 (January 1945), republished in *City Development,* 220.

167. Frederic J. Osborn and Arnold Whittick, *New Towns: Their Origins, Achievements and Progress,* 3d rev. ed., with an introduction by Mumford (London: Leonard Hill; Boston: Routledge and Kegan Paul, 1977), 48–51.

168. Hughes, *The Letters of Lewis Mumford and Frederic J. Osborn,* 4.

169. Mumford, "The Garden City Idea and Modern Planning," introduction to *Garden Cities of To-morrow,* by Ebenezer Howard, 4th rev. ed. (Cambridge, Mass., and London: Massachusetts Institute of Technology Press, 1965), 35.

170. On the events leading up to the passage of the two acts, see Osborn and Whittick, *New Towns,* 38–61.

171. Frederic J. Osborn to Mumford, 30 March 1953, published in Hughes, *The Letters of Lewis Mumford and Frederic J. Osborn,* 213–214.

172. Mumford, "The Sky Line: Old Forms for New Towns," *New Yorker,* 17 October 1953, republished in Mumford, *The Highway and the City* (New York: Harcourt, Brace and World, 1963), 26.

173. Mumford to Frederic J. Osborn, 2 July 1953, published in Hughes, *The Letters of Lewis Mumford and Frederic J. Osborn,* 220.

174. Mumford, "The Sky Line: East End Urbanity," *New Yorker,* 26 September 1953, republished in *Highway,* 20.

175. Mumford, "The Sky Line: The Cave, the City, and the Flower," *New Yorker,* 2 November 1957, republished in *Highway,* 46.

176. Ibid., 50.

177. Mumford, "The Sky Line: The Marseilles 'Folly,'" *New Yorker,* 5 October 1957, republished in *Highway,* 57.

178. Ibid., 65–66.

179. Mumford, "The Sky Line: Philadelphia – I," *New Yorker,* 28 April 1956, 106–115; "The Sky Line: Philadelphia – II," *New Yorker,* 26 May 1956, 110–119; "The Sky Line: [Historic] Philadelphia – I," *New Yorker,* 17 November 1956, 138–148; "The Sky Line: Historic Philadelphia – II," *New Yorker,* 9 February 1957, 100–106; "The Sky Line: Historic Philadelphia – III," *New Yorker,* 6 April 1957, 132–141; and "The Sky Line: Historic Philadelphia – IV," *New Yorker,* 13 April 1957, 155–162. The "Historic Philadelphia" series was republished in *Highway,* 176–214.

180. On the creation of the Independence Park district surrounding Independence Hall, see Constance Greiff, *Independence: The Creation of a National Park* (Philadelphia: University of Pennsylvania Press, 1987).

181. Mumford, *Highway,* 190.

182. Ibid., 203.

183. Ibid., 204.

184. See Charles E. Peterson, "American Notes: Ante-Bellum Skyscraper," *Journal of the Society of Architectural Historians* 9 (October 1950): 27–28.

185. Mumford, "The Sky Line: The Roaring Traffic's Boom – II," *New Yorker*, 2 April 1955, republished in Mumford, *From the Ground Up: Observations on Contemporary Architecture, Housing, Highway Building, and Civic Design* (New York: Harcourt, Brace and Company, 1956), 210.

186. On Moses' life and work, see Robert A. Caro, *The Power Broker: Robert Moses and the Fall of New York* (New York: Alfred A. Knopf, 1974).

187. See, for example, Mumford, "The Sky Line: Meditations on a Zoo," *New Yorker*, 5 January 1935, 50–52; and "The Sky Line: Bridges and Beaches," *New Yorker*, 17 July 1937, 50–52.

188. Mumford to Frederic J. Osborn, 31 August 1947, published in Hughes, *The Letters of Lewis Mumford and Frederic J. Osborn*, 152.

189. On the design of Stuyvesant Town, see Richard Plunz, *A History of Housing in New York City: Dwelling Type and Social Change in the American Metropolis* (New York: Columbia University Press, 1990), 255–260.

190. Mumford, "The Sky Line: Prefabricated Blight," *New Yorker*, 30 October 1948, 49.

191. Robert Moses, letter to the editors of the *New Yorker*, published in Mumford, "The Sky Line: Stuyvesant Town Revisited," *New Yorker*, 27 November 1948, 68.

192. Mumford, "The Sky Line: Stuyvesant Town Revisited," 72.

193. Mumford, "The Sky Line: From Utopia Parkway Turn East," *New Yorker*, 22 October 1949, republished in *From the Ground Up*, 4.

194. Mumford, "The Sky Line: The Great Good Place," *New Yorker*, 12 November 1949, republished in Mumford, *From the Ground Up*, 19.

195. Mumford was particularly opposed to Moses' plan, first announced in the late 1930s, to bridge the Narrows at the entrance to New York harbor, a plan that was finally realized in 1964 with the opening of the Verrazano–Narrows Bridge. See Mumford, "The Sky Line: Growing Pains – The New Museum," *New Yorker*, 3 June 1939, 51; and "The Sky Line: The Skyway's the Limit," *New Yorker*, 14 November 1959, 181–191.

196. Miller, *Lewis Mumford: A Life*, 481.

197. Mumford, "The Sky Line: The Roaring Traffic's Boom – I," *New Yorker*, 19 March 1955, 115–121; "The Sky Line: The Roaring Traffic's Boom – II," *New Yorker*, 2 April 1955, 97–103; "The Sky Line: The Roaring Traffic's Boom – III," *New Yorker*, 16 April 1955, 78–88; "The Sky Line: The Roaring Traffic's Boom – IV," *New Yorker*, 11 June 1955, 86–97. This series was republished in *From the Ground Up*, 199–243.

198. Mumford, *From the Ground Up*, 242.

199. Miller, *Lewis Mumford: A Life*, 483.

200. Mumford, "The Highway and the City," *Architectural Record* 123 (April 1958), republished in *Highway*, 234.

201. Mumford, "The Sky Line: The Disappearance of Pennsylvania Station," *New Yorker*, 7 June 1958, republished in *Highway*, 151.

202. Mumford, "The Modern City," in *Forms and Functions of Twentieth-Century Architecture*, vol. 4, ed. Talbot Faulkner Hamlin, with an introduction by Leopold Arnaud (New York: Columbia University Press, 1952), 775–819.

203. Miller, *Lewis Mumford: A Life*, 459–460.

204. Ibid., 461.

205. For a discussion of *The City in History*, see David Riesman, "Some Observations on Lewis Mumford's *The City in History*," *Salmagundi* 49 (Summer 1980): 80–86.

206. Mumford, *The City in History: Its Origins, Its Transformations, and Its Prospects* (New York: Harcourt, Brace and World, 1961), 46.

207. Ibid., 141.

208. Ibid., 239.

209. Ibid., 551.

210. Ibid., 556.

211. Ibid., 576.

212. Miller, *Lewis Mumford: A Life*, 462.

213. *Lewis Mumford on the City*, produced and written by Ian MacNeill for the National Film Board of Canada and based on *The City in History*, 1963.

214. Frederic J. Osborn to Mumford, 2 April 1961, published in Hughes, *The Letters of Lewis Mumford and Frederic J. Osborn*, 306.

215. Clarence S. Stein to Mumford, 23 June 1961, Mumford Papers, folder 4664.

216. Allan Temko, "How Civilized Can Urban Man Be? In the History of Cities, Mr. Mumford Finds Forces That Have Destroyed the Dwellers," review of *The City in History*, *New York Times Book Review*, 16 April 1961, 1.

217. Ibid., 1, 32.

218. Christopher Tunnard, "The City and Its Interpreters," review of *The City in History*, *Journal of the American Institute of Planners* 27 (November 1961): 348.

219. Henry S. Churchill, "Sticks and Stones *May* Break Our Bones," review of *The City in History*, *Progressive Architecture* 42 (October 1961): 181, 175, 181.

220. Robert Moses, "Are Cities Dead?" *Atlantic Monthly*, January 1962, 55.

221. Jane Jacobs, *The Death and Life of Great American Cities* (New York: Vintage Books, 1961), 25.

222. Mumford, "The Sky Line: Mother Jacobs' Home Remedies," *New Yorker*, 1 December 1962, republished in Mumford, *The Urban Prospect* (New York: Harcourt, Brace and World, 1968), 194.

223. Mumford, *Urban Prospect*, 207.

224. See, for example, Wolf Von Eckardt, "Mrs. Jacobs vs. Mumford: Urban Planning Stirs a Storm," *Washington Post*, 30 December 1962. More recent discussions of the Mumford–Jacobs debate can be found in Goldberger, "Organic Remedies," 92–95; Eric H. Monkkonen, *America Becomes Urban: The Development of U.S. Cities and Towns, 1780–1980* (Berkeley, Los Angeles, and London: University of California Press, 1988), 9–19; and Robert Fulford, "When Jane Jacobs Took on the World," *New York Times Book Review*, 16 February 1992, 1, 28–29, 33.

225. Mumford, preface to *Highway*, v.

226. Mumford, *Urban Prospect*, 226.

227. Mumford, introduction to *New Towns*, xvii.

228. Mumford, "Revaluations I: Howard's Garden City," review of *Garden Cities of To-morrow*, by Ebenezer Howard, *New York Review of Books*, 8 April 1965, 10.

CONCLUSION

1. See, for example, Brendan Gill, "The Sky Line: Homage to Mumford," *New Yorker*, 2 April 1990, 90–93; and Paul Goldberger, "Architecture View: Lewis Mumford: Preacher, Prophet, Romantic," *New York Times*, 4 February 1990, sec. H, 38, 40. On the media's general neglect

of Mumford's death, see Martin Filler, "Mumford Remembered," *Design Book Review* 19 (Winter 1991): 14–19.

2. Mumford, introduction to *The Condition of Man* (New York: Harcourt, Brace and Company, 1944), 13.

3. Mumford, *The Conduct of Life* (New York: Harcourt, Brace and Company, 1951), 235.

4. See Mumford, "Utopia, the City and the Machine," *Daedalus* 94 (Spring 1965): 271–292.

5. For a discussion of *The Myth of the Machine*, see Gale H. Carrithers Jr., *Mumford, Tate, Eiseley: Watchers in the Night* (Baton Rouge and London: Louisiana State University Press, 1991), 78–106.

6. Mumford, prologue to *Technics and Human Development*, vol. 1 of *The Myth of the Machine* (New York: Harcourt Brace Jovanovich, 1967), 12.

7. Mumford, *The Pentagon of Power*, vol. 2 of *The Myth of the Machine* (New York: Harcourt Brace Jovanovich, 1970), 210.

8. Mumford, as quoted in Andrea Oppenheimer Dean, "International Style: A Lively Dissection Fifty Years Later," *Journal of the American Institute of Architects* n. s. 71 (June 1982): 9.

9. Mumford to Catherine K. Bauer [Wurster], published in Mumford, *My Works and Days: A Personal Chronicle* (New York and London: Harcourt Brace Jovanovich, 1979), 304.

BIBLIOGRAPHY

For a published bibliography of Lewis Mumford's writings up to 1970, see Elmer S. Newman, *Lewis Mumford: A Bibliography, 1914–1970*, with an introduction by Lewis Mumford (New York: Harcourt Brace Jovanovich, 1971). See also Jane Morley, "A 'Canvass of Possibilities': A Bibliographic Guide to Lewis Mumford's Life and Work," *Horns of Plenty: Malcolm Cowley and His Generation* 2 (Fall 1989): 63–74. An updated bibliography by Morley is forthcoming.

Ackerman, Frederick L. 1917. "What Is a House? IV." *Journal of the American Institute of Architects* 5 (December): 591–639.

Adams, Thomas. 1932. "A Communication: In Defense of the Regional Plan." *The New Republic*, 6 July.

Alexander, William. 1981. *Film on the Left: American Documentary Film from 1931–1942*. Princeton: Princeton University Press.

Anderson, Robert L. 1942. "The Brown Decades Revisited." *Journal of the [American] Society of Architectural Historians* 2 (July): 14–25.

Balfour, Alan. 1978. *Rockefeller Center: Architecture as Theater*. New York: McGraw-Hill.

Beevers, Robert. 1988. *The Garden City Utopia: A Critical Biography of Ebenezer Howard*. New York: St. Martin's Press.

Benson, Robert. 1983. "Douglas Haskell and the Modern Movement in American Architecture." *Journal of Architectural Education* 36 (Summer): 2–9.

———. 1991. "Douglas Haskell and the Criticism of International Modernism." In *Modern Architecture in America: Visions and Revisions*, edited by Richard Guy Wilson and Sidney K. Robinson. Ames: Iowa State University Press, 164–183.

Beyer, Oskar, ed. 1967. *Eric Mendelsohn: Letters of an Architect*. Translated by Geoffrey Strachan. London, New York, and Toronto: Abelard-Schuman.

Birch, Eugenie Ladner. 1980. "Radburn and the American Planning Movement: The Persistence of an Idea." *Journal of the American Planning Association* 46 (October): 424–439.

Blake, Casey Nelson. 1990. *Beloved Community: The Cultural Criticism of Randolph Bourne, Van Wyck Brooks, Waldo Frank, and Lewis Mumford*. Chapel Hill and London: University of North Carolina Press.

Blake, Peter. 1993. *No Place like Utopia: Modern Architecture and the Company We Kept*. New York: Alfred A. Knopf.

Bluestone, Daniel. 1991. *Constructing Chicago*. New Haven and London: Yale University Press.

Boardman, Philip. 1978. *The Worlds of Patrick Geddes: Biologist, Town Planner, Re-Educator, Peace-Warrior.* London, Henley and Boston: Routledge and Kegan Paul.

Bragdon, Claude. 1918. *Architecture and Democracy.* New York: Alfred A. Knopf.

Bricker, Lauren Weiss. 1990. "The Writings of Fiske Kimball: A Synthesis of Architectural History and Practice." In *The Architectural Historian in America: A Symposium in Celebration of the Fiftieth Anniversary of the Founding of the Society of Architectural Historians.* Studies in the History of Art, vol. 35, edited by Elisabeth Blair MacDougall. Hanover and London: University Press of New England.

Brooks, Van Wyck. 1918. "On Creating a Usable Past." *Dial* 64 (11 April): 337–341.

Bruegmann, Robert. 1991. "The Marquette Building and the Myth of the Chicago School." *Threshold* 10 (Fall): 6–23.

Buder, Stanley. 1990. *Visionaries and Planners: The Garden City Movement and the Modern Community.* New York and Oxford: Oxford University Press.

Carlson, Elizabeth Borden. 1988. "Lewis Mumford: Twentieth-Century Architectural Critic." Ph.D. diss., University of California at Santa Barbara.

Caro, Robert A. 1974. *The Power Broker: Robert Moses and the Fall of New York.* New York: Alfred A. Knopf.

Carrithers, Gale H. Jr. 1991. *Mumford, Tate, Eiseley: Watchers in the Night.* Baton Rouge and London: Louisiana State University Press.

Cavendish, W. Davenant. 1931. "And Who Is Keats?" Letter to the editor with response by Lewis Mumford. *New Republic,* 6 May.

Chappell, George Sheppard. 1926. "The Sky Line: Cheap Architecture – The Aeolian Building – Athletic Club Plans – New York Noises." *New Yorker,* 16 October.

    1928. "The Sky Line: A Pat for the Tiger – Nautical – A Classical Touch." *New Yorker,* 11 February.

Chappell, Sally Kitt, and Ann Van Zanten. 1982. *Barry Byrne, John Lloyd Wright: Architecture and Design.* Chicago: University of Chicago Press.

Churchill, Henry S. "Sticks and Stones *May* Break Our Bones." 1961. Review of *The City in History,* by Lewis Mumford. *Progressive Architecture* 42 (October): 175, 181.

Cole, Mary Susan. 1975. "Catherine Bauer and the Public Housing Movement, 1926–1937." Ph.D. diss., George Washington University.

Condit, Carl W. 1952. *The Rise of the Skyscraper.* Chicago: University of Chicago Press.

Creese, Walter L. 1990. *T.V.A.'s Public Planning: The Vision, the Reality.* Knoxville: University of Tennessee Press.

Dean, Andrea Oppenheimer. 1982. "International Style: A Lively Dissection Fifty Years Later." *Journal of the American Institute of Architects* n. s. 71 (June): 9–11.

Dow, Eddy. 1973. "Van Wyck Brooks and Lewis Mumford: A Confluence in the 'Twenties." *American Literature* 45 (November): 407–422.

    1977. "Lewis Mumford's Passage to India: From the First to the Later Phase." *South Atlantic Quarterly* 76 (Winter): 31–43.

Dudley, George A. 1994. *A Workshop for Peace: Designing the United Nations Headquarters.* New York: Architectural History Foundation; Cambridge, Mass., and London: Massachusetts Institute of Technology Press.

Duffey, Joseph. 1980. "Mumford's Quest: The First Decade." *Salmagundi* 49 (Summer): 43–68.

Duffus, R. L. 1938. "A History of the Urban Life: Mr. Mumford's 'The Culture of Cities' Links Past, Present and Future." Review of *The Culture of Cities,* by Lewis Mumford. *New York Times Book Review,* 17 April.

Egbert, Donald Drew. "The Idea of Organic Expression and American Architecture." In *On Arts in Society: Selections from the Periodical Writings of Donald Drew Egbert*. Watkins Glen, N.Y.: American Life Foundation for the University of Victoria.

Embury, Aymar II. 1924. "Architecture and Life." Review of *Sticks and Stones*, by Lewis Mumford. *Saturday Review of Literature*, 27 December.

The Fair of the Future, 1939: Social Theme, Physical Concept, Design Organization, Summary. 1936. [New York]: Office of the Secretary, 10 February.

Fein, Albert. 1972. *Frederick Law Olmsted and the American Environmental Tradition.* New York: George Braziller.

Filler, Martin. 1991. "Mumford Remembered." *Design Book Review* 19 (Winter): 14–19.

Fishman, Robert. 1977. *Urban Utopias in the Twentieth Century: Ebenezer Howard, Frank Lloyd Wright, and Le Corbusier.* New York: Basic Books.

"Form of Forms." 1938. *Time*, 18 April.

Forty-Seventh Annual Report of the Trustees of the American Museum of Natural History for the Year 1915. 1916. New York: American Museum of Natural History, 7 February.

Fried, Lewis F. 1990. *Makers of the City: Jacob Riis, Lewis Mumford, James T. Farrell, and Paul Goodman.* Amherst: University of Massachusetts Press.

Fulford, Robert. 1992. "When Jane Jacobs Took on the World." *New York Times Book Review,* 16 February.

Geddes, Patrick. 1904 [1973]. *City Development: A Study of Parks, Gardens, and Culture-Institutes, A Report to the Carnegie Dunfermline Trust.* New Brunswick, N.J.: Rutgers University Press.

   1915. *Cities in Evolution: An Introduction to the Town Planning Movement and to the Study of Civics.* London: Williams and Norgate.

   1923. *Dramatisations of History.* Bombay: Modern Publishing Company; Edinburgh: P. G. and Colleagues.

Geddes, Patrick, and Victor Branford. 1919. *The Coming Polity.* London: Le Play House Press.

Geddes, Patrick, and J. Arthur Thomson. 1919. *Evolution.* London: Williams and Norgate.

Giedion, Sigfried. 1967. *Space, Time and Architecture: The Growth of a New Tradition.* 5th rev. ed. Cambridge, Mass.: Harvard University Press.

Gill, Brendan. 1987. "The Sky Line. Prospectus." *New Yorker,* 23 February.

   1990. "The Sky Line: Homage to Mumford." *New Yorker,* 2 April.

Gillette, Howard Jr. 1977. "Film as Artifact: *The City* (1939)." *American Studies* 18 (Fall): 71–85.

Goldberger, Paul. 1980. "Organic Remedies: Building and the City." *Salmagundi* 49 (Summer): 87–98.

   1990. "Architecture View: Lewis Mumford: Preacher, Prophet, Romantic." *New York Times,* 4 February, sec. H.

Greiff, Constance. 1987. *Independence: The Creation of a National Park.* Philadelphia: University of Pennsylvania Press.

Guerard, Albert. 1931. "Mr. Mumford on the Arts." Review of *The Brown Decades*, by Lewis Mumford. *New York Herald Tribune Books,* 11 October.

Hall, Peter. 1988. *Cities of Tomorrow: An Intellectual History of Urban Planning and Design in the Twentieth Century.* Oxford and New York: Basil Blackwell.

Hamlin, Talbot Faulkner. 1924. "Engineering or Architecture?" Review of *Sticks and Stones*, by Lewis Mumford. *Nation,* 3 December.

Hancock, John. 1988. "The New Deal and American Planning: The 1930s." In *Two Centuries of American Planning,* edited by Daniel Schaffer. Baltimore: Johns Hopkins University Press.

Haskell, Douglas. 1931. "The House of the Future." *New Republic,* 13 May.

   1932. "Architecture: What the Man about Town Will Build." *Nation,* 13 April.

1938. "The City, Past and Future." Review of *The Culture of Cities*, by Lewis Mumford. *Nation*, 23 April.

Hazlitt, Henry. 1931. "The Buried Renaissance." Review of *The Brown Decades*, by Lewis Mumford. *Nation*, 11 November.

Hitchcock, Henry-Russell Jr. 1927. "The Decline of Architecture." *The Hound and the Horn* 1 (September): 28–35.

  1928. "Review of *American Architecture*, by Fiske Kimball. *Creative Art* 3 (August): xiii–xv.

  1929 [1972]. *Modern Architecture: Romanticism and Reintegration*. New York: A.M.S. Press.

  1930 [1968]. "Humanism and the Fine Arts." In *The Critique of Humanism: A Symposium*, edited by C. Hartley Grattan. Freeport, N.Y.: Books for Libraries Press.

  1932. "Architectural Criticism." *Shelter* 2 (April): 2.

Hitchcock, Henry-Russell Jr., and Philip Johnson. 1966. *The International Style*. 2d rev. ed. New York: Norton, 1966.

"Housing – One Way to Prosperity." 1930. *New Republic*, 17 September.

Howard, Ebenezer. 1965. *Garden Cities of To-morrow*. Edited by Frederic J. Osborn with an introduction by Lewis Mumford. 4th rev. ed. Cambridge, Mass., and London: Massachusetts Institute of Technology Press.

Hughes, Michael, ed. 1972. *The Letters of Lewis Mumford and Frederic J. Osborn: A Transatlantic Dialogue, 1938–1970*. New York and Washington: Praeger.

Hutchison, Percy A. 1924. "American Architecture the Expression of Our Culture." Review of *Sticks and Stones*, by Lewis Mumford. *New York Times Book Review*, 24 September.

Jackson, Frank. 1985. *Sir Raymond Unwin: Architect, Planner, and Visionary*. London: A. Zwemmer.

Jacobs, Jane. 1961. *The Death and Life of Great American Cities*. New York: Vintage Books.

Jacoby, Russell. 1987. *The Last Intellectuals: American Culture in the Age of Academe*. New York: Basic Books.

Johnson, David A. 1988. "Regional Planning for the Great American Metropolis: New York between the World Wars." In *Two Centuries of American Planning*, edited by Daniel Schaffer. Baltimore: Johns Hopkins University Press.

Josephson, Matthew. 1931. "The Days of the Brooklyn Bridge." Review of *The Brown Decades*, by Lewis Mumford. *New Republic*, 11 November.

Kimball, Fiske. 1922 [1966]. *Domestic Architecture of the American Colonies and of the Early Republic*. New York: Dover.

  1924. "A Machine Age." Review of *Sticks and Stones*, by Lewis Mumford. *New York Herald Tribune Books*, 26 October.

  1928 [1970]. *American Architecture*. New York: A.M.S. Press.

Koenigsberg, Lisa. 1990. "'Lifewriting': First American Biographers of Architects and Their Works." In *The Architectural Historian in America: A Symposium in Celebration of the Fiftieth Anniversary of the Founding of the Society of Architectural Historians*. Studies in the History of Art, vol. 35, edited by Elisabeth Blair MacDougall. Hanover and London: University Press of New England.

Krinsky, Carol Herselle. 1978. *Rockefeller Center*. New York: Oxford University Press.

Lethaby, W. R. 1922. *Form in Civilization: Collected Papers on Art and Labour*. London: Oxford University Press.

Lewis, Thomas S. W. 1980. "Mumford and the Academy." *Salmagundi* 49 (Summer): 99–111.

Lovett, Robert Morss. 1922. Review of *The Story of Utopias*, by Lewis Mumford. *New Republic*, 13 December.

Lubove, Roy. 1963. *Community Planning in the 1920's: The Contribution of the Regional Planning Association of America*. Pittsburgh: University of Pittsburgh Press.

MacFadyen, Dugald. 1933 [1970]. *Sir Ebenezer Howard and the Town Planning Movement*. Cambridge, Mass.: Massachusetts Institute of Technology Press.

MacKaye, Benton. 1928 [1990]. *The New Exploration: A Philosophy of Regional Planning*. With an introduction by Lewis Mumford and foreword by David N. Startzell. Harpers Ferry, W.Va.: Appalachian Trail Conference; Urbana-Champaign: University of Illinois Press.

Marx, Leo. 1990. "Lewis Mumford: Prophet of Organicism." In *Lewis Mumford: Public Intellectual*, edited by Thomas P. Hughes and Agatha C. Hughes. New York and Oxford: Oxford University Press.

Mayer, Albert. 1934. "New Homes for a New Deal – I: Slum Clearance – But How?" *New Republic*, 14 February.

Meller, Helen. 1990. *Patrick Geddes: Social Evolutionist and City Planner*. London and New York: Routledge.

Mendelsohn, Eric. 1926. *Amerika: Bilderbuch eines Architekten*. Berlin: Rudolf Mosse Buchverlag.
   1929. *Russland: Europa: Amerika: Ein Architektonischer Querschnitt*. Berlin: Rudolf Mosse Buchverlag.

"Metropolis: Lewis Mumford's Book Scraps Today's City, Plans a New and Saner U.S." 1938. *Life*, 23 May.

Miller, Donald L. 1989. *Lewis Mumford: A Life*. New York: Weidenfeld and Nicolson.

Molesworth, Charles. 1990. "Inner and Outer: The Axiology of Lewis Mumford." In *Lewis Mumford: Public Intellectual*, edited by Thomas P. Hughes and Agatha C. Hughes. New York and Oxford: Oxford University Press.

Mollela, Arthur P. 1990. "Mumford in Historiographical Context." In *Lewis Mumford: Public Intellectual*, edited by Thomas P. Hughes and Agatha C. Hughes. New York and Oxford: Oxford University Press.

Monkkonen, Eric H. 1988. *America Becomes Urban: The Development of U.S. Cities and Towns, 1780–1980*. Berkeley, Los Angeles and London: University of California Press.

Morrison, Hugh. 1940. "After the International Style – What?" *Architectural Forum* 72 (May): 345–347.

Moses, Robert. 1962. "Are Cities Dead?" *Atlantic Monthly*, January.

Mumford, Lewis. 1912. "An Improved Electrolytic Detector." *Modern Electrics*, April.
   1918. "The Marriage of Museums." *Scientific Monthly*, September.
   1919. "Current Criticism of 'The State,'" *Sociological Review* 11 (Autumn): 136–140.
   1919. "The Heritage of the Cities Movement in America: An Historical Survey." *Journal of the American Institute of Architects* 7 (August): 349–354.
   1919. Review of *Architecture and Democracy*, by Claude Bragdon. *Dial* 67 (4 October): 318.
   1919. Reviews of *Town Improvement*, by Frederick Noble Evans, and *New Towns after the War*, by the New Townsmen. *Dial* 67 (20 September): 274.
   1920. "Miscellany." *Freeman* 1 (31 March): 67–68.
   1920. "Miscellany." *Freeman* 1 (23 June): 356.
   1920. "Miscellany." *Freeman* 1 (4 August): 497.
   1920. "Painting: Standards Old and New." *Freeman* 1 (7 April): 89–90.
   1920. "The Tate Gallery Reopens." *Freeman* 2 (22 September): 38–39.
   1921. "Machinery and the Modern Style." *New Republic*, 3 August.
   1922. "The City." In *Civilization in the United States: An Inquiry by Thirty Americans*, edited by Harold E. Stearns. New York: Harcourt, Brace and Company.

1922. "Ex Libris." Review of *Daniel H. Burnham: Architect, Planner of Cities*, by Charles Moore. *Freeman* 4 (22 February): 574–575.

1922. Review of *The Enjoyment of Architecture*, by Talbot Faulkner Hamlin. *Freeman* 4 (8 March): 622.

1922 [1959]. *The Story of Utopias*. Gloucester, Mass.: Peter Smith.

1923. "American Architecture: The Medieval Tradition." *Freeman* 8 (19 December): 344–346.

1923. "Architectural Piety." *Journal of the American Institute of Architects* 11 (August): 304–306.

1923. "Beauty and the Industrial Beast." *New Republic*, 6 June.

1923. "Community Planning and Housing." *Journal of the American Institute of Architects* 11 (December): 492.

1923. "Early American Architecture." Review of *Domestic Architecture of the American Colonies and of the Early Republic*, by Fiske Kimball. *New Republic*, 7 March.

1923. "Herzl's Utopia." *Menorah Journal* 9 (August): 155–169.

1924. "American Architecture: The Classical Myth." *Freeman* 8 (9 January): 418–420.

1924. "American Architecture: The Diaspora of the Pioneer." *Freeman* 8 (13 February): 538–540.

1924. "American Architecture: The Heritage of the Renaissance." *Freeman* 8 (2 January): 394–396.

1924. "American Architecture: The Realization of Industrialization." *Freeman* 8 (27 February): 584–586.

1924. "Architecture and History." *Journal of the American Institute of Architects* 12 (April): 191–192.

1924. "Architecture and the Machine." *American Mercury*, September.

1924. "The Autobiography of an Idea." Review of *The Autobiography of an Idea*, by Louis H. Sullivan. *New Republic*, 25 June.

1924. "The Imperial Age." *Journal of the American Institute of Architects* 12 (August): 366–371.

1924. "Report of Committee on Community Planning." *American Institute of Architects: Proceedings of the Fifty-Seventh Annual Convention*.

1925. "Architecture and Broad Planning: II. Realities vs. Dreams." *Journal of the American Institute of Architects* 13 (June): 198–199.

1925. "The Bricks of Baltimore." *[Baltimore] Evening Sun*, 1 December, sec. 2.

1925. "Decoration and Structure." *Commonweal* 2 (7 October): 532–533.

1925. "Deserts versus Gardens." *[Baltimore] Evening Sun*, 4 December, sec. 2.

1925. "The Fourth Migration." *Survey Graphic* 54 (1 May): 130–133.

1925. "Houses – Sunnyside Up." *Nation*, 4 February.

1925. "How to Ruin Baltimore." *[Baltimore] Evening Sun*, 10 December, sec. 2.

1925. "Modern Public Buildings." *[Baltimore] Evening Sun*, 8 December, sec. 2.

1925. "The Poison of Good Taste." *American Mercury*, September.

1925. "Report of Committee on Community Planning." *American Institute of Architects: Proceedings of the Fifty-Eighth Annual Convention*.

1925. "The Social Back Ground [sic] of Frank Lloyd Wright." *Wendingen* 7: 65–79.

1925. Untitled cartoon. *Survey* 55 (15 December): 336.

[1925]. *Vom Blockhaus zum Wolkenkratzer: Eine Studie über Amerikanische Architektur und Zivilisation*. Translated by M. Mauthner. Berlin: Bruno Cassirer Verlag.

1926. "Amerikanische Baukunst." *Die Form* 1 (February): 102–104.

1926. *Architecture*. Chicago: American Library Association.

1926. "The Destruction of the Shelton." *Commonweal* 3 (28 April): 689–690.

1926. "Downfall or Renewal?" Review of *The Decline of the West: I. Form and Actuality*, by Oswald Spengler. *New Republic*, 12 May.

1926. *The Golden Day: A Study in American Experience and Culture.* New York: Boni and Liveright.

1926. "Magnified Impotence." *New Republic,* 22 December.

1926. "The New Municipal Building." *[Baltimore] Evening Sun,* 11 February, sec. 2.

1926. "The Pageant of American Architecture." Review of *The American Spirit in Architecture,* by Talbot Faulkner Hamlin. *Journal of the American Institute of Architects* 14 (September): 410–411.

1927. "American Architecture." *American Federationist* 34 (December): 1479–1484.

1927. "American Taste." *Harper's,* October.

1927. "The Barclay-Vesey Building." *New Republic,* 6 July.

1927. "The Fate of Garden Cities." *Journal of the American Institute of Architects* 15 (February): 37–39.

1927. "Is the Skyscraper Tolerable?" *Architecture* 55 (February): 67–69.

1927. "That Monster – The Machine: Lewis Mumford vs. Genevieve Taggard: The Bourgeois Girls Like Their Ham Sliced Thin." *New Masses* 3 (September): 23.

1927. "New York *vs.* Chicago in Architecture." *Architecture* 56 (November): 241–244.

1928. "American Architecture To-day: II." *Architecture* 57 (June): 301–308.

1928. "The Little Testament of Bernard Martin Aet. 30." In *The Second American Caravan: A Yearbook of American Literature,* edited by Alfred Kreymborg, Lewis Mumford, and Paul Rosenfeld. New York: Macaulay Company.

1929. "The Economics of Contemporary Decoration." *Creative Art* 4 (January): xix – xxii.

1929. "Form in Modern Architecture: I. The Breakup of Form." *Architecture* 60 (September): 125–128.

1929. "Form in Modern Architecture: II. The Beginnings of Modern Form." *Architecture* 60 (December): 313–316.

1929. "Frank Lloyd Wright and the New Pioneers." Review of *Frank Lloyd Wright,* by Henry-Russell Hitchcock Jr. *Architectural Record* 65 (April): 414–416.

1929. "On Judging Art." Review of *Ananias, or the False Artist,* by Walter Pach. *New Republic,* 20 March.

1929. "Patrick Geddes: Insurgent." *New Republic,* 30 October.

1929. "A Philosopher of History." Review of *The Decline of the West: II. Perspectives of World History,* by Oswald Spengler. *New Republic,* 20 March.

1930. "The American Dwelling-House." *American Mercury,* April.

1930. "Art in America." Review of *Art in America,* by Suzanne La Follette. *New Republic,* 5 March.

1930. "Bourgeois Culture and Machine Art/Bürgerliche Kultur und Maschine." Translated by Ethel Talbot Scheffauer. *Die Form* 5 (7 June): 322–326.

1930. "The Chance for Civilized Housing." *New Republic,* 17 September.

1930. "The City of Tomorrow." Reviews of *The Metropolis of Tomorrow,* by Hugh Ferriss; *Our Cities Today and Tomorrow: A Survey of Planning and Zoning Progress in the United States,* by Theodora Kimball Hubbard and Henry Vincent Hubbard; and *The City of Tomorrow and Its Planning,* by Le Corbusier. *New Republic,* 12 February.

1930. "Form in Modern Architecture: III. The Social Contribution." *Architecture* 61 (March): 151–153.

1930. "Form in Modern Architecture: IV. The Community as a Source of Form." *Architecture* 62 (July): 1–4.

1930. "Form in Modern Architecture: V. The Wavy Line versus the Cube." *Architecture* 62 (December): 315–318.

1930. "Mass Production and the Modern House [Part One]." *Architectural Record* 67 (January): 13–20.

1930. "Modern Architecture." Review of *Modern Architecture: Romanticism and Reintegration*, by Henry-Russell Hitchcock Jr. *New Republic*, 19 March.

1930 [1968]. "Towards an Organic Humanism." In *The Critique of Humanism: A Symposium*, edited by C. Hartley Grattan. Freeport, N.Y.: Books for Libraries Press.

1931. "The Brooklyn Bridge." *American Mercury*, August.

1931. "The Brown Decades." *Scribner's*, February.

1931. "The Brown Decades: Architecture." *Scribner's*, April.

1931. "The Brown Decades: Art." *Scribner's*, October.

1931. *The Brown Decades: A Study of the Arts in America, 1865–1895*. New York: Harcourt, Brace and Company.

1931. "The Flaw in the Mechanical House." *New Republic*, 3 June.

1931. "Frozen Music or Solidified Static? Reflections on Radio City." *New Yorker*, 20 June.

1931. "Housing versus Ownership." *New Republic*, 16 December.

1931. "Notes on Modern Architecture." *New Republic*, 18 March.

1931. "Two Chicago Fairs." *New Republic*, 21 January.

1932. "The Decline of Spengler." Review of *Man and Technics: A Contribution to a Philosophy of Life*, by Oswald Spengler. *New Republic*, 9 March.

1932. "England's Two Million Houses, New." *Fortune*, November.

1932. "Housing." In *Modern Architecture: International Exhibition*. New York: Museum of Modern Art.

1932. "Notes on Germany." *New Republic*, 26 October.

1932. "The Plan of New York [I]." *New Republic*, 15 June.

1932. "The Plan of New York: II." *New Republic*, 22 June.

1932. "The Sky Line: Organic Architecture." *New Yorker*, 27 February.

1932. "The Sky Line: The Regional Plan." *New Yorker*, 21 May.

1933. "The Art Galleries: Early Americans – Ben Shahn and Tom Mooney – Mr. Rivera's Mural." *New Yorker*, 20 May.

1933. "Machines for Living." *Fortune*, February 1933.

1933. "The Sky Line: Two Theatres." *New Yorker*, 14 January.

1933. "Taxes Into Houses." *Fortune*, May.

1934. "The Art Galleries: Portrait of the Mechanic as a Young Man – Newcomers in Retrospect." *New Yorker*, 31 March.

1934. "New Homes for a New Deal – III: The Shortage of Dwellings and Direction." *New Republic*, 28 February.

1934. "A New York Childhood: Ta-Ra-Ra-Boom-De-Ay." *New Yorker*, 22 December.

1934. "The Sky Line: The New York Lunchroom." *New Yorker*, 19 May.

1934. *Technics and Civilization*. New York: Harcourt, Brace and Company.

1935. "Civilized History." Review of *A Study of History*, vols. 1–3, by Arnold J. Toynbee. *New Republic*, 27 November.

1935. "The Sky Line: Meditations on a Zoo." *New Yorker*, 5 January.

1935. "The Sky Line: Mr. Wright's City – Downtown Dignity." *New Yorker*, 27 April.

1936. "Giants of Modern Architecture." Reviews of *The Architecture of H. H. Richardson and His Times: 1838–1886*, by Henry-Russell Hitchcock Jr.; and *Louis Sullivan: Prophet of Modern Architecture*, by Hugh Morrison. *New Republic*, 26 February.

1937. "A New York Adolescence: Tennis, Quadratic Equations, and Love." *New Yorker*, 4 December.

1937. "The Sky Line: Bridges and Beaches." *New Yorker,* 17 July.

1938. *The Culture of Cities.* New York: Harcourt, Brace and Company.

1938. "The Sky Line: Bauhaus – Two Restaurants and a Theatre." *New Yorker,* 31 December.

1938. "The Sky Line: Paxe in Urbe." *New Yorker,* 21 May.

1938. *Whither Honolulu? A Memorandum Report on Park and City Planning.* Honolulu: City and County of Honolulu Park Board.

1939. *Regional Planning in the Pacific Northwest: A Memorandum.* Portland, Oreg.: Northwest Regional Council.

1939. "The Sky Line: Growing Pains – The New Museum." *New Yorker,* 3 June.

1939. "The Sky Line in Flushing: Genuine Bootleg." *New Yorker,* 29 July.

1939. "The Sky Line in Flushing: West Is East." *New Yorker,* 17 June.

1940. "The Sky Line: Rockefeller Center Revisited." *New Yorker,* 4 May.

1940. "Transcendental Dissolution." Review of *A Study of History,* vols. 4–6, by Arnold J. Toynbee. *New Republic,* 1 April.

1941 [1967]. *The South in Architecture.* With a foreword by A. W. Vaughan. New York: Da Capo Press.

1943. *The Social Foundations of Postwar Building.* Rebuilding Britain Series no. 9. London: Faber and Faber.

1944. *The Condition of Man.* New York: Harcourt, Brace and Company.

1945. *City Development: Studies in Disintegration and Renewal.* New York: Harcourt, Brace and Company.

1945. "Lewis Mumford on the Future of London." *Architectural Review* 97 (January): 3–10.

1947. "Communitas." Reviews of *When the Cathedrals Were White: A Journey to the Country of Timid People,* by Le Corbusier; and *Communitas: Ways of Livelihood and Ways of Life,* by Percival Goodman and Paul Goodman. *Virginia Quarterly Review* 23 (Summer): 439–443.

1947. "The Sky Line: Status Quo." *New Yorker,* 11 October.

1947. "The Sky Line: United Nations Headquarters: The Ground Plan." *New Yorker,* 25 October.

1947. "The Sky Line: United Nations Headquarters: Buildings as Symbols." *New Yorker,* 15 November.

1948. "The Sky Line: Prefabricated Blight." *New Yorker,* 30 October.

1948. "The Sky Line: Stuyvesant Town Revisited." *New Yorker,* 27 November.

1949. "Monumentalism, Symbolism and Style, Part One." *Magazine of Art,* October.

1949. "Monumentalism, Symbolism and Style, Part Two." *Magazine of Art,* November.

1949. "The Sky Line: From Utopia Parkway Turn East." *New Yorker,* 22 October.

1949. "The Sky Line: The Great Good Place." *New Yorker,* 12 November.

1951. *The Conduct of Life.* New York: Harcourt, Brace and Company.

1951. "The Sky Line: Magic with Mirrors – I." *New Yorker,* 15 September.

1951. "The Sky Line: Magic with Mirrors – II." *New Yorker,* 22 September.

1952. *Art and Technics.* New York: Columbia University Press.

1952. "The Modern City." In *Forms and Functions of Twentieth-Century Architecture,* vol. 4, edited by Talbot Faulkner Hamlin. With an introduction by Leopold Arnaud. New York: Columbia University Press.

1952, ed. *Roots of Contemporary American Architecture: A Series of Thirty-Seven Essays Dating from the Mid-Nineteenth Century to the Present.* New York: Reinhold.

1952. "The Sky Line: House of Glass." *New Yorker,* 9 August.

1953. "The Sky Line: East End Urbanity." *New Yorker,* 26 September.

1953. "The Sky Line: Old Forms for New Towns." *New Yorker,* 17 October.

1953. "The Sky Line: A Phoenix Too Infrequent – I." *New Yorker*, 28 November.

1953. "The Sky Line: A Phoenix Too Infrequent – II." *New Yorker*, 12 December.

1953. "The Sky Line: United Nations Assembly." *New Yorker*, 29 (14 March): 72–81.

1953. "The Sky Line: Workshop Invisible." *New Yorker*, 17 January.

1954. "The Life, the Teaching and the Architecture of Matthew Nowicki [Part I]." *Architectural Record* 115 (June): 139–149.

1954. "The Life, the Teaching and the Architecture of Matthew Nowicki, Part II: Matthew Nowicki as an Educator." *Architectural Record* 116 (July): 128–135.

1954. "The Life, the Teaching and the Architecture of Matthew Nowicki, Part III: His Architectural Achievement." *Architectural Record* 116 (August): 169–175.

1954. "The Life, the Teaching and the Architecture of Matthew Nowicki, Part IV: Nowicki's Work in India." *Architectural Record* 116 (September): 153–159.

1954. "The Napoleon of Notting Hill." Review of *A Study of History*, vols. 7–10, by Arnold J. Toynbee. *New Republic*, 8 November.

1954. "The Sky Line: Crystal Lantern." *New Yorker*, 13 November.

1955. *The Brown Decades: A Study of the Arts in America, 1865–1895.* 2d rev. ed. New York: Dover.

1955. "Garden Civilizations: Preparing for a New Epoch." *Town and Country Planning* 23 (March): 138–142.

1955. "The Sky Line: The Roaring Traffic's Boom – I." *New Yorker*, 19 March.

1955. "The Sky Line: The Roaring Traffic's Boom – II." *New Yorker*, 2 April.

1955. "The Sky Line: The Roaring Traffic's Boom – III." *New Yorker*, 16 April.

1955. "The Sky Line: The Roaring Traffic's Boom – IV." *New Yorker*, 11 June.

1955. *Sticks and Stones: A Study of American Architecture and Civilization.* 2d rev. ed. New York: Dover.

1956. *From the Ground Up: Observations on Contemporary Architecture, Housing, Highway Building, and Civic Design.* New York: Harcourt, Brace and Company.

1956. "The Sky Line: [Historic] Philadelphia – I." *New Yorker*, 17 November.

1956. "The Sky Line: Philadelphia – I." *New Yorker*, 28 April.

1956. "The Sky Line: Philadelphia – II." *New Yorker*, 26 May.

1957. *The Golden Day: A Study in American Literature and Culture.* 2d rev. ed. Boston: Beacon Press.

1957. "The Sky Line: Historic Philadelphia – II." *New Yorker*, 9 February.

1957. "The Sky Line: Historic Philadelphia – III." *New Yorker*, 6 April.

1957. "The Sky Line: Historic Philadelphia – IV." *New Yorker*, 13 April.

1957. "The Sky Line: The Cave, the City, and the Flower." *New Yorker*, 2 November.

1957. "The Sky Line: The Marseilles 'Folly.'" *New Yorker*, 5 October.

1958. "The Highway and the City." *Architectural Record* 123 (April): 179–186.

1958. "The Sky Line: The Disappearance of Pennsylvania Station." *New Yorker*, 7 June.

1958. "The Sky Line: The Lesson of the Master." *New Yorker*, 13 September.

1959. "The Sky Line: The Skyway's the Limit." *New Yorker*, 14 November.

1959. "The Sky Line: What Wright Hath Wrought." *New Yorker*, 5 December.

1961. *The City in History: Its Origins, Its Transformations, and Its Prospects.* New York: Harcourt, Brace and World.

1962. "The Case against 'Modern Architecture.'" *Architectural Record* 131 (April): 155–162.

1962. "The Sky Line: Mother Jacobs' Home Remedies." *New Yorker*, 1 December.

1963. *The Highway and the City.* New York: Harcourt, Brace and World.

1965. "Revaluations I: Howard's Garden City." Review of *Garden Cities of To-morrow*, by Ebenezer Howard. *New York Review of Books*, 8 April.

1965. "Utopia, the City and the Machine." *Daedalus* 94 (Spring): 271–292.

1967. *Technics and Human Development*. Vol. 1 of *The Myth of the Machine*. New York: Harcourt Brace Jovanovich.

1968. *The Urban Prospect*. New York: Harcourt, Brace and World.

1970. *The Pentagon of Power*. Vol. 2 of *The Myth of the Machine*. Harcourt Brace Jovanovich.

1971. *The Brown Decades: A Study of the Arts in America, 1865–1895*. 3d rev. ed. New York: Dover.

1975. *Architecture as a Home for Man: Essays for Architectural Record*, edited by Jeanne Davern. New York: Architectural Record Books.

1975. *Findings and Keepings: Analects for an Autobiography*. New York and London: Harcourt Brace Jovanovich.

1979. *My Works and Days: A Personal Chronicle*. New York and London: Harcourt Brace Jovanovich.

1982. *Sketches from Life: The Autobiography of Lewis Mumford, The Early Years*. New York: Dial Press.

Mumford, Lewis and Benton MacKaye. 1931. "Townless Highways for the Motorist: A Proposal for the Automobile Age." *Harper's*, August.

Mumford, Lewis, Albert Mayer and Henry Wright. 1934. "New Homes for a New Deal – IV: A Concrete Program." *New Republic*, 7 March.

Newhouse, Victoria. 1989. *Wallace K. Harrison, Architect*. New York: Rizzoli.

Novak, Frank G. Jr. 1975. "Lewis Mumford as a Critic of American Culture." Ph.D. diss., University of Tennessee.

1987. "Lewis Mumford and the Reclamation of Human History." *Clio* 16 (February): 159–181.

1988. *The Autobiographical Writings of Lewis Mumford: A Study in Literary Audacity*. [Honolulu]: University of Hawaii Press.

1989. "Master and Disciple: Selections from the Patrick Geddes–Lewis Mumford Letters." *Horns of Plenty: Malcolm Cowley and His Generation* 2 (Fall): 45–62.

Osborn, Frederic J., and Arnold Whittick. 1977. *New Towns: Their Origins, Achievements and Progress*. With an introduction by Lewis Mumford. 3d rev. ed. London: Leonard Hill; Boston: Routledge and Kegan Paul.

Oud, J. J. P. 1926. *Hollaendische Architektur* (Munich: Albert Langen, 1926), 76.

Palmer, A. Emerson. 1922. "Utopias That Make the World Tolerable." Review of *The Story of Utopias*, by Lewis Mumford. *New York Times Book Review*, 24 December.

Parsons, Kermit C. 1990. "Clarence Stein and the Greenbelt Towns: Settling for Less." *Journal of the American Planning Association* 56 (Spring): 161–183.

1994. "Collaborative Genius: The Regional Planning Association of America." *Journal of the American Planning Association* 60 (Autumn): 462–482.

Perry, Clarence Arthur. 1929. "The Neighborhood Unit: A Scheme of Arrangement for the Family-Life Community." In *Regional Plan of New York and Its Environs*, vol. 7. New York: Committee on Regional Plan of New York and Its Environs.

Peterson, Charles E. 1950. "American Notes: Ante-Bellum Skyscraper." *Journal of the Society of Architectural Historians* 9 (October): 27–28.

Plunz, Richard. 1990. *A History of Housing in New York City: Dwelling Type and Social Change in the American Metropolis*. New York: Columbia University Press.

Report of the Commission of Housing and Regional Planning to Governor Alfred E. Smith. 1926. Albany: New York [State] Commission of Housing and Regional Planning, 7 May.

Review of *The Brown Decades,* by Lewis Mumford. 1932. *Architectural Forum* 56 (February): 17.

Riesman, David. 1980. "Some Observations on Lewis Mumford's *The City in History.*" *Salmagundi* 49 (Summer): 80–86.

Riley, Terence. 1992. *The International Style: Exhibition 15 and the Museum of Modern Art.* New York: Rizzoli.

Samson, Miles David. 1988. "German-American Dialogues and the Modern Movement before the 'Design Migration,' 1910–1933." Ph.D. diss., Harvard University.

Schaffer, Daniel. 1982. *Garden Cities for America: The Radburn Experience.* Philadelphia: Temple University Press.

Schapiro, Meyer. 1938. "Looking Forward to Looking Backward." Review of *The Culture of Cities,* by Lewis Mumford. *Partisan Review* 8 (July): 12–24.

Scheffauer, Herman George. 1921. "Dynamic Architecture: New Forms of the Future." *Dial* 70 (March): 323–328.

Schuyler, Montgomery. 1961. *American Architecture and Other Writings,* 2 vols., edited by William H. Jordy and Ralph Coe. Cambridge, Mass.: Belknap Press.

Searing, Helen. 1990. "Henry-Russell Hitchcock: The Architectural Historian as Critic and Connoisseur." In *The Architectural Historian in America: A Symposium in Celebration of the Fiftieth Anniversary of the Founding of the Society of Architectural Historians.* Studies in the History of Art, vol. 35, edited by Elisabeth Blair MacDougall. Hanover and London: University Press of New England.

Shay, Howell Lewis. 1931. "Modern Architecture and Tradition." *T-Square Club Journal* 1 (February): 14.

Simpson, Michael. 1985. *Thomas Adams and the Modern Planning Movement: Britain, Canada and the United States, 1900–1940.* London and New York: Alexandrine Press.

Spiller, Robert E., ed. 1970. *The Van Wyck Brooks–Lewis Mumford Letters: The Record of a Literary Friendship, 1921–1963.* New York: E. P. Dutton and Company.

Stein, Clarence S. 1922. "Amsterdam – Old and New." *Journal of the American Institute of Architects* 9 (October): 310–327.

⸻ 1966. *Toward New Towns for America.* With an introduction by Lewis Mumford. 3d rev. ed. Cambridge, Mass., and London: Massachusetts Institute of Technology Press.

Stephens, Suzanne. 1990. "Architectural Criticism in a Historical Context: The Case of Herbert Croly." In *The Architectural Historian in America: A Symposium in Celebration of the Fiftieth Anniversary of the Founding of the Society of Architectural Historians.* Studies in the History of Art, vol. 35, edited by Elisabeth Blair MacDougall. Hanover and London: University Press of New England.

Stern, Robert A. M., Gregory Gilmartin, and Thomas Mellins. 1987. *New York 1930: Architecture and Urbanism between the Two World Wars.* New York: Rizzoli.

Stunkel, Kenneth R. 1989. "Lewis Mumford: Guardian and Critic of Civilization." *Horns of Plenty: Malcolm Cowley and His Generation* 2 (Fall): 30–44.

Stunkel, Kenneth R., and Vincent DiMattio. 1989. "Lewis Mumford's Life in Art Comes to Light." *Horns of Plenty: Malcolm Cowley and His Generation* 2 (Fall): 29–30.

Sullivan, Molly. 1992. *Lewis Mumford's New York: A Personal View.* New York: City College of New York.

Sussman, Carl, ed. 1976. *Planning the Fourth Migration: The Neglected Vision of the Regional Planning Association of America.* Cambridge, Mass., and London: Massachusetts Institute of Technology Press.

"Symposium: The International Architectural Exhibition." 1932. *Shelter* 2 (April): 3–9.

Taggard, Genevieve. 1927. "That Monster – The Machine: Lewis Mumford vs. Genevieve Taggard: Do You Kill Your Own Hogs Too?" *New Masses* 3 (September): 23–24.

Temko, Allan. 1961. "How Civilized Can Urban Man Be? In the History of Cities, Mr. Mumford Finds Forces That Have Destroyed the Dwellers." Review of *The City in History*, by Lewis Mumford. *New York Times Book Review*, 16 April.

Thomas, John L. 1988. "In Retrospect: Lewis Mumford: Regionalist Historian." *Reviews in American History* 16 (March): 158–172.

———. 1990. "Lewis Mumford, Benton MacKaye, and the Regional Vision." In *Lewis Mumford: Public Intellectual*, edited by Thomas P. Hughes and Agatha C. Hughes. New York and Oxford: Oxford University Press.

Trachtenberg, Alan. 1979. *Brooklyn Bridge: Fact and Symbol*. 2d ed. Chicago and London: University of Chicago Press.

———. 1980. "Mumford in the Twenties: The Historian as Artist." *Salmagundi* 49 (Summer): 29–42.

Tschachler, Heinz. 1994. *Lewis Mumford's Reception in German Translation and Criticism*. Lanham, Md., New York, and London: University Press of America.

Tunnard, Christopher. 1961. "The City and Its Interpreters." Review of *The City in History*, by Lewis Mumford. *Journal of the American Institute of Planners* 27 (November): 346–350.

Twombly, Robert C. 1973. *Frank Lloyd Wright: An Interpretive Biography*. New York, Evanston, San Francisco, and London: Harper and Row.

———. 1979. *Frank Lloyd Wright: His Life and His Architecture*. New York, Chichester, Brisbane, and Toronto: John Wiley and Sons.

Unwin, Raymond. 1912. *Nothing Gained by Overcrowding! How the Garden City Type of Development May Benefit Both Owner and Occupier*. London: P. S. King.

Vale, Lawrence J. 1990. "Designing Global Harmony: Lewis Mumford and the United Nations Headquarters." In *Lewis Mumford: Public Intellectual*, edited by Thomas P. Hughes and Agatha C. Hughes. New York and Oxford: Oxford University Press.

Veblen, Thorstein. 1899 [1973]. *The Theory of the Leisure Class*. With an introduction by John Kenneth Galbraith. Boston: Houghton Mifflin Company.

Von Eckardt, Wolf. 1960. *Eric Mendelsohn*. New York: George Braziller.

———. 1962. "Mrs. Jacobs vs. Mumford: Urban Planning Stirs a Storm." *Washington Post*, 30 December.

———. 1963. "Changing Our Unnatural Habitat." Review of *The Highway and the City*, by Lewis Mumford. *New Republic*, 1 June.

Von Moos, Stanislaus. 1990. "The Visualized Machine Age: Or: Mumford and the European Avant-Garde." In *Lewis Mumford: Public Intellectual*, edited by Thomas P. Hughes and Agatha C. Hughes. New York and Oxford: Oxford University Press.

Ward, Stephen V., ed. 1992. *The Garden City: Past, Present and Future*. London, Glasgow, New York, Tokyo, Melbourne, and Madras: E. and F. N. Spon.

Weimer, David R. 1962. "Lewis Mumford and the Design of Criticism." *Arts and Architecture* 79 (September): 14–15, 30–31.

"What Is Happening to Modern Architecture?" 1948. *Museum of Modern Art Bulletin* 15 (Spring): 4–21.

Whittick, Arnold. 1987. *F.J.O. – Practical Idealist: A Biography of Sir Frederic J. Osborn*. London: Town and Country Planning Association.

Williams, Rosalind. 1990. "Lewis Mumford as a Historian of Technology in *Technics and Civilization*." In *Lewis Mumford: Public Intellectual*, edited by Thomas P. Hughes and Agatha C. Hughes. New York and Oxford: Oxford University Press.

Wilson, Richard Guy. 1979. "The Early Work of Charles F. McKim: Country House Commissions." *Wintherthur Portfolio* 14 (Autumn): 235–267.

Wilson, Richard Guy, Dianne H. Pilgrim, and Dickran Tashjian. 1986. *The Machine Age in America, 1918–1941.* New York: Harry N. Abrams.

Winsten, Archer. 1939. "Movie Talk: 'The City' Opens Saturday at the World's Fair: Documentary of Unqualified Excellence Shows the Way to New Achievements." Review of *The City. New York Post,* 23 May.

Wojtowicz, Robert. 1990. "Lewis Mumford: The Architectural Critic as Historian." In *The Architectural Historian in America: A Symposium in Celebration of the Fiftieth Anniversary of the Founding of the Society of Architectural Historians.* Studies in the History of Art, vol. 35, edited by Elisabeth Blair MacDougall. Hanover and London: University Press of New England.

———. 1991. "The Critic as Propagandist: Lewis Mumford and the 'Radburn Idea.'" In *Proceedings of the Fourth National Conference on American Planning History.* Richmond, Va.: Society for American City and Regional Planning History.

Woods, Mary. 1989. "The First American Architectural Journals: The Profession's Voice." *Journal of the Society of Architectural Historians* 48 (June): 117–138.

"A World's Fair Film." 1939. Review of *The City. Architectural Review* 86 (August): 93–94.

[Wurster], Catherine K. Bauer. 1932. "Exhibition of Modern Architecture: Museum of Modern Art." *Creative Art* 10 (March): 201–206.

———. 1934. *Modern Housing.* Boston and New York: Houghton Mifflin.

———. 1965. "The Social Front of Modern Architecture in the 1930s." *Journal of the Society of Architectural Historians* 24 (March): 48–52.

Wright, Frank Lloyd. 1941. "Mumford Lectures." Review of *The South in Architecture,* by Lewis Mumford. *Saturday Review of Literature,* 23 August.

———. 1943. *An Autobiography.* New York: Duell, Sloan and Pearce.

Wright, Henry. 1934. "New Homes for a New Deal – II: Abolishing Slums Forever." *New Republic,* 21 February.

———. 1935. *Rehousing Urban America.* New York: Columbia University Press.

Zeublin, Charles. 1899. "The World's First Sociological Laboratory." *American Journal of Sociology* 4 (March): 577–592.

Zimmern, Alfred. 1923. "Post-War Utopianism." Review of *The Story of Utopias,* by Lewis Mumford. *Literary Review* 4 (20 January): 397.

INDEX

Abercrombie, Patrick, 145–146
Ackerman, Frederick, 75, 115–116, 119, 122, 126–127, 128, 133, 142–143
Adams, Charles Francis, 54
Adams, Thomas, 121–123, 145
Addams, Jane, 19
Adler, Dankmar, 56
Adler and Sullivan, 56
Adshead, S. D., 33
Ahearn, Nellie, 7
airplane, the, 100, 119, 127, 135, 139
Alabama College, 68
Alger, Horatio, 8
Allen, Collens and Willis, 103
Allies, 4, 68, 105
"Alpha Transparency Company," 23
Amenia, N.Y., 150
America, 2, 3, 4, 6, 12, 16, 29, 32, 37, 38, 39, 40, 41, 43, 44, 47, 51, 52, 56, 58, 59, 60, 64, 70, 71, 72, 79, 85, 86, 87, 90, 91, 92, 95, 109, 114, 115, 119, 123, 124, 127, 134, 148, 161
American Federationist, The, 126
American Institute of Architects, 29, 118
American Institute of Planners, 142
American Journal of Sociology, The, 29
American Mercury, The, 45, 60, 74, 85, 101
American Museum of Natural History, 8, 27
Amsterdam, 156, 157, 160
Anderson, Robert, 66
Andreae, Johann Valentin, 36–37
Appalachian Trail, 116, 144
Appleton's, 20
Architectural Forum, The, 65

architectural history, 1, 45, 46, 47, 48, 50, 55, 58, 61, 65, 68, 71, 72
architectural profession, 3, 29, 31, 75, 83, 91, 107, 111, 123, 124
Architectural Record, The, 72, 76, 77, 102, 108, 123
Architectural Review, The, 143, 145, 147
architectural theory, 74
Architecture, 56, 77, 89
architecture, 1, 7, 16, 17, 19, 22, 24, 25, 26, 28, 30, 31, 35, 37, 39, 43, 44, 45, 46, 47, 49, 51, 52, 53, 56, 57, 58, 59, 60, 61, 62, 63, 64, 65, 66, 68, 69, 72, 74, 76, 77, 78, 79, 80, 82, 83, 84, 85, 87, 88, 89, 92, 94, 95, 96, 97, 98, 104, 112, 113, 118, 127, 129, 134, 147, 152, 157
    American, 3, 17, 23, 31, 40, 44, 45, 48, 50, 53, 55, 57, 59, 62, 64, 66, 67, 79, 80, 82, 85, 86; books about, 87; development of, 56, 71; of the early republic, 51; historiography of, 66; history of, 45, 48; modern tradition in, 71; native tradition in, 58; revisionist studies of, 67
    arranged, 31
    British, 30
    classical style of, 79
    contemporary, 47, 49, 52, 63, 76, 107
    country house, 37, 48
    destruction of, 68
    eclectic, 51
    European, 56, 62
    Federal, 46
    functionalist, 131
    Georgian, 46

Printed in Great Britain
by Amazon.co.uk, Ltd.,
Marston Gate.